The First Generation of Electronic Records Archivists in the United States: A Study in Professionalization

The First Generation of Electronic Records Archivists in the United States: A Study in Professionalization

Richard J. Cox, PhD, MA

The Haworth Press, Inc.
New York • London • Norwood (Australia)

The First Generation of Electronic Records Archivists in the United States : A Study in Professionalization has also been published as *Primary Sources & Original Works*, Volume 3, Numbers 3/4 1994.

The Haworth Press, Inc., 10 Alice Street, Binghamton, NY 13904-1580 USA

Library of Congress Cataloging-in-Publication Data

The First generation of electronic records archivists in the United States : a study in professionalization / Richard Cox.
p. cm.
"Has also been published as Primary sources & original works, volume 3, number 3/4, 1994"–T.p. verso.
Based on the author's dissertation.
Includes bibliographical references.
ISBN 1-56024-644-8 (alk. paper)
1. Archivists–Training of–United States. 2. Information technology–United States. I. Cox, Richard J.
CD987.F57 1994
025'.00285–dc20 94–17961
CIP

INDEXING & ABSTRACTING

Contributions to this publication are selectively indexed or abstracted in print, electronic, online, or CD-ROM version(s) of the reference tools and information services listed below. This list is current as of the copyright date of this publication. See the end of this section for additional notes.

- ***Abstracts in Anthropology***, Baywood Publishing Company, 26 Austin Avenue, P.O. Box 337, Amityville, NY 11701
- ***America: History and Life,*** ABC-CLIO, Inc., 130 Cremona Drive, Santa Barbara, CA 93117
- ***Bulletin Board for Libraries ("BUBL"),*** The Andersonian Library, Curran Building, 101 St. James Road, Glasgow G4 ONS Scotland
- ***GEO Abstracts (GEO Abstracts/GEOBASE)***, Elsevier/GEO Abstracts, Regency House, 34 Duke Street, Norwich NR3 3AP, England
- ***Historical Abstracts,*** ABC-CLIO Library, 130 Cremona Drive, Santa Barbara, CA 93117
- ***Index to Periodical Articles Related to Law***, University of Texas, 727 East 26th Street, Austin, TX 78705
- ***Information Science Abstracts***, Plenum Publishing Company, 233 Spring Street, New York, NY 10013-1578
- ***Int Zeitschrift fur Bibelwissenschaft und Grenz (Bible Studies)***, Universitat Paderborn IZBG, FB 1 Warburger Str 100, D-33098 Paderborn, Germany
- ***Library & Information Science Abstracts (LISA)***, Bowker-Saur Limited, Maypole House, Maypole Road, East Grinstead, East Sussex RH19 1HH, England
- ***Library Hi Tech News***, Pierian Press, P.O. Box 1808, Ann Arbor, MI 48106

(continued)

- ***Newsletter of Library and Information Services***, China Sci-Tech Book Review, Library of Academia Sinica, 8 Kexueyuan Nanlu, Zhongguancun, Beijing 100080, People's Republic of China
- ***Sage Urban Studies Abstracts***, Sage Publications, Inc., 2455 Teller Road, Newbury Park, CA 91320
- ***Social Work Research & Abstracts***, National Association of Social Workers, 750 First Street NW, 8th Floor, Washington, DC 20002
- ***The Informed Librarian,*** Infosources Publishing, 140 Norma Road, Teaneck, NJ 07666

SPECIAL BIBLIOGRAPHIC NOTES

related to special journal issues (separates) and indexing/abstracting

- ❑ indexing/abstracting services in this list will also cover material in the "separate" that is co-published simultaneously with Haworth's special thematic journal issue or DocuSerial. Indexing/abstracting usually covers material at the article/chapter level.
- ❑ monographic co-editions are intended for either non-subscribers or libraries which intend to purchase a second copy for their circulating collections.
- ❑ monographic co-editions are reported to all jobbers/wholesalers/approval plans. The source journal is listed as the "series" to assist the prevention of duplicate purchasing in the same manner utilized for books-in-series.
- ❑ to facilitate user/access services all indexing/abstracting services are encouraged to utilize the co-indexing entry note indicated at the bottom of the first page of each article/chapter/contribution.
- ❑ this is intended to assist a library user of any reference tool (whether print, electronic, online, or CD-ROM) to locate the monographic version if the library has purchased this version but not a subscription to the source journal.
- ❑ individual articles/chapters in any Haworth publication are also available through the Haworth Document Delivery Services (HDDS).

ABOUT THE AUTHOR

Richard J. Cox is Assistant Professor in Library Science at the University of Pittsburgh, School of Library and Information Science. Prior to his current position he was Associate Archivist, External Programs, New York State Archives and Records Administration; Head of the Archives and Records Division at the Alabama Department of Archives and History; Archivist and Records Manager for the City of Baltimore; and Curator of Manuscripts at the Maryland Historical Society. Dr. Cox was also a visiting lecturer, teaching archives and manuscripts administration, at the School of Information Science and Policy, State University of New York at Albany in 1986 and 1987.

Through the years Dr. Cox has been very active in professional archival associations. He chaired the Society of American Archivists (SAA) committee that drafted new graduate archival education guidelines adopted by its Council in 1988, served for four years as a member of that association's Committee on Education and Professional Development, and was a member of the Society's governing Council from 1986 through 1989. He served on the Society's Committee on Institutional Development and Evaluation and edited the newsletter for the Society's Archival Educators' Round Table. In addition to his work with SAA, Dr. Cox has served: on the Steering Committee of the Mid-Atlantic Region Archives Conference, as a member of the editorial board for *The Public Historian*, and as book review editor for *Manuscripts*. Recently, he was one of five plenary speakers at the 1992 International Council on Archives meeting in Montreal. Presently, he is Editor of the *American Archivist*.

Dr. Cox has written extensively on archival and records management professional issues, publishing articles in such journals as the *American Archivist*, *Provenance*, *Mid-Western Archivist*, *Archivaria*, *Journal for Library History*, *Libraries and Cultures*, *Journal of Library Administration*, *Public Historian*, *Library and Archival Security*, and the *ASIS Proceedings*. He was also principal author of a major evaluation of Alabama's historical records, *Assessing Alabama's Archives* (1985), and a self-study guide for New York's historical records programs, *Strengthening New York's Historical Records Programs* (1988), winner of the Arline Custer Memorial Award given by the Mid-Atlanic Region Archives Conference for publishing excellence in the field of archival administration. Dr. Cox also won the Custer Award in 1979. In 1989 the American Association for State and Local History also published his annotated bibliography on archives and manuscripts management and in 1990 he had published a book, *American Archival Analysis: The Recent Development of the Archival Profession in the United States*, on the development of archival professionalism in the United States in the 1980s; this book won the Waldo Gifford Leland Award given by the Society of American Archivists. More recently, Greenwood Press published his *Managing Institutional Archives: Foundational Principles and Practices.* His main areas of interest include the history of record keeping and the archival profession, archival education and professional development, the management of archival institutions, and archival appraisal and documentation.

He holds an MA in history from the University of Maryland and has additional training in archival administration and records management and a PhD in Library Science from the University of Pittsburgh. He is a member of the Academy of Certified Archivists and was named a Fellow of the Society of the American Archivists, that association's highest honor, in 1989.

The First Generation of Electronic Records Archivists in the United States: A Study in Professionalization

CONTENTS

∞ ALL HAWORTH BOOKS & JOURNALS
ARE PRINTED ON CERTIFIED
ACID-FREE PAPER

The First Generation of Electronic Records Archivists in the United States: A Study in Professionalization

Preface

Richard Cox's *First Generation of Electronic Records Archivists in the United States* is the first single-authored monograph in *Primary Sources & Original Works.* It expands the notion of the primacy of source material to include the curator, archivist, librarian, and interpreter as integral to the identification, preservation, and provision of access to primary sources . . . in this case, records in electronic form.

The series now has several volumes published:

Bibliographical Foundations of French Historical Studies, edited by myself;

Bibliographic Access to Medieval and Renaissance Manuscripts, guest edited by Wesley Stevens;

and

Discovery in the Archives of Spain and Portugal: Quincentenary Essays, 1492-1992, edited by myself.

Forthcoming titles will explore such issues as further discussion of methodologies and adoption of information technology for access to medieval and Renaissance manuscripts; electronic data archives and historical quantification studies; the experience of commercial documentary publishers in the archives of Europe and the former Soviet Union; sources for the study of the Pacific Rim and Oceania; the dimension of Time in historical research and interpretation of sources; and communications theory and analysis of human dialogue and texts.

[Haworth co-indexing entry note]: "Preface." McCrank, Lawrence J. Co-published simultaneously in: *Primary Sources & Original Works* (The Haworth Press, Inc.), Volume 3(3/4), 1994, pp. xiii-xiv; and: *The First Generation of Electronic Records Archivists in the United States: A Study in Professionalization*, Richard J. Cox, The Haworth Press, Inc., 1994, pp. xiii-xiv. Multiple copies of this article/chapter may be purchased from The Haworth Document Delivery Center [1-800-3-HAWORTH; 9:00 a.m. - 5:00 p.m. (EST)].

We would like to hear from authors and potential guest editors who would be interested in monographic and collected studies about newspaper collections as sources, and peculiarities of newspapers as sources; new analytical bibliographic methodologies and documentation for verification of electronic texts and images; access to archeological artifacts as original sources and in electronic facsimile; the implications of new technologies on the dissemination of source material such as holographic replication, computer simulation, and virtual reality; the applications of scanning, machine-translation, and expert systems to documentary editing; etc. And, as in the case of Cox's study, we are interested in the professional, organizational aspects of everything that makes humanistic and historical research possible, e.g., institutional profiles and histories, studies of the professions and disciplines as these relate to research based on primary sources, and methodologies related to codicology, analytical bibliography, paleography and diplomatics, numismatics and museology, archeology, and source criticism (all forms of media).

Overtures to the editor and board for consideration of inclusion in this series are relatively simple. Send a letter describing the project, its scope, intended audience, timetable for completion, and a tentative outline of a table of contents. Attach a resume of the author or proposed guest editor of a volume of collected studies, and in the latter case sketch out a preliminary list of topics and possible contributors. Allow approximately one month for a proposal review. If the proposal is supported by the editor, members of the editorial board, and sometimes external reactors, then details are negotiated, and a contract proposal is forwarded to the publisher. If a contract is offered, a timetable is established, and publication is usually about six months after submission of a completed manuscript, its electronic form, and camera-ready artwork.

So one might read Richard Cox's contribution for personal edification, but also as a model and case study to see if you, the reader, might be interested in engaging the issues of primary sources and research as a contributor to this public forum.

Lawrence J. McCrank, PhD
Editor, Primary Sources & Original Works

Foreword

This monograph is a revision of Richard Cox's doctoral dissertation which investigates a critical issue in the broader topic of primary sources and research: as more records are electronically produced and their use is primary in electronic form, how will they be conserved for future research without electronic archives or without professional archivists adequately educated and trained to preserve them, and create access to them for such research? In attacking his subject, Cox uses documents that are often overlooked as primary sources, namely job position advertisements, which are actually self-characterizations of the profession he investigates. Finally, rather than merely presenting data and their interpretation, Cox weaves his findings into essays that critically assess the archival profession, the changing nature of archival work commensurate with the changed mix of media in records production, and the response or lack thereof of archival professional education to the impact of electronic records production and documentation. He concludes with an assessment of one important recent attempt to confront the challenge of electronic records, the NAGARA Institute, before suggesting avenues for future research and curricular changes in professional education for modern archives.

I have professional and personal interest in presenting this study to the archivist and historical communities. First, as an historian and information professional who has devoted more than a decade to the education of archivists, rare book librarians, museum curators, and historians interested in research methodology and source criticism, I have long been an advocate of reform in the educational programs

[Haworth co-indexing entry note]: "Foreword." McCrank, Lawrence J. Co-published simultaneously in: *Primary Sources & Original Works* (The Haworth Press, Inc.), Volume 3(3/4), 1994, pp. xv-xix; and: *The First Generation of Electronic Records Archivists in the United States: A Study in Professionalization*, Richard J. Cox, The Haworth Press, Inc., 1994, pp. xv-xix. Multiple copies of this article/chapter may be purchased from The Haworth Document Delivery Center [1-800-3-HAWORTH; 9:00 a.m. - 5:00 p.m. (EST)].

and curricula for these professional fields. Second, I was one of the earlier pioneers who over two decades ago engaged natural language computing for creating access to archives, manuscripts, and rare book collections, and for electronic publishing of traditional finding aids and catalogs as well as innovative access tools involving new indexing strategies and the burgeoning role of terminological studies in information science. My generation of electronic text and reference tools, and working with computer centers then unaccustomed to large-scale and long-term humanities and social science computing, taught me how necessary it was to engage the field of electronic archives even to control intellectually my own research projects and to be able to have adequate information storage and retrieval technologies and documentation strategies to access my own files.

Such first-hand experience from 1972 onward was shared with my graduate students at the University of Maryland's College of Library and Information Services (1974-) where I developed the joint masters degree program between information science and historical studies (1976). We had few teaching materials and I recall working with colleagues such as David Batty, Irene Travis, Hans Wellish, and Dagobert Soergel, to interject archival methodologies into courses on cataloging, information storage and retrieval, indexing and thesaurus construction, etc., and to bring these subjects into archives education where the very idea of such inclusion was novel. Our courses were self-designed as we went along, and out of our classroom experiences came a series of essays, research articles, and monographs, which seemed never to penetrate the archives community and its narrowly focused professional reading habits. I was exposed to the problems addressed by Richard Cox over and over again in working between history and information science, with one field's lack of receptivity to the other and an incredible lack of professional ecumenism and multidisciplinary intellectual curiosity. Not only did we forge new programs, revolutionize curricula, generate instructional materials and innovative textbooks, but we applied theory to practice in testing such technologies as machine-readable cataloging to rare books and manuscripts *before* the MARC standard was promulgated. I experimented with permutation and rotational indexing, authority control, and thesauri for intellectual access to manuscripts and archives, and to generate totally electronically new forms of catalogs, several years before any other electronically published tools were available. In workshops for the Society of American Archivists (1978-79), I attempted to introduce basic indexing concepts to historians *qua* archivists who were just beginning to envision the impact of such technologies and methodologies for new possibilities in the future. Finally, I attempted to create the synergism between the archives and information science communities we were achieving in our graduate seminars by convening at UMCP the first conference (1980) where archivists and information scientists scrutinized each other's work and applied such new thinking to archives problems. It was in this incubus that the idea of a national information task force for archival information exchange was born. All of this was done in the early years studied by Richard Cox (1976-), when the first electronic archivists were re-educating and retooling themselves and were rethinking archival education so that a future generation might be trained more effectively both in managing electronic records and also in applying new information technologies to archival work.

It was difficult for me to read Richard Cox's assessment of this pioneer era and its aftermath, not only because it made me uncomfortable about my own aging and how much time had lapsed between these experimental days and now, but also because his conclusions are less than flattering of the archives profession and indicate just how slow progress has been pervasively and nationally overall. It somehow made me feel as though my efforts and those of my colleagues in the reform of archives education and our early confrontation of information technology and electronic records was somehow unsuccessful or was limited to an immediate impact and isolated development. I suppose I knew this without his assessment and ushering of data to illustrate what I experienced after leaving UMCP to enter academic library administration, in founding two university archives and attempting to rehabilitate another, when I hired archivists into the faculties of two universities and removed one from another. The lack of adequate education in modern information technologies and electronic archives was revealed repeatedly in interviews and in performance evaluations.

I understand what Cox is talking about from sobering experiences in working with institutions with considerable computing capabilities and extensive automated information systems but no integration of archival information systems in their operations or programs. I have been confronted by remarkable ignorance of academic administrators who have no concept of information resource management or regard for the empowerment offered their institutions by administrative information systems that include archives in any form, say nothing of electronic archives. And when I have preached the cause in national and international forums (1979, 1980, 1985-87, 1990, 1993), and introduced such concepts as the life cycle of records and the recycling of databases as electronic archives, such ideas were difficult to comprehend, too theoretical for application, and certainly too costly to be practical. Resistance to such innovation continues. Thus, I was confronted with Cox's study of developments from 1976 when I enthusiastically entered a new academic arena, to the early 1990s when my perspectives are now tempered by a decade of senior administration in higher education, that confirmed my worst suspicions and created in me both the feelings of saddening *déjà vue* and an unsettling *angst*.

More positively and personally, however, I take pleasure in presenting this study by a longtime associate, friend and colleague, whose cordial advice, critical insights, and biting wry humor I have learned to value over the years. I met Richard in 1974 when he was curator of manuscripts at the Maryland Historical Society. When I coordinated the History-Information and Library Science program at the University of Maryland, I recall urging him into doctoral studies in the information field rather than traditional history. So it was ironic and with some personal satisfaction that I found myself editing his doctoral dissertation for publication some years later. Of course, in the meantime I have continued to be edified by him during long telephone conversations and lunches together at numerous conferences, and reading his continuing track of valuable contributions to archival literature.

Our mutual mentoring has resulted in cross stimulation more than either of us probably realizes. When I approached Richard to work with me in establishing a new cross-disciplinary forum, *Primary Sources & Original Works*, we discussed many aspects about publishing and reading circuits, improvements needed in professional literatures, and the idea of comparative reviewing of multiple titles in a series (like the RAMP studies) and related titles in a subject area or developmental trends. Since then we have had to laugh together about our roles as editors, e.g., his contributions as editor of *The American Archivist* and as a member of the *PSOW* Board of Editors. And we had to keep friendship subservient to professionalism as coincidentally we found ourselves criticizing and editing each other's work at the same time, i.e., my editing this monograph while he was editing a contribution of mine to *The American Archivist*. We each survived both of our red pens with egos, professional good will, and humor intact!

It is, therefore, with mixed personal feelings and professional perspectives that I offer to you, the readers, this study of electronic archives, professionalization, and educational reform. I am pleased to include this title in *Primary Sources & Original Works* and provide such a substantial contribution to the current debate from a respected archivist and educator, friend and colleague.

Lawrence J. McCrank
Editor, Primary Sources

Introduction: Archival Professionalization in the United States and This Study; Personal Notes and Acknowledgements

A PERSONAL VIEW OF A PROFESSIONAL RESEARCH AGENDA

In the early 1970s, not long after I started my career as an archivist, I became interested in the origins, development, and nature of the American archival profession which I have written about elsewhere (Cox, 1990c, pp. vii-xv). This interest has been both part of my own professional odyssey and an element of my commitment to the discipline. I turned to this topic in an effort to determine who I was as a professional, a process necessary for many who came into the archival community when I did.[1]

This present work is a continuation of a series of such studies that I have embarked upon, examining the development of archival institutions, the formation and continued progress of the archival profession, and an analysis of the needs of the archival community. As a personal research agendum, it was largely formed in my own mind twenty years ago as I reached to determine my own professional self-identity. It will likely occupy much of my next two decades.

My first major work was the preparation of a collection of essays on the recent development of the American archival profession in

---

[Haworth co-indexing entry note]: "Introduction." Cox, Richard J. Co-published simultaneously in: *Primary Sources & Original Works* (The Haworth Press, Inc.), Volume 3(3/4), 1994, pp. 1-21; and: *The First Generation of Electronic Records Archivists in the United States: A Study in Professionalization,* Richard J. Cox, The Haworth Press, Inc., 1994, pp. 1-21. Multiple copies of this article/chapter may be purchased from The Haworth Document Delivery Center [1-800-3-HAWORTH; 9:00 a.m. - 5:00 p.m. (EST)].

the past two decades, bringing together many essays written in the decade before (Cox, 1990c). This was followed by an extended essay on the management of institutional archives (Cox, 1992b), both as a basic primer and an argument for a renewed emphasis on the fostering of such programs *rather* than the continuing focus on *collecting*. One purpose of this latter volume was to present my view that while there is a body of timeless principles and methods, there are also many aspects of archival science that are constantly being reformulated, reconsidered, rejected, revised, and, even, rediscovered.

Two other major works are also being completed that explore related themes in the professionalization of archivists in America and which have some bearing on this current volume. Another extended essay is being finished on the development of an archival community in one state, Maryland, and yet another on the concept and process of documenting localities, both very different in substance but related in purpose and by distinct autobiographical features as far as my own career is concerned.

The Maryland study considers the formation of archival institutions over a three century period and tries to develop a model of development for such programs that can be used for the writing of institutional history in this profession. It also pulls together some earlier research and writing from the 1970s, updated to reflect my current thinking, which began to emerge as I first became interested in the historical foundations of archival science and its practice. This is also a case study in the *value* of American archival history which I have written about earlier (Cox, 1990c, chapter eight). Since I am now more convinced than ever that our archival programs are, in some sense, trapped by historical traditions and other circumstances which limit their ability to handle the new challenges of historical records in electronic form, this kind of historical analysis needs to be undertaken to gain a greater understanding of the problems archivists have created for themselves that serve as barriers to working effectively with electronic records. In one sense, then, this is a study to refute the notion of progress in my other earlier research and writing which has been criticized sometimes (see, for example, Gilliland-Swetland, 1991).

The volume on the documentation of localities is an extension of my own continued work on archival appraisal, building on the documentation strategy concept introduced a decade ago, but also trying to relate the need to develop institutional archives with the seemingly competing need to document society and its various aspects. For a considerable period the archival community has seen the public archives and historical manuscripts traditions as somehow competing, or even contrary efforts (Berner, 1983), but I am convinced that the continuing professionalization of the field is bringing us to see how the various elements fit together. While there are purists who argue that there is a distinct archival science that separates us from the work of historical manuscript curators (see, for example, Eastwood, 1993), archivists in the United States continue to be pragmatic, if often unsystematic, in their approaches. While I, too, believe in an archival science, I also think this science encompasses many of the aspects of what Europeans have defined to be the work of "documentalists," those concerned with the broader goals of documenting society. My own work on documenting localities and teaching archival appraisal is intended to contribute to this sort of approach.

Despite this, I also believe that American archivists have failed to capitalize on the work of other disciplines, and this is reflected in their struggles to cope with the impact of electronic information technology. Lawrence McCrank's series of essays (1979, 1981, and 1985) when he was an archival educator argued in a similar fashion, but they have generally been overlooked by the American archival profession, at least as regards any practical implementation. I hope my study demonstrates some of these problems, although I think the matter of the interdisciplinarity of archival science is a topic deserving another kind of analysis.[2]

Finally, I am also engaged in new research, assisted by a major grant from the National Historical Publications and Records Commission (NHPRC), on recordkeeping requirements and electronic information systems. The primary purpose of this project is to define and then test the possibility of integrating appropriate recordkeeping functions into software design in a variety of organizational types, taking into consideration such variables as the organization's responsibilities, interests, and corporate culture; the regulatory requirements that govern or affect the organization; and the technical capabilities of the software being examined. The impetus for this project emerged from the National Historical and Publications Commission's leadership (1991) in defining a research agenda for electronic records in the first few years of the 1990s. This project, and the definition of a research agenda, represent a severe break with what has occurred up to this point and what is described in this study. Terry Cook's description (1991-92) of a "second generation" of electronic records archivists also reflects this as well and this is the reason for the title of this study. What is described in the following study is largely an analysis of false starts, wrong approaches, experimentation, poor professional priorities, inadequate leadership, and other problems that have prevented American archivists from embarking on more meaningful research and application to preserve records with archival value in electronic form.[3]

THE IMMEDIATE AIMS OF THIS CURRENT STUDY

This work on electronic records management in North America has several essential aims. It is, first and foremost, part of my continuing study on the professionalization of North American archivists, a continuing effort which gets more complex, as my foregoing commentary conveys. By examining one portion of the archival community and a segment of its work, electronic records archivists and the management of these records, this present study is intended to demonstrate how the professionalization process is still malformed in many aspects. The study also tries to correct one omission (there are others, of course), evident in my *American Archival Analysis* (Cox, 1990c). In this volume I did not consider directly any of the efforts by American archivists to deal with the increasing impact of the computer in society and on their own work and institutions; this omission was somewhat intentional, because I viewed *American Archival Analysis* as laying a foundation for inspecting the condition of the archival profession (the origins of that volume came in my work in 1985-86, partly supported by a fellowship at the Bentley Historical Library, University of Michigan, to absorb the sociological and historical research on the nature of disciplines as a means of evaluating the state of the American archival profession).

This present research is also a mark of my own transition as a professional archival practitioner and, now, archival educator. Through the 1980s I became increasingly aware of the archival community's work with electronic records and harnessing the use of computers to manage their own activities and their holdings. Like most archivists, my initial exposure to this came through the practical efforts to administer archival description in an automated process which would strengthen its management, standardization, and utility to researchers (a topic deserving of a full study as well). When I assumed the role of an archival educator in 1988, I became more aware of my own need to re-tool for reconsidering how to introduce students to the precepts of archival science and its relevant applications to the vast constellation of the uses of information and evidence, and to the preservation of historical records. When I arrived at the University of Pittsburgh, I found that I had become involved in an effort by state government archivists themselves to figure out how to cope with the growing government information policy practices and increasing use of electronic information technology. (Representatives of the National Association of Government Archives and Records Administrators had approached my school to serve as a host for an institute on electronic information technology and information policy in government.)

The advanced institute, described in more detail in chapter five of this study, provided both a personal opportunity and was the immediate genesis of this study, building on my own earlier work on the changing nature of the archival profession. As I sat through four years of this institute, I became more convinced of some serious weaknesses in the infrastructure of the archival profession, weaknesses which severely limited the profession from resolving many of the problems it knew must be faced as a result of the continuing transition from a print to an electronic culture.

This study on electronic records management is also intended to correct the still prevailing notion that the archival practitioner is, and ought to be, a generalist. As an educator, this is precisely how I am viewed by the archival profession, although my library and information science colleagues see me as a specialist without any hesitancy on their part. If nothing else, I have become convinced about several matters. A fundamental aspect of the professionalization of the archival discipline is its becoming a community of *specialized* professionals. While American archivists seem to view the primary measure of graduate education programs as the hiring of a single qualified archival educator, it is more than obvious to the small group of such educators that they cannot teach everything that their students need to know. I believe this present study reflects this challenge. While the worldwide archival profession has clearly identified the notion that archival science is based both on core knowledge and interdisciplinary knowledge, its institutions and individual practitioners operate in a way that conveys a much more limited scope to their work. How else could it be that both Luciana Duranti (1993) and John Roberts (1987 and 1990) seem to co-exist in the same profession? This study is offered in the hope that it will assist the archival profession in the United States to resolve what I see as some of its most critical weaknesses in education, perspective, and organization.

I have explored a few of these themes in more detail below in this preface as a way of introducing this work and enunciating its own limitations. This is not intended to defend this work against its critics before it is even distributed to or read by them, but I hope it will assist readers to understand what I have endeavored to accomplish in the volume. And, I should note at the outset, that I consider this a *preliminary* analysis of the development of American archival approaches to electronic records management. The lack of prior investigation on related issues requires this to be more an exploratory than definitive study.

THE PROFESSIONALIZATION OF ARCHIVISTS IN THE UNITED STATES: REVISITING AN OLD THEME

The purpose of this study is to address issues of professionalization by re-examining two major aspects of the archival community: its institutional forms and structures (as specifically revealed by position descriptions and advertisements–chapters two and three), and the basic educational foundations (graduate and continuing education–chapters four and five) that are important aspects of any profession (see Table One).[4]

The archival community is considered to be a part of the modern information professions, even though its origins and development might give it some atypical characteristics. For example, the archival community has strong roots in *both* academic history and library and information science. Not only has this given the archival profession a schizophrenic identity, but these fields have traditionally held very different views about the notion of professions. Academic historians have tended to be more skeptical about credentials, standards, accreditation, and other common aspects of professionalism. Librarians have been among the strongest advocates of such elements.

Looking at these two elements is essentially a process of investigating the opposite ends of a professional spectrum. The archival repository–and its descriptions of positions and the way it recruits prospective archivists–represents the ultimate *present* manifestation of the nature, health, values, and concerns of the profession. The archival institution, like any institution affected by tradition and its cultural and other contexts, is perhaps the last aspect of a profession to reflect change. Cultural forms can remain, indeed, long after their reason for existence passes.[5] Since faculty and academic researchers are often forces for change and innovation, the education of archivists is a likely predictor of where the profession is heading and how it is equipping its future practitioners. In any applied profession such as archival administration, there is some continuing debate and tension between academic educators who are often portrayed as tending to be more theoretical, speculative, and forward-looking in orientation, and professional practitioners who are sometimes typecast as being concerned only with immediate application and daily management matters (Richardson and Hernon, 1981; White and Paris, 1985). While this relationship is cast here in overly simplistic terms, it is nevertheless true that a fundamental re-orientation in the education of archivists will help to determine the profession's development and whether, in fact, the viability of the profession will be ensured or even lost.[6] This study will examine some of the essential aspects of archival institutions and education in the increasingly information technology-oriented society of the

TABLE 1. Characteristics of a Profession Compared to Its Education and Institutions

Characteristic	*Education*	*Institutions and Positions*
Specialized Knowledge or Systematic Theory	Distinctive Graduate Program and Curriculum; Thesis or Other Research Requirement; Preappointment Education, Well-Defined Continuing Education	Distinctive Position Descriptions; Stringent Entry and Other Level Requirements; Discernible Entry, Middle, and Upper Level and Specialized Positions; Institutional Support for Research; Concern for Principles and Theoretical Applications
Community Sanction	Accredited Graduate Education Programs; Regular Graduate Faculty Specialists; Availability of Grant Funding for Research	Accredited Institutions; Support for Hiring of Certified Practitioners; Technical Standards
Professional Cohesion or Organization	Presence and Influence of Educators in Professional Associations; Guidelines for Graduate Programs Sanctioned by Associations; Support for Continuing Education	Behavioral Standards or Guidelines; Certified Practitioners; Accreditation Program
Professional Culture	Sufficient Profile to Attract Prospective Employees as Students; Agreed-Upon Professional Terminology	Concern for and Distinction Between Professional and Institutional Concerns; Professional Memberships and Activities
Institutionalized Altruism	Specific Required Qualifications for Educators; Concern for Quality Manifested in Interest in Accreditation of Education Programs	Specific Guidelines for Performance Evaluations Based Upon Professional Standards and Principles; Interest in Adoptio n and Incorporation of Professional Standards and Principles; Self-Study and Planning Emphasis; Support of Individual Certification and Institutional Accreditation

late twentieth century in an effort to suggest where the archival profession may be heading and ways for this profession to strengthen itself for a surely more complex twenty-first century. The ability to preserve recorded information to understand the past and the present as an important mission in any society, is taken as a given in this study.

THE COMPUTER, ARCHIVAL WORK, AND TECHNOLOGICAL DETERMINISM

In my comments thus far, I have noted that this study is part of my larger body of work on the fundamental nature of archival work. As is indicated in the first chapter, archivists have debated for decades the impact of information technology on archival principles and practice, and this debate has generated considerable discussion that seems intent on dredging up ancient arguments on technological determinism and countervailing viewpoints.

Hopefully, readers will not perceive this study to be yet another salvo in an endless debate or the handiwork of a technological determinist. I believe the study is eminently consistent with the fundamental precepts of archival science. The mission of the archival profession is to identify, preserve, and make available records of continuing or enduring value. The basic functions are (in the right-hand column) as follows:

Mission:	*Function:*
identify	appraisal
preserve	preservation management and conservation
make available	arrangement, description, reference, public programs and outreach.

All of these functions require the ability to understand the nature of the documentation, the contexts of its creation, and the procedures needed to maintain the record in a usable form. There are, of course, important differences between a traditional eye-readable record on paper and a machine-readable record in digital form, and that is the crux of the need for archivists to understand the nature of the electronic information technology. On the other hand, it is imperative that archivists know their own concepts so that they may be applied, where appropriate, to the management of electronic information that possesses continuing value.

Let me re-emphasize that this study is not intended to suggest that everything will change because of new technology. This is not only a deterministic view, but an ahistorical one inappropriate for a study that endeavors to provide the historical skeleton of a critical period of activity (1960-1990) in the American archival profession. There is a vast literature that baldly states that technology drives or leads society, ignoring the many other cultural, economic, political, and social elements that always have some impact on the manner in which technology is used and incorporated into its milieu. I do not accept that at all, and I constantly adhere to long-term historical trends and other societal events and characteristics that mitigate the impact of technology, much in the manner described by Arnold Pacey (1983) and adhered to in the writings of such electronic records archivists as Margaret Hedstrom (1991a).

How should information technology be viewed by archivists, who are, after all, concerned with records and their informational content? In this study, it is assumed that archivists must be concerned with the technology as it affects records creation; a portion of electronic records can always be identified as having at least continuing value to their institutional creator and to society in general. This is certainly the case because a larger portion of formerly paper-based records is being created in electronic form.[7] Frank Webster and Kevin Robins, in an intriguing analysis of the impact of technology on recent society, provided a useful definition of information technology that can be used as a starting point for this study:

> Information technology . . . is a neologism . . . coined to describe a tendency for computing and telecommunications to integrate and converge. It is a generic term which encompasses word processors, office equipment, electronic mail, cable television, videotext, robotics, television games, computer networks, and satellite communications. Its growth is being promoted by the rapid rise of microelectronics, which is

> the source of dramatically cheapened computing capacity that is the enabling technology behind recent developments. (Webster and Robins, 1986, p. 10)

While the focus of this study is on the modern (i.e., the past half-century) information technology, built on a foundation of computing and telecommunications hardware and software, used by individuals and in offices that affect record-keeping, it is also important to remember that other forms of technology created for the management of information have long had an impact on the institutional office and record-keeping.

The reason for such a focus is primarily twofold. First, since archivists are primarily interested in transactional records that capture an organization's activity and provide ample evidence and information about its existence and work, all records generated in the office place must be scrutinized (in some manner) by the archivist and records manager. Second, the impact of electronic information technology poses the most serious challenges to the mission and work of the archivist and records manager. Such electronic office information systems are increasingly decentralized, confronting the archivist and records manager with the specter of having to consider such records long after the system has been designed and when information and evidence has been lost. A recent meeting at the Brookings Institution concluded that not only a policy framework, but an implementation framework, is needed (Bearman, 1990c).

This can be seen historically. The advent of the manual typewriter in the late nineteenth century (to name only one form of earlier information technology) was a major contributor to the feminization of the office work place and was also utilized by pioneer scientific managers to standardize and make more efficient office work (Schlereth, 1989). It is also important to consider that "modern information technology" brings into play not only technology but the concept of "modern." One American historian has seen modernization as "patterns of thought, behavior, and organization" (R. Brown, 1976, p. 9) where the use and view of technology is an inherent aspect of the modern age, but where technology does not necessarily drive such a society. "Dynamism" is a major characteristic, where "change, in all spheres of life, is a characteristic feature of the modern society, and from this reality flow many of its distinctive elements" (Brown, 1976, p. 12). In effect, the modern archivist is trying to adapt the archival mission in the midst of such dynamism, perhaps best reflected by the efforts to contend with the computer and its products. Finally, it is necessary to keep in mind that writing is at the heart of institutional communication and record keeping and, hence, the continuing focus of the archivist/records manager. All writing is a technological exercise, although the kinds of technology supporting it (from pencil to computer) have undergone considerable change and brought fundamentally different implications. Jay David Bolter has stated that

> ancient and modern writing is a technology . . . It is a method for arranging verbal thoughts in a visual space . . . Writing with quill and parchment is a different skill from writing with a printing press, which in turn differs from writing with a computer. However, all writing demands method, the intention of the writer to arrange ideas systematically in a space for later examination by a reader. (Bolter, 1991, p. 35)

The archivist, concerned with the identification and preservation of records that possess continuing or enduring value, has, as a result of this mission, long had an interest in information technology, or at least so it seems. This general interest is seen in the writings of a relatively small cadre of archivists who have been interested in electronic information technology. Margaret Hedstrom, as an example of one of the recent leaders in examining and managing electronic information technology from the archival point-of-view, has used a definition of this technology as being the "machines, processes and know-how used to create, store, manipulate, disseminate, and retrieve information," sketching a definition that ranges from pens to computers and through a wide range of processes from the most routine to the most exotic (Hedstrom, 1991b, p. 339). For Hedstrom, and other archivists like her, it is the impact of this technology on the office and, more broadly, the organization, that is of fundamental interest, for it is in these places that the archival record is formed and derives its importance. Another archivist, Richard Kesner, wrote that "EDP and telecommunications products are altering the way people create, distribute, file, and retrieve information," urging archivists to understand better these changes and to adapt their institutional activities to cope with them (Kesner, 1984-85, pp. 163, 165). It is these places (the offices where the technology is most prevalent) that the archivist must ultimately reach in influence to ensure that the archival record is identified and preserved.

Major foci of this study are, then, the institutional records creator, that creator's use of technology to originate records, and the archivist's ability to work with these creators and electronic records. This study's emphasis is on transactional records formed in the normal course of an organization's operation and not library materials (although electronic publishing has brought many of the same problems to librarians and libraries that other technologies have brought to institutions and their archivists) (Gurnsey, 1985; Bolter, 1991). This study assumes that if we were in a true Information Age, then this era itself would have gone through some substantive and significant changes in its own right. The world, as perceived by some, has seen a variety of "information ages" concentrated around spoken language, writing, paper production, and telecommunications. But the current Information Age has also brought the decentralization of computer intelligence and networking, much lower costs, intelligent products and systems, and information deemed as a strategic asset or resource. These changes have presented a variety of new challenges, primarily because of the advent of the computer and transformations to the computer's capabilities; these challenges are much different from ones earlier archivists faced. In the early 1980s, for instance, one observer stated that "until the 1970s, the relationship between the user and the computer was so remote that it could be compared more to correspondence by letter than to a conversation. Today, users and computers usually interact directly, in a similar fashion to a conversation" (Fischer, 1984, p. 57).

The question of adequate preparation of the archival repository to manage such records has to do with such concerns as the knowledge of archivists, the educational preparation of the archivists, the structure and administrative placement of the repositories, and the resources and facilities of the repositories to handle and make available such records. This study is examining, obviously, two of these major aspects.

THE FUTURE OF SOCIETY, TECHNOLOGY, INSTITUTIONS, AND ARCHIVISTS

In my book on institutional archives (Cox, 1992b, Chapter 8) included a chapter entitled "The Changing Contexts of Institutional Archives: Some Speculations" in which I presented the case that the archival profession is changing. There I also noted that institutions are changing as is their context, such as represented by information technology. I stated the following:

> For the institutional archivist, it is, in some ways, merely an extension from managing earlier technology changes, such as the typewriter or the electrostatic photocopier, and their shaping of the institutional record. Nevertheless, the modern computer has speeded up the rate of change, altered expectations for the arrangement of records and information, and even transformed certain fundamental concepts of information. Modern information technology suggests the need for a certain rethinking of the nature and roles of the institutional archives and its staffing that should be carefully considered by any individual occupying the archivist's position. (p. 228)

Following this statement, I then briefly speculated on the implications of such change for the archivist.

It is always difficult, especially for archivists, it seems, to project very far in the future. Still, the prospects of technological change promise great changes for information repositories such as archives and libraries. Eldred Smith, a former academic librarian, has noted that (1990, p.35): "because electronic communication of text is becoming so easy, it is no longer necessary to use traditional channels for the distribution of scholarly information. Every scholar can, in effect, broadcast findings as he or she wishes. This threatens to overwhelm the procedures established over several centuries to control and validate scholarly communication" (see also Michelson and Rothenberg, 1992). Or, as another commentator has suggested, "in Western economies, the telephone may be the most common method of *transmitting* information . . . But the computer, now a half-century old, has revolutionalized methods for *accumulating*, *processing*, and *distributing* information" (Jacobsen, 1989, p. 10). Tom Forester, in his excellent one volume description of the "high-technology society," (1988, pp. 1-2) has noted that there are "three broad economic, technological and political trends [that] provide the main driving forces behind the high-tech revolution": rapidly declining computing costs, the "convergence of voice, image and data" systems, and immense "entrepreneurial and corporate activity." The nature of information technology changes, then, possesses great potential for transforming what archivists do and need to know (see, for example, Durrance, 1989).

Technology is contributing, in unique and novel ways, to new concepts of information and records which seem to challenge the archivist's (and others') efforts to identify and preserve the portion of these records that possesses continuing or enduring value. We know that systems, such as hypermedia, are transforming the notion of the document; we possess documents written jointly by thousands of people or that are frequently revised and updated with text, graphics, and images. While the archivist's traditional definition of a record or document as "recorded information regardless of medium or characteristics" (Evans, 1974, p. 421) seems to have some usefulness in this context, it is also apparent that a full understanding of the complexities of the electronic document was absent when this definition was prepared.

The changing notion of the document is reflective of how technology is also fundamentally transforming the ways that organizations work. Some of this is directly tied to the basic nature and perceived values of documents and information. Organizations become, for example, "information refineries." This refinery is an "electronic, computer-based process that takes undifferentiated volumes of raw information . . . converts them into electronic form, extracts the content units and recombines them into a new form that can be distributed in a variety of ways" (Cloppinger and Konsynski, 1989, p. 74). This notion of refineries is not inconsistent with another's idea that "as electronic databases become more sophisticated, they resemble information 'pools' rather than discrete records" (U. S. Congress, Office of Technology Assessment, 1988, p. 207). While information refineries and pools are images that could be applied to non-automated organizations, it nevertheless appears that the computerized environments show more evidence of such characterizations. Modern information technology, most recently in the form of office automation, has helped to stimulate the decentralization of the work place, the creation of satellite offices, increased specialization, and a greater reliance on technical consultants (Diebold, Duffy, and Levy, 1987; Chandler, 1977; and Yates, 1989). Information technology is also prompting the development of flatter (horizontal rather than hierarchical information and decision flows) organizations, as seen from the perspective of management, because of the increased access to information by upper and middle level managers. Managers routinely use electronic mail and other employees have more efficient access to institutional information stores (Radding, 1989).

While some of these comments are clearly predictions of *future* directions, it is important for archivists to focus on the here and now in meaningful ways. The research agenda published by the National Historical Publications and Records Commission (NHPRC) reflected this concern in his articulation of ten priorities for research. The ninth question, after more practical and immediate items on recordkeeping functions, technological implications for electronic capture of archival records, the use of data dictionaries, and so forth, was "What barriers have prevented archivists from developing and implementing archival electronic records programs?" (NHPRC, 1991, pp. 20-21). This is essentially the topic of this current study, but it is clearly a more applied historical analysis that seeks to understand what has prevented archivists from advancing much more than they have in their work with electronic records. This is the kind of analysis needed to be undertaken as a way of helping the profession to cope in the present and future with the continuing dramatic shifts in information technology.

This study is also intended to emphasize the need for archivists, as professionals and people, to make changes in attitudes and behaviors. The stress on institutions and educational venues is seen, hopefully, as a reflection of individual professionals and a community of professionals. Economist Robert Reich's study (1992) on the change to multi-national corporations and international economies expressed this view quite well:

> In the high-value enterprise, only one asset grows more valuable as it is used: the problem-solving, -identifying, and brokering skills of key people. Unlike machinery that gradually wears out, raw materials that become depleted, patents and copyrights that grow obsolete, and trademarks that lose their ability to comfort, the skills and insights that come from discovering new linkages between technologies and needs actually increase with practice. (p. 108)

While it is evident that there are some individuals in the American (United States) archival community who reflect this–David Bearman, Thomas Brown, Margaret Hedstrom and her staff, Richard Kesner, Avra Michelson, and Lisa Weber, to name a few–the lack of strong educational programs and electronic records operations in archives have minimized the opportunity to provide very many any chance to "practice" or to attract the "key" people the profession needs. If only five state government archives advertised for one electronic records archivist each, these institutions would be hard-pressed to find qualified applicants. And, finding aspects about which the electronic records archivists themselves agree, can sometimes still be a challenge.

Modern information technology then brings to the archivist a host of challenging and interesting questions and implications. How should the archivist deal with what seems to be a new emerging concept of record and information? How do organizations function in the modern information age and how should archivists work within these environments? How does the archivist work in what still can be termed a transition period from the paper to electronic information age? How can the archivist manage effectively great quantities of historical and evidential information in both electronic and paper forms? Are the records problems generated by computers managed by archivists similar to the more traditional paper-based systems? It seems, however, that American archivists have become transfixed by concepts and theories rather than the consideration of the practical management of the information technology. The lack of experience, coupled with the lack of applied research and a lack of experience with information technologists and policy-makers, has weakened the profession's ability to work with electronic records.

CONCLUSION AND ACKNOWLEDGEMENTS

A work like this brings with it many obligations. I am making no exceptions in making acknowledgments, including the caveat that none of the people mentioned here share any of the blame for my mistakes or other miscues in this study.

The origins of this work were as a dissertation, and I must mention first the individuals I forced to suffer with me in this endeavor. Professor R. Stephen Almagno at the University of Pittsburgh School of Library and Information Science guided me from course work through the final dissertation; he was available for good advice and gentle reminders, usually over relaxing lunches, when it was time for me to move on to the next stage. Professor Ellen Detlefsen and Dean Toni Carbo Bearman also played useful roles by asking hard questions and making suggestions for revisions in my interpretation and writing. Frank Zabrosky of the Archives of Industrial Society at the University of Pittsburgh pushed for the practical implications of my study for the working archivist. Last, but not least, Dr. James M. O'Toole of the Department of History at the University of Massachusetts at Boston brought his deep knowledge of archival theory and practice and his sharp editorial eye to my study and made it much better. Jim's sense of humor was always timed to get me to focus on the chase for finishing the degree–letters wondering if this week I had become a Marxist, another speculating on whether I had become a technological determinist, and, one in French after a week-long vacation in Paris, in the middle of the dissertation writing. He will still have questions to which he wants better, or different, answers, but he at least prodded me to ask some of the right questions.

Over the past decade, especially in the past five years, I have accumulated numerous intellectual debts regarding the archival management of electronic records. My discussions with David Bearman and his writings on the topic have always been helpful, even though I have different perspectives on these issues. Likewise,

I have had many discussions with Luciana Duranti, Margaret Hedstrom, John McDonald, Avra Michelson, Fred Stielow, Lee Stout, and Lisa Weber about this issue, and I have always been edified by their viewpoints and their experience. Others have influenced me more through their writings. Terry Cook's essays have always helped me, and I wish I had more opportunity to relate to him in person; his essays, primarily in *Archivaria*, on archival theory and practice are among the most thoughtful and enlightening that any North American archivist has produced in the past two decades. Charles Dollar's work was also available to me through his publications, and I find them extremely useful–especially as benchmarks for where the archival profession is at any given point. Other prolific authors, such as F. Gerald Ham and Hugh Taylor, have had an influence on me as well. Last, but not least, I am grateful to Lawrence McCrank, his essays on a wide range of theoretical and practical issues in the archival discipline, and his comments to guide my revision of this study for publication; his perspective is unique and useful, and he has often been somewhat ahead of many of us in his ideas and practices.

There are numerous others who could be mentioned as well. For all the archivists who have first-hand experience in trying to manage electronic records, and who wrote on the topic or made presentations at professional conferences, or who talked with me about what they do or wish they could do, I express gratitude. You are among a group of hardy pioneers, and we have always needed more of you. Then, there are those seeking answers to electronic records management. From 1989 through 1992 I shared a classroom with groups of government archivists and records administrators to discuss, argue, plan, and contemplate the challenges of electronic records for their institutions and the archival profession. At the end, I think we ended in very different places–I saw a failure to build an adequate professional superstructure and to be bolder and more innovative in program design and implementation, and they saw progress and movement towards building better approaches to the management of electronic records. While I hope they are right, I do not think that is the case. Only time will tell, but in the short run I can at least thank them for providing a forum in which I was able to reflect on the study that is presented in the remainder of this publication.

ENDNOTES

1. While there is no formal study of this, what I am referring to is the entrance into the American archival profession from the mid-1960s through the 1970s of many individuals with education in history or related disciplines and, at best, a course or two in archival science. Many of these individuals discovered the archival community as an alternative means of employment or fell into it by chance. This trend probably had a significant impact on archivists' ability to work with electronic records; the low status of disciplinary education weakened a knowledge of archival science and contributed to a confusion of professional self-awareness.

2. In fact, I am planning to prepare a volume of essays which explores this theme, considering the relationship of history, library and information science, material culture studies, management, preservation, and other areas of knowledge or formalized disciplines to the core of archival science. The current proposal to the Society of American Archivists for a Masters of Archival Studies degree builds on such a notion (Society of American Archivists, 1993), but it is an idea that has not been practiced by the archival community, as reflected in its literature with narrow citations to its own professional literature and the holding of professional meetings that attract only mainstream archivists. The writings of individuals such as Michael Buckland, Terry Cook, and Lawrence J. McCrank demonstrate the need to push forward the concept of interdisciplinarity.

3. One exception, approaching this problem from somewhat the opposite direction, is the work of Anne Kenney and her associates at Cornell University in digitizing images of traditional paper-based records for preservation purposes. This has led to considerations of the capture of provenancial information and other such basic archival concerns, much the same issues as being discussed by electronic records archivists (refer to Kenney and Personius, 1992).

4. The elements described in Table 1 for discussion purposes are drawn from my previous work on the sociology of professions and its value for the archival community (see Cox, 1990, chapter two, and Cox, 1990d).

5. To borrow an example of this from the archival field itself, one could consider the importance and use of seals on documents. In the early medieval period, when illiteracy was high, seals were probably used as symbols of authority or as substitutes for signatures. Later, seals came to be seen as the main method of authenticating a document, especially in a time when the maintenance of government and legal records was more haphazard. More recently, seals have probably returned to their largely symbolic importance, since the official record generally is that maintained by the government or other official body. The same may be true for institutions. In colonial America, for example, the centrality of the county courthouse (located in the middle of the county seat with a green in front) had much to do with the manner in which official decrees were issued and the economic and social life of the community functioned. The construction today of the county courthouse would probably follow the same pattern for symbolic reasons. What are the implications of this for libraries and archives? Will these institutions continue to remain in the cultural forms they have long retained or will the changing patterns of information creation, need, and use alter them?

6. Abbott (1988) provides a rich and complex analysis of the nature of professions and provides the appropriate intellectual framework for examining the respective places of education and employers of professionals in any discipline. Viewing professions as an ecological system, Abbott sees a profession's base of theoretical and abstract knowledge (and its perpetuation through university programs and researchers) as very fundamental to a profession's ability to remain viable.

7. In this study I have isolated my attention to electronic records produced in the course of an organization's or individual's business or transaction, defining, as was done in the initial chapter of this study, an archival record as a transactional record. Many manuscript collections, acquired by historical societies and other collecting repositories, are themselves organizational or personal archives consisting of transactional documents. I have not considered either an archival repository's use of automation to manage its holdings or the increasing use by researchers of automation to analyze texts and apply new research techniques. Both have, of course, numerous additional implications for the archival profession, its theory and techniques, and its repositories.

Chapter One

Prolegomenon

THE CHALLENGE OF ELECTRONIC RECORDS

Recently, within the space of a few weeks, two important essays appeared which demarcated (or at least seemed to do so) the shift of generations of archivists involved with machine-readable (as they used to be called) or electronic (as they are now more commonly referred to) records.[1] Terry Cook (1991-92, p. 203), reviewed in his essay, eight publications from 1990-91 which revealed according to him, the "arrival of the second generation of electronic records archives." Cook sees the first generation as having been generally isolated from the mainstream archival profession, and, as a result, in need of assistance from other fields which had experience with electronic records. Moreover, the first generation archivists were primarily involved with electronic datafiles of aggregate statistics. But, Cook argues, this array of new reports and studies reveals more integration of electronic records into the archival profession and its institutions as well as reflecting archivists' grappling with the more sophisticated electronic hardware and software. For Cook, his reading of these recent publications causes him to write optimistically that archivists are in an excellent position to work, both theoretically and practically, with electronic records: "Facing such a banquet with eight courses [the reports and studies he reviews] on the table, there is no excuse for any archivist to hesitate biting into this electronic food" (T. Cook, 1991-92, p. 215).

[Haworth co-indexing entry note]: "Prolegomenon." Cox, Richard J. Co-published simultaneously in: *Primary Sources & Original Works* (The Haworth Press, Inc.), Volume 3(3/4), 1994, pp. 23-51; and: *The First Generation of Electronic Records Archivists in the United States: A Study in Professionalization,* Richard J. Cox, The Haworth Press, Inc., 1994, pp. 23-51. Multiple copies of this article/chapter may be purchased from The Haworth Document Delivery Center [1-800-3-HAWORTH; 9:00 a.m. - 5:00 p.m. (EST)].

The other essay is Margaret Hedstrom's statement (1991a) of an archival research agenda for electronic records, originally presented at a 1991 conference on this theme. Hedstrom's interesting title, (1991a, p. 335), "Understanding Electronic Incunabula," is a play on her perception that "electronic records are in their infancy," as is the archival profession's work with and management of such records. The tone of Hedstrom's essay is significantly different from that of Cook's. She bluntly states that despite three decades of concern for such records, "archivists have made little progress toward developing specialized programs for electronic records or integrating them into core functions" (Hedstrom, 1991a, p. 336). Hedstrom then articulates her agenda for research on electronic records, suggesting that archivists still have many questions to answer about how to deal with electronic information technologies and their products. While it could be argued that virtually any aspect of archival administration lacks sufficient research, it is particularly disturbing here because of the prevalence of the technology and its influence on the way that organizations and society function. Implicit in such calls for research is a sense that if archivists fail to come to terms with this technology, then they fail to come to terms with their relevance to society. Nevertheless, the mere fact that archivists are now defining a research agenda for electronic records management can be considered additional evidence for a shift to a new generation of archivists and programs.

There are, of course, larger issues at play in the world of archives and electronic records. Archivists in the United States have been engaged since the mid-1960s, in the challenge of managing records created by electronic information systems. Despite three decades of activity, few archival institutions have developed programs to administer and preserve these special records. This study is an effort to understand why American archivists seem to have fared so poorly by addressing the primary research question, *Is the archival profession prepared to carry out its mission in the modern electronic information technology environment?*

This study concludes that the archival profession in the United States has not done well in structuring itself to manage electronic records. Five aspects of this American professional community suggest this conclusion. First, the professional literature seems to lack consensus on the nature of the impact of electronic records on archival theory and practice and how such records should be administered. Second, state government archives' position descriptions do not generally reflect knowledge and skill requirements needed for the management of electronic records. Third, there were virtually no job advertisements from 1976 through 1990 for electronic records specialists. Fourth, graduate archival education programs have offered only a few full courses on electronic records management, and the size and nature of these programs provide little opportunity for educating future archivists in electronic records work. Fifth, and finally, the advanced institute on electronic records and information policy offered to state government archivists at the University of Pittsburgh School of Library and Information Science from 1989 through the present suggests some of the weaknesses in the archival profession's reliance on continuing education for electronic records administration training.

Despite the findings of this study, however, there are recent indications that the American archival profession is improving its ability to deal with electronic records. New publications, courses, programs, and research grant funds have appeared in the early 1990s. The impact of these recent developments on the American archivist's management of electronic records is, however, too early to determine. Still, while the world of information technology is extremely fluid and dynamic, there is substantial evidence that the American archival profession is much less flexible. Technologist Mark Weisner (1991, p. 94) has stated that the "most profound technologies are those that disappear. They weave themselves into the fabric of everyday life until they are indistinguishable from it." This study reveals that technology has only begun to "weave" itself into American archival practice and theory.

THE ARCHIVIST'S RESPONSE TO INFORMATION TECHNOLOGY: THE PRESENT

There has been little research, model-building, or even practical suggestions that have provided much assistance to the archivist needing to cope with an institution's (and society's) full-range of information technologies–from pen and paper to computer and expert system. The first conference devoted to developing a research agenda for electronic records from the archival perspective (for which the Hedstrom paper was originally prepared) was held in early 1991, a half-century after the advent of the computer. This conference's report indicated that the "techniques that archivists have developed [for working with electronic records] reflect the centralized, ubiquitous mainframe computing environments of the 1960s through the early 1980s"; the computing environment is now "far more complex" (NHPRC, 1991, p. 2). The reason for this omission may have as much to do with the archival profession's general lack of interest in research as it does with the particular challenges posed by electronic records.

At present, archivists have been largely content to react to the hardware, software, and storage media after they have been developed, reached the market, and gained a foothold in institutions, and already affect organizations' records and information creation and use. Part of the reason for archivists being content with this situation is that they have generally operated that way in assessing other records forms; in other words: after the records have been created and their active use by the records creator has come to an end. Calls for control of the technology, through citizens' involvement in an open planning process that molds a useful information policy, indicate the changing nature of records and information that requires a much enhanced activism by all concerned with such matters. The dilemma has been captured in a report to the National Historical Publications and Records Commission, which is concerned with the maintenance of a national documentary heritage. This report stated that

> we are totally dependent upon constantly changing computer technology to be able to understand and use electronic information. Concomitantly, users have no control over the development or the continued availability of that technology. A highly competitive marketplace drives its creation and sales. (NHPRC, 1990, p. 3)

As many have observed, the view of information as a commodity has occurred primarily because of its use in the marketplace, industry, bureaucracy, government, advertising, and the like. Information is, in such a perspective, both a commodity and a means of social control (Mosco, 1989; Mosco and Wasko, 1988).

This fact has implications for how archivists will need to control electronic records; it requires professional knowledge and skills, political acumen, and financial and other resources. In fact, as some observers have pointed out, the problem rests in the failure of the policy makers to understand the new technology. Peter Hernon and Charles McClure (1987, p. 172) have argued that "many existing laws and regulations related to information technology are based on interpretations of paper or 'print' information" and these views are outmoded because the technology brings with it fundamental changes (see also de Sola Pool, 1983).

Despite such alarming scenarios, a caveat has to be raised about putting too much faith in the degree to which information technology affects organizations and society. It is, after all, difficult to know what the long-term impact of new notions of document creation and use will be on the archival or documentary heritage which is at the heart of the archivist's task (Hedstrom, 1991, pp. 33-34). Still, it is possible that many archivists have tended, for a variety of reasons, to hold onto more conservative views about the impact of the electronic information technology.

It must be realized, however, that one of the main underlying assumptions for many archivists is that the parameters of the human record keeping and information systems will not be greatly affected from generation to generation and even century to century. Transactional records might be recorded on different media and stored and retrieved in more diverse ways, but the reasons for the creation of such documents are unchanging and, in fact, quite natural (Jenkinson, 1980, pp. 322-23). Archivists have often tried to manage electronic records as if they were no different from other information media. The impact of electronic records on archival principles and practices continues as a point of debate for archivists.

The matter that must be considered continuously by the archivist is, however, how the information technology of the past fifty, especially the past twenty, years differs from the technology used during preceding centuries. In other words, there have been continuous changes in information technology (even at the heyday of the development of the basic archival principles); how, then, have these affected the ways that organizations work and the way that individuals work with those organizations to ensure that their records of archival value have been identified and preserved (Cox, 1990a)?

THE ARCHIVIST'S RESPONSE TO INFORMATION TECHNOLOGY: THE HISTORICAL CONTEXT

The above brief description of the present American archivist's approach to information technology seems to suggest a profession that has not yet adequately positioned itself for dealing with electronic records. A late 1960s statement stressing, for example, that the "first problem" with the archivist relating to computer technology was the "term itself," suggests some fundamental attitudes widely held by archivists at the time.[2] "The archivist is not a technologist. His preoccupation is with content and value. Technique is only a means to an end" (Fisher, 1969, p. 216). While this reflects a notion of the primacy of archival principles over record form, it also suggests a tendency to avoid focusing on specific characteristics of the technology carrier. In many ways, while some of the specific terms may have been disguised, this attitude may still be held in the 1990s by a sizeable portion of the profession. This type of statement shows that the issue of working with electronic records is a matter not only of technical competence and knowledge but professional identity and mission.[3] Of course, the 1969 statement was also written when the technology was generally restricted to use in managing large numerical databases.

Many currently practicing archivists date the origins of the modern North American archival profession with the founding of the National Archives and the Society of American Archivists in the mid-1930s. It was roughly during the same period that the computer age dawned, and it was not too many years prior that computers were being used, in practical ways, in large corporate and government applications. The seminal writings on the concepts underlying electronic computing were being published in these years and the first working models of computers were in place not long after that (Augarten, 1984; Forester, 1988). While the advent of the modern archival profession is certainly squarely in the midst of the modern

Information Age, it is also true that the profession lagged in its acknowledgement of this reality.

An examination of the indexes of the *American Archivist* for the years 1938 through 1967 revealed only three articles that concerned the management of electronic records. The first relevant essay, published in 1965, focused on trends in American political history and included a brief reference to the fact that historians and political scientists were then working on establishing a new kind of archival repository for quantitative political data. Interestingly, this article called for the necessary participation of archivists in the creation of data archives, a call that was, at best, only partially answered (Hays, 1965). In a far more important essay in 1966, buried within the "technical notes" section of the Society of American Archivists' journal, Morris Rieger noted (p. 109) that because "it has become increasingly clear that creating agencies rely on parts of their ADP documentation for record purposes–preserving them for long periods or indefinitely and referring to them frequently in connection with official operations–archival attitudes are now changing, certainly at the national level."

The emphasis here should be, of course, on "*changing*" attitudes, as the debate on this matter has continued for many years down to the present. In the same year that Rieger's brief article appeared, the Society of American Archivists' annual meeting included a session on the "Application of Automation to the Control of Archives and Manuscripts," noted by one of its participants (Wood, 1967, p. 311) as the "first time a full session of the annual meeting reported accomplishments as distinguished from speculation with regard to automated information handling." While this session focused on archival automated techniques, it still marked a newly emerging attitude by the archival profession about the computer. In fact, prior to the mid-1970s the Society of American Archivists did not even have a structure to deal with the matter of electronic records (T. Brown, 1984); see Table 1.1 for a listing of the early important activities by the archival profession in regards to electronic records. Lawrence McCrank, also reviewing the early work of the archival profession in this area, had a broader reflection of why the archivists had failed to deal with the computer more effectively: "Although the impact of the computer may seem radi-

TABLE 1.1. Selected Milestones in the American Archival Profession and Electronic Records, 1956-1984

1956	Schellenberg's "The Appraisal of Modern Public Records" contends that "machine-readable records" should be considered as records by archivists
1966	Morris Rieger, "Archives and Automation," *American Archivist* reflects changing opinions by archivists toward electronic records
1966-68	National Archives' Committee on the Disposition of Machine-Readable Records recommends that electronic records be officially considered as records
1969	National Archives establishes Data Archives staff in Office of Records Management
1972	Meyer Fishbein, "Appraising Information in Machine Language Form," *American Archivist* is the first major writing on the technical aspects of appraisal
1972	National Archives issues General Records Disposition Schedule for automated records
1978	Charles Dollar's essay on appraisal of electronic records in *American Archivist* summarizes decade of experience by National Archives with electronic records
1979	Ann Arbor conference on automated records in archives is the first major focused conference on this topic in North America
1979/83	Publication of Richard Kesner's bibilographies by the Society of American Archivists
1984	Harold Naugler, *The Appraisal of Machine-Readable Records: A RAMP Study with Guidelines*, summarizes state of art appraisal theory and practice for large automated statistical databases
1984	Margaret Hedstrom's *Archives & Manuscripts: Machine-Readable Records* provides the first comprehensive manual for North American archivists on the care of electronic records

cal for those who never experienced really or intellectually similar transformations in scribal or print technology, electronic forms are extensions of previous technologies" (McCrank, 1987, p. 274).

It was also true, in fact, that the profession would begin to struggle with how to approach electronic records. A generation ago, in the 1970s, archivists seemed to be still somewhat ambivalent about the impact of electronic information technology on the records of society's institutions. In 1972, Meyer Fishbein stated (p. 36) that "many archivists continue to question the record character of information in machine language form. This medium, they argue, merely transcribes and processes data from one traditional form, the source documents, to another traditional form, a publication or report."[4] Fishbein, drawing on his experience of working with computers in the federal government on behalf of the National Archives, offered a different view of the impact of the technology on archives. Reviewing in a summary fashion some of the changes in technology and the its use, especially the increasing need of officials and researchers for large data sets to make decisions and examine trends, he noted (1972, p. 36) the technology would have a "revolutionary impact on archives." This impact was, he assumed, due to the need of these individuals to include archival information in their statistical files. This assumption led the National Archives to establish in 1969 a Data Archives staff in the Office of Records Management to locate tape files that should be accessioned by the federal archival agency for preservation and continued use.

Among other things, Fishbein foresaw a time when "archives will communicate and transfer their information to researchers by remote control circuits," transforming the very nature of the manner in which archivists would facilitate research in their holdings.[5] It should be noted that Fishbein, in this period, was writing in a generally optimistic vein. In a 1975 bibliography he stated (p. 33) that while "only a few archival establishments are developing programs for accessioning records in machine-readable form . . . within the next decade . . . most large depositories will have either an active program for receiving and servicing such records or will be planning the establishment of machine-readable archival units." This prophecy has *yet* to be fulfilled. In truth, Fishbein's optimism swam against the tide of his own experience. In 1974 Fishbein offered a course on electronic records through the National Archives that was, however, canceled due to a lack of response from the archival profession (only four individuals expressed an interest in the course) (T. Brown, 1984, pp. 373-74).

Just a short time after Fishbein's article, the Society of American Archivists' presidential address suggested some shift in thinking in the American archival community. Wilfred Smith noted that at "one time it was thought that computer-generated information worthy of permanent retention could be preserved in the forms of printouts on paper. We have, however, advanced beyond that stage, and it is apparent that machine-readable records have become a normal archival medium" (Smith, 1974, p. 7). In the same address, however, Smith expressed his concern (p. 8) that "many archivists have abdicated their responsibilities in this field because of unfamiliarity with the technology." As if to give credence to Smith's concerns, the same issue of the *American Archivist* featured an essay on the creation of electronic records in businesses and concluded that, in one corporation at least, "there are no plans to store machine-readable records permanently . . . [because] the information recorded in this form is not a kind for archival retention . . . The storage of valuable records in this form is too expensive" (Thexton, 1974, p. 41). A brief analysis of changing notions of the appraisal of electronic records reflected that all electronic records were destroyed on the precept that they were non-records before 1960, that by the late 1960s electronic records were considered to be records but were appraised only for their informational value, and that it was not until the early 1980s that electronic records were to be appraised for evidential, legal, and informational values (T. Brown, 1987).

Evidence of the difficulties that the archival profession was having can be found in continued spotty record of appearance of articles on the management of electronic records in the *American Archivist* (the main professional journal for archivists in the United States) and other professional journals. Despite some of Smith's and others' optimism about the programmatic incorporation of electronic records, it was not until 1978 that another essay on the topic appeared in this journal. Charles Dollar, then Director of the National Archives' Machine-Readable Archives Division, prepared in

1978 the first truly systematic analysis of the appraisal of electronic records. Carolyn L. Geda (1979) followed Dollar's essay with a description of the procedures used in maintaining research data generated by social scientists and other researchers in electronic form, and indicated some of the implications that this experience revealed for the increasing creation of transactional and other records in electronic form.

For the next few years, articles and other studies continued to trickle slowly into professional journals such as the *American Archivist* until several major changes occurred in the mid-1980s that put a new face on the archival profession's consideration of electronic records. Most of these changes stemmed from the work of a small band of archivists (like Dollar and Geda) operating through the Society of American Archivists' Task Force on Automated Records and Techniques–a task force that would eventually become the current Committee on Automated Records and Techniques.

The publication of the proceedings of a 1979 conference on the archival management of electronic records, Richard M. Kesner's bibliography on the topic in 1979 (updated in 1983), and Margaret Hedstrom's manual on electronic records in 1984, all provided a new foundation for the consideration by the archival profession of what to do with electronic records and the implications of these activities; they were the foundation for the first generation of electronic records archivists in the United States. The 1979 conference was important because it provided the opportunity to examine a variety of crucial topics from a diversity of perspectives: research opportunities, archival programs, information technology developments, confidentiality, privacy, and the implications of the technology for archival practice and historical research (Geda, Austin, and Blouin, 1980). As one critical commentary about the volume suggested, it represented an important contribution to an "inadequate literature" reflecting that, at least, some "exploration" of the archival management of electronic records had begun (McCrank, 1983).

Kesner's bibliography was another important contribution, in that it brought together a disparate literature to bear on the issue of electronic records, and provided a convenient gathering point for archivists to see what was available for guidance (Kesner, 1983). Margaret Hedstrom's manual for the Society of American Archivists, *Archives & Manuscripts: Machine-Readable Records*, published in 1984, represented, perhaps, one of the most important milestones in the American archival profession's work with electronic records.

Hedstrom's manual was the first major effort to create a practical guide to the issue of managing electronic records.[6] However, as she noted in the volume's preface, this guide had some severe limitations because of what archivists had not accomplished with these record types. "Many of the examples in this manual reflect the state of the art among archivists for handling machine-readable records," she wrote (p. 7), "yet they do not address some of the complex, contemporary aspects of information technology. This limitation is due in part to the fact that archivists have not developed techniques for preserving some of the most advanced and technically sophisticated machine-readable records." As she noted in this publication, "the guidelines [in this manual] are most applicable to numeric data files stored on magnetic tape and accessed sequentially." She pointed out that these "relatively simple methods for recording and storing information" were changing and that archivists would need to be aware of these changes and to transform their techniques accordingly (Hedstrom, 1984, p. 60). Despite Hedstrom's efforts (and successful efforts they were) to describe the practical aspects of an electronic records program, there were relatively few archives that opted to establish such programs.

In the past decade, especially in the years since the appearance of the Hedstrom manual, there have been some noticeable changes in how North American archivists approach the matter of electronic records (see Table 1.2 for a representation of these changes). First, there have been some specific case studies relative to how archivists must deal with the technology from their perspective. These case studies have been on geographic information systems (Ahlgren and McDonald, 1981/82), automated case files (Cameron, 1983; Kowlowitz, 1988), evaluation of the reliability of legislation covering electronic records (T. Brown, 1986), downloading electronic data for access (Harrison and Hedesheimer, 1987), and the use of computers in specific record-keeping applications and subsequent challenges to the management of these systems (Harrison, 1987 and 1989). Second, there was at last some progress made within specific

TABLE 1.2. Selected Milestones in the American Archival Profession and Electronic Records, 1985-Present

1985	Committee on the Records of Government issues report that stresses the danger of electronic records for the nation's documentary heritage
1987	*Archival Informatics Newsletter* (later *Archives and Museum Informatics*) starts publication, providing the first major outlet for discussion about electronic records form an archival perspective
1988	National Archives creates the Center for Electronic Records
1988	Society of American Archivists College and University Section forms Automated Records Planning Committee, reflecting spread of interest in electronic records outside of government
1989	National Archives of Canada symposium on "Converging Technologies in the Management of Recorded Information" is held
1989-91	University of Pittsburgh School of Library and Information Science/National Association of Government Archives and Records Administrators Institute is held
1990	*Taking A Byte Out of History* is published by the U.S. House Committee on Government Operations, criticizing lack of progress made by National Archive in working with electronic records
1990	Meeting on Electronic Office Records is held at the Brookings Institution
1990	Symposium on the Preservation of Microcomputer Software is held
1990	*Electronic Records Issues: A Report of the Commission* is delivered to the National Historical Publications and Records Commission, identifying electronic records as a priority for funding by the Commission
1991	Electronic Records Research Agenda Conference, co-sponsored by the Minnesota Historical Society and the National Historical Publications and Records Commission, is held
1991	Society of American Archivists Committee on Automated Records and Techniques Curriculum Conference is held
1991	National Archives issues reports on expert systems and optical disk technology and implications for archival profession

state governments (and the North American national governments as well) so that reports of substantial work could be released to the archival profession, although the nature of such progress reports remained rather limited when considered in the broader context of the immensity of the electronic information technology challenge (Belding and Fortson, 1985; Gavrel, 1988; Harrison, 1986; Hedlin and Harrison, 1988; Hedstrom and Kowlowitz, 1988; New York State Archives and Records Administration, 1988). Third, because of case studies such as these, and the development of electronic records programs at the National Archives in the United States and Canada and a few state archives, there has also been the preparation of more detailed manuals in certain specific archival functions as applied to electronic records, such as in appraisal (Cunliffe and Miller, 1989; Hedstrom, 1989b; McDonald, 1985; and Naugler, 1984), the acquisition of software (Bearman, 1987), the use of database management systems to administer electronic records with archival value (T. Brown and Reader, 1987), and general summaries of how to administer archival records in electronic form (Ambacher, 1989; NARA, 1990; United Nations, 1989). Fourth, the 1980s has also been characterized by more deliberate efforts in continuing education and conferences devoted to the topic of electronic records, in North America and throughout the world (Anderson, 1985; Association of Canadian Archivists, 1987; M. Cook, 1987; and Durrance, 1989). Only recently has there been any effort to evaluate the effectiveness of these efforts, or to develop any coherent curriculum, that can be applied to both continuing and graduate education programs.

Finally, increased activity by archivists with electronic records and concern about the requisite knowledge of such archivists led to some early, independent, efforts to define curriculum content and approaches (Fishbein, 1985). Such efforts have been sparse, however, because of other problems that the American archival profession has not resolved. Still, the literature tends to reflect more evidence of substantial work and experimentation with electronic records than in the previous decade, although the matter of a consensus for action in this area remains somewhat problematic.

Despite an obviously higher level of activity by the archival profession in addressing the impact of electronic information technology, it is still clear that progress has been far from what it should be. This can be detected in at least two major ways. First, it can be seen in the series of reports that have been coming out in the past half-dozen years about the impact of information technology on the American federal government's historical documentation. In 1985 the Committee on the Records of Government, the creation of a consortium of organizations, declared that the "United States is in danger of losing its memory," at least partly owing to the impact of the new technologies:

> The danger of losing historically valuable records is greatly increased by the changeover to electronic recordkeeping. Under current procedure, records created on tapes or disks are erased or lost before anyone exercises judgement about their possible value. In addition, given the rapidity of technological change, even information recognized as valuable can be lost because the equipment and skills necessary to retrieve it become obsolete or unavailable. (pp. 9-10)

The report called for more authority and responsibility for the Archivist of the United States and the National Archives. Four years later the U. S. National Academy of Public Administration (NAPA) prepared, on behalf of the National Archives, a report on the impact of electronic recordkeeping on the federal government's archival documentation; this report concluded that federal agencies were generally retaining policy and other potentially archival records in traditional paper formats, but the consulting firm also concluded that this would change rapidly over the next decade. NAPA (1989) also urged that the National Archives take on a more aggressive role in developing strategies and programs for managing electronic records.

Slightly more than a year later, another report from the U.S. House Committee on Government Operations (1990) charged that progress by the National Archives had not been sufficiently substantial. This report, and the previous reports, carefully portrayed the changing electronic nature of federal records, but was even more blunt in its assessment that the National Archives' "current policies are inadequate to assure the long-term preservation of electronic records. Both evolutionary and revolutionary changes in

NARA's policies, methods, and procedures may be needed to respond to the challenge of preserving electronic records" (p. 5). The report laid out a series of recommendations that, in some ways, summarized the thinking of a generation of archivists about electronic records. These recommendations included charges to the National Archives to review its work with electronic records, undertake the re-evaluation of the "technical characteristics of electronic recordkeeping systems" relative to the preservation of their information, conduct "more long-range planning" by the Federal government in the preservation of electronic records, integrate "records management and preservation functions with information resources management staffs and activities," incorporate "recordkeeping rules and procedures" into "major electronic information systems from the outset," and make amendments to federal legislation "to reflect the changes in recordkeeping practices resulting from the widespread use of computers in the Federal Government" (pp. 5-6). All of these reports reflect mounting concern and the need for more deliberate action on the part of the archival community in the United States.

INFORMATION TECHNOLOGY AND ARCHIVAL PRINCIPLES: THEORY, PRINCIPLES, AND PRACTICES.

Some suggestions were made earlier about how recent technological developments have affected the concepts of records and information. Now it is appropriate to suggest the implications of these changes for archival concepts, principles, and practices or, at least, how archivists have grappled with the potential implications. As also has been suggested earlier, the debate on the degree of impact continued for nearly three decades. In 1966, Morris Rieger (p. 109) noted that:

> there is no special problem in determining the eligibility of ADP-type records for archival preservation. In principle, their physical form is irrelevant; like records of conventional form they should be appraised in terms of the standard criteria of archival value and, to the extent they meet these criteria, be considered accessionable.

In an article published the following year, Elizabeth Wood (1967, p. 314) noted that archivists must play a more active role with such electronic records: "Heretofore archivists have gratefully received records as handed to them. I believe that eventually they must be empowered to determine the form of permanent records." A decade later, in 1979, Robert M. Warner and Francis X. Blouin, Jr. stated that the "concepts we use in the handling of records on paper–arrangement, description, appraisal–will be useful and applicable to records in machine-readable form. However, the ways we apply these concepts to this new form of record will be different." Warner and Blouin were careful to point out (pp. 242-43), however, that "archival theory cannot be equated with present archival practices." As if to build upon Warner and Blouin's caveat, British archivist Michael Roper noted (1980, p. 146) that "it must be admitted that machine-readable records present problems which differ from those encountered in respect of conventional written records," although Roper viewed this mainly within the technical realm, being content to see more of the similarities between electronic and other traditional records. Hedstrom, in her important 1984 manual (p. 7), noted that "although archivists need new skills, experience, and confidences to manage machine-readable records, existing archival techniques provide a firm foundation for handling these records.

In that same year Trudy Huskamp Peterson wrote the most thorough analysis at the time about archival principles and theory in the light of modern information technology and concluded that the principles and theory remained valid. Peterson's article was more candid (1984, p. 385), however, in its assumptions about the technology, believing that the "computer has been very imperfectly integrated into institutional life" and that the function of the computer is "simple," being only "to assist the institution in conducting its business." Why is it, then, that the American archival profession has lagged in its ability to manage electronic records? Peterson noted (p. 392) that "archivists will be specialists within the larger community of information resource managers, but there will continue to be a distinct need for our skills." The problem may be twofold: the technology is not as simple as some would like, and the archivist has resisted learning as much about the technology as she or he needs to fulfill the professional mission and mandate.

While through the mid-1980s there appeared to be a consensus regarding the applicability of archival principles to the management of electronic records, the past five or more years has seen a more spirited debate about this issue.[7] There was, for example, the debate generated by an article by Richard Kesner. In late 1984 Kesner published an essay in the Canadian journal *Archivaria* that seriously challenged some of the prevailing views concerning the archivist's work with electronic records. In this essay Kesner asked the question, "In the era of automated information systems, where the accurate and timely delivery of data in the most economical fashion has become big business for many companies operating in the industrialized West, is there a place for archivists?" He answered in the negative. "If we do not change the way we view the purpose and nature of our performance within our parent organization, I expect that before too long we will be relegated to the antiquarian curatorial role that we have heretofore rejected as a misplaced 'popular' notion of what an archivist does for society" (Kesner, 1984/85, p. 163). Kesner (p. 164) argued that archivists "must cease to act as archivists in the traditional sense" and "become information specialists drawing upon a wide array of automated tools and analytical techniques." Kesner advocated changes in training, knowledge, and attitudes that stopped short of confronting basic archival principles, but it was interesting that this article was a dramatic departure from one he had written only a few years before, which was, in fact, more in the mainstream of archival thinking about electronic records (Kesner, 1981). The reason may be his (and others) increasing sense that the American archival profession had not moved very far forward in its management of electronic records.

Terry Cook, writing in the same issue of *Archivaria* attempted to answer individuals such as Kesner and those who had generally argued for more radical re-orientations to electronic records. Cook stated (1984-85, p. 32) that "while it is true . . . that archivists need to sharpen their tools, develop new procedures, and hone new approaches to cope with the information revolution and computerization, it does not follow that the historical basis and training for archival work should therefore be overthrown." Cook partially answered Kesner and other critics by noting that certain basic archival principles and approaches remain relevant and extremely valuable for the modern information age. These principles include understanding "records in the aggregate," that is, following through with such basic archival principles as provenance and context of records creation and use; the "appraisal, description, and careful understanding of the informational value found in individual documents"; and, finally, the "development of archival theory within the broader humanities and social science" (T. Cook, 1984-85, pp. 40-48). In the latter area, Cook argued (p. 47) the necessity of understanding records and information, suggesting that "while the archivist is not an historian as the term is generally understood, he must nevertheless be an historian, if a special kind of historian, in order to fulfil the essential and unique challenges of the *archival* profession."

In Kesner's response to Cook, he further described the relevance of basic archival principles. He used the verb "complicate" in this regard. He stated that his

> emphasis on the need to learn the new technologies and how they influence the creation of contemporary records is in fact grounded in [his] commitment to the traditional values of the archivist and [his] view that a failure to come to grips with EDP-generated documents will ultimately result in the mismanagement and ultimately the loss of some of the evidentially and informationally important records of our age. (Kesner, 1985, p. 144)[8]

While Kesner seemed to take a middle road regarding the importance of traditional archival principles, he also reiterated the need for archivists to intervene in the creation of electronic records, arguing that archivists "cannot look to the nineteenth century . . . [because] there is no precedent for dealing with EDP records. We must forge new techniques and seek fresh approaches" (Kesner, 1985, p. 145). Kesner maintained (p. 147) that he was not "advocating a 'redefinition' of the archivist and his role, but rather calling for the archivist to recognize the changes going on around him and to adapt accordingly."

Shortly thereafter a similar debate occurred about the preservation of electronic records. In 1986, John Mallinson wrote a brief essay that described from a preservation viewpoint problems with information technology and concluded (in agreement with the recommendations of a National Archives and Records Administration committee) that "human-readable microfilm" be used to preserve the archival records produced in electronic form. The reasons were generally straightforward: "It provides a hardware and software independent mode of preservation. It is amenable to mechanization . . . . It is risk-free. It provides a basis for a totally integrated modern records management and preservation system" (Mallinson, 1986, p. 152). Again, Mallinson does not explicitly deal with the matter of archival principles and modern information technology, but it is obvious that his solution is to reduce electronic records to a problem that can be managed within the parameters of traditional archival approaches. Sue Gavrel replied to Mallinson's perspective, noting that to follow such ideas means the loss of important information from electronic records. As Gavrel wrote,

> Inherent in the archival value of EDP records is the fact that these records can be analyzed and re-analyzed in their present form. Three special characteristics of these records must be considered during the appraisal process:
>
> 1. *The manipulability of EDP records.* There have been many occasions when records in paper form have been too cumbersome to use for statistical purposes and have been assessed as not having archival value. The same information in machine-readable form, however, may present endless potential for research.
>
> 2. *Non-aggregate data have more value than aggregate data.* This is a particular feature of EDP records; in appraisal of paper records the opposite is true. The non-aggregated form provides researchers with the basis from which they can do their own analysis.
>
> 3. *Linkage of EDP records.* With more standardization of data elements in EDP records, the possibility exists of linking records in one file to records in other files and this increases the informational value of all the records. (Gavrel, 1986, p. 154)

While Gavrel's comments certainly do not stray far from basic archival principles, they also indicate that there are inherent differences in electronic records that require new approaches and thinking by archivists.

Other debates have continued, including, as just one example, the evolving discussion on the matter of information technology technical standards and their applicability to the archival profession. In 1989, the National Institute for Standards and Technology issued *Framework and Policy Recommendations for the Exchange and Preservation of Electronic Records: A Report to NARA*, arguing that such standards were useful for the National Archives' efforts to manage electronic records (Law and Rosen, 1989). A year and a half later, however, the National Archives (1990b) issued a response that took a more conservative view, arguing for tracking to see what standards would emerge as the most essential ones. David Bearman, perhaps a little too critically, characterized the differences in these two reports as follows:

> Where NIST advocated a brave and ambitious program to seize control of electronic records in the government through the imposition of standards for a national information resources directory, definition of standards for content interchange of documents and databases, and development of standard functional specifications for archives and records management in an electronic environment, NARA has opted for cautious study, usually deferring action because standards are not yet fully in place or software to implement has yet to be fully proven. The NARA response is so bureaucratically predictable and so symptomatic of what is wrong with NARA's entire approach to archives that it is hard to find a place to begin to criticize it. On its own terms, the response is a major step forward for NARA. It is also almost certain to be inadequate both technically and politically. (Bearman, 1990a, pp. 11-12)

NARA's report went against what some archivists had previously determined to be a consensus regarding the importance of electronic information technology standards. In 1988 Margaret Hedstrom, buttressed by a decade of experience with electronic records, wrote that

> standards for encryption, compaction, storage, and data or document interchange are essential to enable future access to records stored on magnetic and optical media, to make their

> preservation affordable, and to permit migration of information between generations of storage and retrieval technologies.

Hedstrom (1988, p. 53) went on to say that "archivists need to respond to new information technologies when they are introduced rather than waiting until large backlog of records become irretrievable because they are stored in an obsolete format." She considered, however, that the archival profession had learned a "lesson," "that archivists waited too long to address the problems that this changing technology posed."

There still seems to be, however, a general consensus within the North American archival profession that in the face of emerging trends in modern information technology basic archival principles remain rock-steady. The first graduate archival thesis on the topic, completed in 1988 by Catherine Aileen Bailey, may be the primary testimony to this view (cf., 1989-90). Tom Brown, when reviewing the thesis (1989), wrote:

> Bailey attempts to deal globally with the application of archival theory to automated records, rather than with a single archival function or with practical solutions to specific problems. Her conclusion is that archival theory remains valid for the archival administration of all records regardless of physical medium. Differences in approach are a result of practical application of theory: 'Archival science does not, therefore, need to be redefined, but merely expanded.'[9]

Less satisfactory is Bailey's characterization of the different achievements between United States and Canadian archivists working with electronic records. The main value of the thesis rests, however, on its review of the literature and ultimate credo in support of traditional archival practice. Brown suggests, in fact, that there is considerable need for further research, especially on what is the most effective institutional administrative approach to electronic records. Despite the prevailing view of archivists about the validity of archival principles, this too requires considerably more research and analysis. David Bearman (1990b, p. 14), writing about Bailey's work, for example, stated that she "may be making as good a case as can be made with the traditional framework, but unfortunately the case, based on our past record in the management of electronic records, fails."

The kinds of debate characterized above are precursors of the more intensive debate now forming. One reason for the relatively late emergence of these debates is that the amount of direct work by archivists with electronic records and modern information systems has still been relatively limited. But the flavor of the new kinds of discussion can be seen in the writings of Charles Dollar, who has worked with electronic records and related issues at the National Archives since the mid-1970s. Dollar is one of the archivists who has thought about the relationship of archival principles to the electronic information technology. He developed this in some detail in a paper originally presented in Italy in 1990, and used later in 1991 as the basis for an international effort to reconcile archival theory with electronic records.

Dollar first noted the challenges for the basic archival concepts of original order and original record. These concepts have been important because they are crucial to the notion of documenting transactions and for authenticating genuine records. But, suggested Dollar, electronic records challenge these concepts because these records are actually signals that can be easily altered with implications for sustaining records in a constantly changing form. Archivists must transfer their attention from a fixation with the physical form and content to considering the transactions and systems (Dollar, 1986, 1992; Bearman, 1991a).

According to Dollar, archival provenance is another concept that is threatened by the modern electronic record. Provenance is the principle that upholds the maintenance of the records' context, arguing that records are generally less valuable (or, sometimes, not useful at all) if they are removed from their transactional and organizational contexts. Pioneer archival theorist Jenkinson provided one version of the principle of provenance in the following statement:

> Archives normally pass through three phases. In the first they are the current Files . . . which may be needed at any moment for reference: the Archive at this stage has not as a rule attained its full stature–the document is written but is not yet

> placed. In the second phase the File may still be wanted on occasion, but for the purposes of precedent and the historical background of the work of the Office rather than for current reference: they are relegated morally . . . to a kind of Limbo where they lie half-forgotten and sometimes–for storage space and staff are expensive things–wholly neglected. Finally, if they survive, they reach the third stage; in which their value for the purposes of Research is recognized and becomes the governing factor in their preservation. There is no fixed period for the endurance of the first two phases: it varies with circumstances and in the past the "Limbo" phase has sometimes lasted for centuries. (Jenkinson, 1980, p. 240)

In this description, Jenkinson has portrayed the natural progression of the creation, use, re-use, and description of records–all in accord with the needs of the records creators. As Dollar and other archivists have pointed out, however, electronic records have the potential to lose such features because they can be used as signals apart from any institutional context.

Another cherished archival principle has been that of centralizing records with archival values into repositories for preservation, arrangement, description, reference and use. Archival records are often accumulated to ensure their integrity and because it seems to be more cost-effective for their maintenance and subsequent uses. It is difficult to imagine these aims and aspects being very practical with electronic records. Migrating data from system to system is extremely expensive, as is any archival repository's need to maintain appropriate equipment to allow the records to be used. Some archivists have urged their colleagues to develop procedures that will allow them to have the electronic records used in the originating offices with these offices also taking responsibility to maintain the records in a useful state. As Dollar suggests (1992), centralization of archival records in electronic form should only be done as a measure of last resort.

Moving to the basic archival practices leaves considerable room for change and improvement. Dollar has noted that, generally, appraisal work has been devoted to considering issues of evidential and informational values that are closely related to a view of records reflecting administrative hierarchies. Archivists have made additions to the appraisal process when devoted to electronic records, looking at things such as manipulability, computer linkage, and other technical considerations–opening up a consideration of the need to incorporate appraisal at the information systems design process rather than some later point. Dollar (1992) similarly reevaluates other basic archival practices. Archival arrangement and description have to be moved from merely a reflection of physical and informational content and organizational structure to a focus on information systems design and the possibilities of full text searching. Archival reference needs to move from a "supply-driven" concept in which records are acquired because it is thought they will be used by researchers, to one in which records are maintained by their creators in their original software environment–the archivist becoming a facilitator of access to archival records. And, finally, the notion of archival preservation must rest upon the idea of continuing rather than permanent value (Dollar, 1992).

More substantively, views such as Dollar's have been incorporated in records management and archival guidelines developed for specific kinds of institutions. In 1987, the United Nations, through its Advisory Committee for the Coordination of Information Systems, initiated a study on the impact of electronic records on UN organizations. The main driving force behind the study was the "worry that traditional approaches to archives and records management are not keeping pace with changes in information technology and in the way people perform knowledge-based work today–and that the gap between the two is growing" (R. Barry, 1989, p. 4). The result of this study was a series of recommendations re-affirming the value of the life-cycle concept of records and information, the need for cooperation between archivists/records managers and other information resources managers, the appraisal of electronic records at the point of records creation, consideration that the "physical management of records may more sensibly be assigned to substantive managers responsible for automated systems in their fields of responsibility," the need to preserve not just electronic records but "systems functionality–context as well as content," the adoption of the Open Systems Interconnection Reference Model group of information standards, and the need for the UN to "conduct periodic surveys of its organizations to keep abreast of shifts in the use of information technology and the electronic records implications" (Barry, 1989, p. 4).

Dollar's ideas, and those of others like him, directly challenge many of the precepts that have been derived from traditional archival practice and theory. While some other archivists have argued that Dollar's own definitions of archival theory and principles are weak, it is nevertheless true that the kinds of questions and issues that he raises will characterize the substance of one of the most central of debates within the North American archival profession over the next decade. These kinds of concerns have been appearing in a variety of settings, such as a group of papers presented at the 1990 annual meeting of the National Association of Government Archives and Records Administrators–which reflected the entire range of potential views about how archivists should approach the matter of electronic records. Kenneth Thibodeau and David Bearman presented papers on the opposite side of the issue of whether electronic records should be accessioned into archival repositories or maintained by the systems' originators. Thibodeau took the more traditional view, while Bearman stated that the "archival repository is as a strategy for the electronic age what the walled city became with the invention of gunpowder, an indefensible bastion and a liability" (Bearman, 1991b, p. 24; Thibodeau, 1991, p. 13).

In the same vein, Alan Kowlowitz and Michael L. Miller delivered papers on the matter of appraising electronic records. Kowlowitz did not question archival principles, but noted that the "most pressing issues facing electronic records appraisal today are not narrowly technical and methodical, but are broad program development and information management issues that will ultimately determine the configuration of government electronic records programs, including appraisal" (Kowlowitz, 1991, p. 31). In fact, Kowlowitz went so far as to say (p. 35) that "through electronic records appraisal archivists and records managers have . . . advanced the theory and practice of archival appraisal in general," although he never really explained what was meant by this claim. Miller, on the other hand, took a view more in keeping with the conservative position that archivists have brought to the matter of electronic records, "stressing that what archivists know, or don't know about appraising government records in paper form has a great deal to do with how they appraise electronic ones" (Miller, 1991, p. 38). Still, Miller suggested that "archivists need to be involved in systems design," since database by database, or system by system scheduling is too labor-intensive and new approaches are needed. This needs to occur because electronic records must be considered "in the context of the information system that created them and the overall documentation of the creating agency," and problems in technological concerns will diminish and archivists will increasingly view technology as representing an opportunity (Miller, 1991, pp. 40-42). More important than either of these two related papers was Terry Cook's commentary in which he stated that "those responsible for machine-readable records must come out of their isolationist electronic cloisters, and accept the archival implication of information resource management." Cook also stated that, "It is information, not records; it is a corporate resource, not a media specialty; and it is a contextual, functional, and holistic approach, not a technocratic preserve for cybernetic gurus" (T. Cook, 1991, p. 53). Cook's comment, in fact, is a harbinger of what is being considered in the remainder of this study.

SUMMARIZING THE PROLEGOMENON TO THIS STUDY

In the recent 1990 staff report on electronic records to the National Historical Publications and Records Commission a pointed statement was made concerning the archival profession's ability to deal with the modern information technology of the late twentieth century:

> Although the obstacles that exist for archivists to preserve and provide access to electronic information are enormous, they are not insurmountable. The primary strategy upon which everyone agrees is that archivists must take an active approach and not wait to take action at the conclusion of the active life of electronic records systems. Archivists must acquire the knowledge and develop the expertise to become involved in the system development life cycle to ensure that information of archival value is preserved. But how to develop successful-

ly and implement this strategy is not yet clear. (NHPRC, 1990, pp. 5-6)

As the review of literature in this chapter has endeavored to demonstrate, the lack of clarity about an appropriate strategy for the American archival profession may be due to the substantial structural problems within the archival community and its institutions, and to a still general problem about the relevance of archival theory, principles, and practices to modern information technology. These structural problems include the lack of relevant research on electronic records and the often poor profiles of archival institutions within their environments. The next four chapters–looking more closely at position descriptions, employment advertisements, and continuing and graduate archival education programs–intend to show to what degree this may or may not be the case.

ENDNOTES

1. There has been no consistency in the use of the terms "electronic records" or "machine-readable records" except that the former has begun to be more consistently used by North American archivists over the past decade, nearly replacing the latter term that dominated from the 1960s through the mid-1980s; for that reason, I have used the term "electronic records" throughout this work. An etymological analysis of the phrase would be useful and illuminating, but it is beyond the scope of this study; furthermore, it is very possible it would not discover any specific reasons for the shift in terminology other than convention. The more important point is that despite a shift in the way such records have been described is their continuing treatment as a "special" record, suggesting that the North American archival community (and, in fact, the international profession) has not really integrated such records into their normal operations. The most recent basic manuals on archival science (Dearstyne, 1992; Ellis, 1993) still relegate a discussion of electronic records to a separate chapter after introducing all the primary or basic archival functions. This study is one explanation of the reasons why this lack of integration has occurred. And, it is my thesis that this lack of integration is symptomatic of the general failure of the North American archival profession to manage effectively such records.

2. This discussion is a much reduced analysis reflected in my dissertation (Cox, 1992d, chapters one and two). Readers interested in the literature might also want to examine a recent annotated bibliography compiled by myself for another publication (Cox, 1993).

3. I am not meaning to imply in this that the archivist should master all the technical aspects of electronic information systems. What is the concern is when

such statements are used as rationales for not dealing with electronic records. The archivist must know enough to be able to work with the information professions to ensure that electronic records possessing archival value are identified, preserved, and accessible for use.

4. For statements that collaborate the concept as a prevailing one, see Mitchell, 1970, pp. 168-69.

5. As he elaborated in an earlier essay, this prediction was based both upon the nature of uses of the computer by records-creating organizations and the then rapidly spreading rise of quantification in historical research (see Fishbein, 1970).

6. Harold Naugler (1984), published at the same time as the Hedstrom manual, was written from the Canadian perspective and experience and has been generally considered to be the finest description of dealing with large automated statistical and related systems. Its impact has been limited to a small group of archivists in the United States, however, mainly because the RAMP studies have not been widely used by most practicing archivists in this country (for this refer to Cox 1990b).

7. A number of authors, such as Morris Rieger and Terry Cook, have clearly written that the management of electronic records can occur within a framework of existing archival principles. Others, such as Charles Dollar, have argued that the use of information technology requires the development of new principles. Many others fall within the opposite ends of this spectrum.

8. This article was also a response to comments made by Tom Nesmith in his editorial preface of no. 19 of *Archivaria*, but I have chosen to focus on the fuller comments of Cook.

Chapter Two

State Government Archives and Position Descriptions: A Case Study of Archivists and Archival Work in the Information Age

INTRODUCTION

To date, archivists have tended to discuss their work as if they had to possess a comprehensive knowledge about all aspects of archival administration and management, law, personnel management, financial administration, and other areas. Archival certification, graduate and continuing archival education, and other archival activities have usually reflected a pre-occupation with *basic* or *general* archival competencies.[1] Failing this, archival employers have sought out individuals with attributes such as "imagination, intuition, and initiative" or a "keen desire to do *archival* work, not teaching, research, library cataloging, or being a bureaucrat" (Society of American Archivists, 1982, 1984c, and 1985). A recent impressionistic effort to examine employers' expectations for their archivists concluded that:

[Haworth co-indexing entry note]: "State Government Archives and Position Descriptions: A Case Study of Archivists and Archival Work in the Information Age." Cox, Richard J. Co-published simultaneously in: *Primary Sources & Original Works* (The Haworth Press, Inc.), Volume 3(3/4), 1994, pp. 53-96; and: *The First Generation of Electronic Records Archivists in the United States: A Study in Professionalization*, Richard J. Cox, The Haworth Press, Inc., 1994, pp. 53-96. Multiple copies of this article/chapter may be purchased from The Haworth Document Delivery Center [1-800-3-HAWORTH; 9:00 a.m. - 5:00 p.m. (EST)].

> because of the variety of demands placed upon an archivist, the broader the background, the better. In addition to academic proficiency, the position demands a wide variety of skills, such as public relations, management, detective work, reference service, computer literacy, fundraising, interviewing, solicitation, grantsmanship, preservation, and supernatural power. The latter is required because an archivist is often challenged to create space out of nothing! (Murrah, 1990, p. 173)[2]

What is missing, it seems, is any articulation of differing responsibilities or educational, knowledge, and skill requirements for archivists (working as generalists, specialists, technicians, or administrators). This posture may be especially problematic in the late twentieth century as the archival profession strives to re-tool itself to work with complex information technology and its by-products of electronic records. Can archival generalists be expected to be proficient in managing the specific technical demands of electronic records?

There are, of course, historical explanations for this attitude. The malformed nature of archival education–consisting of a few basic graduate courses, institutes, and workshops and seminars–has contributed to a preoccupation with *basic* knowledge and skills.[3] The origins of archival administration in other professional disciplines such as history and librarianship have tended to subjugate the work of the archivist to practice rather than theoretical knowledge. Finally, the public image of archivists has been a weak one. Employers and others have simply not understood the differences (subtle and otherwise) between what archivists do and the labor of historians or librarians and other information professionals. There is a continuing perception that anyone with a minimum of in-service training and practice can function adequately as an archivist. Even though the last decade or two has been a time of immense change in the archival profession, these long-held views and attitudes continue to prevail and change seems destined to be a slow process.[4]

The recent dramatic changes in society and its institutions have certainly strained the archivist's preoccupation with in-service training and practice, suggesting both the need for greater specialization in areas such as information technology, broader management knowledge and competencies, and a moving away from a vision of the archivist as a generalist. Archivists are now confronted with myriad information creators, forms, and users that stretch their abilities to cope with the problems caused by this diversity. An archivist confronting the preservation of electronic records will face very different issues from those confronted by the archivist working with paper records or photographic materials. Attitudinal changes and educational restructuring, a topic that will be returned to later in this study, should equip the archivist to administer increasingly complex institutions and to cope with such institutions' equally difficult environments and information forms.[5] A recent issue of the *American Archivist* included an article which noted that the "challenge for archivists . . . is to prepare for the increasingly rapid changes [archivists] will encounter in coming years" and asked whether archivists "will become quaint anachronisms in a world of instant data communication, high technology, and rapid change" (Jimerson, 1989, p. 333). The question has been asked before and will be asked again. While there has been a much-needed call for more research in this area (McCarthy, 1988), the continuing lack of research on archival administration hinders the archival profession's ability to strengthen the basic management of its institutions.

JOB DESCRIPTIONS RESEARCH

The purpose of the research presented in this chapter is to examine systemically the position descriptions that exist for professional archivists and related professionals (such as records managers and conservators) in American state government archives; and to consider the research question that archival position descriptions are very general in content and requirements. These descriptions are written documents that provide a profile of the position's responsibilities, examples of work, knowledge and skill requirements, and educational and experiential requirements; and they are essential to the administration and adequate staffing of any organization.[6] The research question being considered, in this part of the study, is whether the current position descriptions reflect the trends in specialization (in responsibilities and requirements) that would assist the state archival programs to operate effectively within the modern electronic information environment, the institutions' rapidly increasing volume of records, and the new demands for information access. This research was conducted with the expectation that the positions would be found to be traditionally described with a stress on general archival responsibilities (the ones that have long been reflected in articles and studies about archival administration and education). The state archives position descriptions examined in this chapter were current as of 1989, although some had been originally developed a decade or more before or were in the process of being revised.

Descriptions of positions in the state archives were examined in a variety of ways: range of duties (whether general or specialized in areas such as arrangement and description or appraisal), administrative responsibilities, skills and knowledge requirements, and educational and experiential requirements. Hopefully, this analysis will help to provide some increased understanding about how archival institutions are trying (or failing) to cope with their changing demands. In fact, since this profession has not conducted such research about its own institutional patterns, profiles, and performances, the data presented in this chapter are unusual for the archival profession. Specifically, the following questions have been asked of the position descriptions:

1. Do they contain work examples that extend beyond basic traditional archival functions (appraisal and accessioning, arrangement and description, preservation, reference, and public outreach)?
2. What knowledge, abilities, or skills do they mention that are not central to archival administration? Are these traditional for archives positions (e.g., knowledge of history) or for civil service classifications (such as the ability to communicate effectively both orally and in writing)?
3. Are there any patterns in archival position descriptions reflecting the administrative placement (such as in a historical society or library) of the state archives?
4. Are there any patterns in archival position descriptions reflecting the position level (senior, middle, entry) or specializa-

tions (public records or manuscripts, photographs or cartographic records)?

Since it is assumed that the state archivist or state deputy archivist positions will be managerial and/or appointed positions that encompass responsibilities such as planning, budgeting, and the like, they have been excluded from this analysis. Also, only a few of the state archives provided descriptions for these positions.

State archives have been chosen because they are the largest and oldest of archival institutions, and traditionally one of the primary sources of leadership in the archival profession. The manner in which they are defining their professional positions may indicate, with some limitations, something about overall trends in the profession. The archival repository represents a vision of the way in which the profession sees its own self (values, issues, and concerns); the institution employing professional archivists may be the last vestige of a discipline to reflect change. State archives, both because of their position of long-held leadership within the archival profession and because they also work within a broader and better-defined information policy environment, should be an excellent focus for this study. In fact, of twenty-four state archives approached, the seventeen that responded to the request for position descriptions represented the diversity of region, form, and size that generally characterize these institutions (see Table 2.1).

State archives have also been selected because of some preliminary research by an archival educator in this area that provides a convenient starting point for this research. This educator, Constance Schultz, analyzed state archives' hiring practices to determine needs for graduate and continuing archival education. Although she also looked at position descriptions, Schultz made no effort to determine similarities in position qualifications and responsibilities.[7] However, the Schultz study provides an excellent springboard by which to determine whether the archives profession is reflecting changes in information technology, research patterns, and the general political and economic milieu of the late twentieth century.

There are, however, some distinct limitations to the study presented in this chapter. It is clearly a one dimensional effort. Position descriptions can be effective managerial tools, but they also can be

TABLE 2.1. State Archives Included in This Study by Organizational Type, Region, and Staff Size

n = 17

Organizational Type	
Part of Larger State Agency	6
State Historical Society	6
Independent State Agencies	5
Region	
Northeast	4
Southeast	5
Midwest	5
West	3
Professional Staff Size	
1-5	5
6-10	4
11-20	3
21 plus	5

extremely unreliable. Philip Grant, a human resources management expert, has written (1988a, p.53) that "most job descriptions are too simplistic: they lack detail; they are out of date; they neglect many key structural elements of the job; and they are unclearly written." He contends that position descriptions need to be more specific about the percentage of time spent on specific tasks and on the priority of the task to the organization (Grant, 1988b). None of the state archives positions provide any such information.

Moreover, in terms of analyzing positions in any organization, a review of written position descriptions can be considered to be only a portion of the task. One method, Integrated Job Analysis, follows a series of steps that include on-site visits, group meetings between job experts and workers, and analysis by job experts of observed work and listed knowledge, skills, and attitudes–all resulting in more precise position descriptions and requirements for the positions (Veres, Lahey, and Buckly, 1987). The intention of this research effort is to provide some preliminary results and from them to pose some possible additional research on state archives professional positions. The other parts of this study (especially the chapter on archival job advertisements) will provide some additional insights that enable the development of a broader context for an analysis of state government position descriptions.

THE RESEARCH DESIGN

The research design for this portion of the research effort is unpretentious. Twenty-four state archives (the same ones used by Schulz in her study) were asked to send examples of currently used professional position descriptions. Seventeen states complied with this request and afforded a well-rounded and representative sample of these kinds of archival institutions (refer to Table 2.1). The position descriptions were grouped according to position type (entry, mid-level, upper level, and related fields such as records management and preservation/conservation) and then compared in a variety of aspects (job responsibilities, knowledge requirements, skills and abilities requisites, and educational and experience requirements) in order to determine if there were any notable similarities or differences in the ways that state archives are staffing (or seeking to staff) their institutions[8] (of course, this analysis was also an effort to consider whether or not these institutions are adequately prepared to support their mission in the modern information technology environment). The position descriptions were also examined for information technology literacy, experience, and work assignments.

The matter of defining knowledge, as opposed to skills and abilities, has proved to be a difficult issue, requiring some compromise and assumptions in order to facilitate comparison between positions. The main problem encountered in these definitions is what one state archives characterizes as knowledge, skills, or attitudes may be different from that of another state. This probably has much to do with the individual traditions of the state government civil services that produced the descriptions. For the purpose of this study, the definitions of knowledge, skills, and attitudes as used in the Griffiths-King report on library and information science were adopted as a guide (Griffiths and King, 1986, pp. 30-34). And, in an effort to be consistent, variations were made in configuring the arrangement of the state archives position descriptions. The Griffiths-King report used the following definitions:

> Knowledge is having information about, knowing, understanding, being acquainted with, being aware of, having experience of, or being familiar with something, someone or how to do something.
>
> Skill is the ability to use one's knowledge effectively.
>
> Attitude is a mental or emotional approach to something or someone. (Griffiths and King, 1986, pp. 30-34)

Finally, the study was placed within the context of other research completed within the last few years, projecting personnel position descriptions and competency changes in related information professions (particularly librarians and records managers in the state government environment). Unfortunately, because of a lack of research on this *and* archival position descriptions no serious comparison can be made. This study does, however, suggest additional research (a topic briefly treated in the final section of this essay and the concluding chapter in this study) that could be carried out. In order to suggest both the limitations and possibilities for change of the presently-defined state archives archival positions, two case studies concerning how state archives have successfully developed electronic records programs have been included in this portion of the study. A follow-up survey with the state archives was completed concerning how state archives perceive and use their position descriptions.

THE FINDINGS

State archives positions were divided into three main groups, these divisions based upon common characteristics.[9] *Entry-level archivist positions* within the state archives were defined as those positions used to hire individuals for the most basic and general archival work, or clearly described as being the junior professional positions. These positions were variously described as Manuscripts Curator, Assistant Archivist, Archivist I, Archivist, Archives Assistant, Archives Technician, Processing Archivist, and Government Records Analyst.

Mid-level archivist positions were loosely defined as positions that fall between entry-level and senior administrative posts, and while the distinction is more impressionistic than scientific, nevertheless it serves a useful role in categorizing the archival positions that are advancements but not necessarily specialized. In the state archives, such positions are called Archivist II, III, and IV, Senior Archivist, Senior Archivist II, Archives Administrator I, Assistant Archivist, Archival Supervisor I and II, Supervising Archivist, Archival Program Supervisor, Principal Archivist, and Advanced Archivist. Some of these positions are generally described as being for specific units in the state archives or for more specialized activities, but the position descriptions are handled in a rather broad manner to serve a variety of purposes for archivists who have progressed beyond entry-level work.

There are at least three basic types of *specialized archivist positions*, the third group, within state archives. The first type or group is concerned with special records formats or topical expertise. These tend to be individuals who are responsible for records such as labor archives and manuscripts, industrial records, African-American source materials, photographic and audio-visual archives, newspapers, local government records, and cartographic and land records. The second type or group represents the records management positions. This group is more the result of the hiring of members of a related discipline, than the matter of a basic function; although (as will be looked at in chapter five of this study) the question as to whether records management is a function of archives administration or vice versa continues to be a matter of some debate. The third and final type or group consists of positions responsible for preservation activities within the state archives. This is a specialization in a basic archival function, although evidence from the position descriptions actually suggest otherwise.

What follows is a description of the findings for each of these types or groups of position descriptions.

Entry-Level positions

These positions appear to be viewed primarily as places for individuals to arrange and describe archival materials and to provide reference services to such materials (see Table 2.2), tasks which are not only very traditional activities for archivists but often identified by American archivists as those which primarily define their role in their institutions and society. When these positions are examined for evidence of responsibility in any of the five basic segments of archival administration (arrangement and description, reference, appraisal, preservation, and public outreach), arrangement and description and reference appear as the predominant responsibilities. Although these positions emphasize arrangement and description, only one state specifies that the U.S. MARC Archives and Manuscripts Control (AMC) format–rapidly emerging as the standard for this professional work–will be required. This not only suggests a lag behind corresponding technological advancements in the profession, but evidence that these positions will be filled by individuals requiring additional on-the-job education, and that in-service training is expected; or, it may simply suggest that these position descriptions originated at a much earlier date.[10] Appraisal and preservation functions and responsibilities also appear in approximately half the positions, but they are much more loosely defined. The sense of preservation in use here, for example, is that individuals performing arrangement and description should be able to both identify documents with basic preservation needs and to perform basic preservation practices such as cleaning and mending. Public outreach duties, except as may occur in the reference room, are rarely required.

Knowledge requirements reveal a broader range and less agreement than archival responsibilities (Table 2.3). Entry-level archivists are most often required to know the basics of archival work and the appropriate state and local history. Beyond that, there is little agreement as to knowledge requirements. American history and records management, very diverse knowledge areas, appear in a little less than half of the position announcements. Historical research, preservation, and library and information science complete the diversity of knowledge requirements. The emphasis on historical knowledge certainly reveals that many state archives view themselves as part of the historian's world.

Skills and attitudes likewise show a more diverse range in these position descriptions (Table 2.4). The ability to communicate, orally and in writing, is most often mentioned. Skills in interpersonal

TABLE 2.2. Ranking of Top Five Responsibilities in State Archives Positions
n = 146

ENTRY n = 26	MIDDLE n = 42	SPECIALIZED n = 15	PRESERVATION n = 16	RECORDS MGT. n = 47
1 Arrangement & Description (15; 57.7%)	1 Administration of Unit (15; 35.7%)	1 Appraisal; Reference (8; 53.3%)	1 Conservation Treatment (11; 68.8%)	1 Appraisal & Scheduling (28; 59.6%)
2 Reference (13; 50%)	2 Specialization in Archival Function (13; 31%)	2 Arrangement & Description; Preservation; & Supervision (7; 46.7%)	2 Micrographics & Reformatting (10; 62.5%)	2 Education & Training (18; 38.3%)
3 Preservation (10; 38.5%)	3 Performance of More Complex Work (12; 28.6%)	3 Education & Training (5; 33.3%)	3 Education & Training (8; 50%)	3 Research; Micrographics (17; 36.2%)
4 Appraisal (8; 30.1%)	4 Reference (4; 9.5%)	4 n/a	4 Administration (5; 31.3%)	4 Administration (16; 34.0%)
5 Public Outreach; Records Management (1; 3.8%)	5 Education & Training (2; 4.8%)	5 n/a	5 Research (3; 18.8%)	5 Inventorying; Systems Analysis (11; 23.4%)
Total = 26	Total = 42	Total = 15	Total = 16	Total =47

TABLE 2.3. Ranking of Top Five Knowledge Requirements in State Archives Positions

n = 146

ENTRY	MIDDLE	SPECIALIZED	PRESERVATION	RECORDS MGT.
n = 26	n = 42	n = 15	n = 16	n = 47
1 Archival Administration (10; 38.5%)	1 Archival Administration (24; 57.1%)	1 State & Local History (5; 33.3%)	1 Micrographics & Reformatting (9; 56.3%)	1 Records Management (23; 48.9%)
2 State & Local History (7; 26.9%)	2 State & Local History (18; 42.9%)	2 Archival Administration (3; 20%)	2 Conservation Techniques (7; 43.8%)	2 State & Local Government; Law (13; 27.7%)
3 Records Management (5; 19.2%)	3 Research Methods (13; 31%)	3 Automated Information Systems; Photography; Research Methods; and Preservation (2; 13.3%)	3 Supervision; Archival Administration; Office Procedures; Chemistry (2; 12.5%)	3 Micrographics & Reformatting; Research; & Information Systems (10; 21.3%)
4 American History; Research Methods; Library Science (4; 15.4%)	4 Management (8; 19%)	4 Education & Training; Journalism & Writing (1; 6.7%)	4 Management (1; 6.3%)	4 Computer Systems; Management (7; 14.9%)
5 Preservation (2; 7.7%)	5 Preservation; Records Management (7; 16.7%)	5 n/a	5 n/a	5 Statistics (4; 8.5%)
Total = 26	Total = 42	Total = 15	Total = 16	Total = 47

TABLE 2.4. Ranking of Top Five Skills and Attitudes in State Archives Positions

n = 146

ENTRY	MIDDLE	SPECIALIZED	PRESERVATION	RECORDS MGT.
n = 26	n = 42	n = 15	n = 16	n = 47
1 Communication (11; 42.3%)	1 Communication (25; 59.6%)	1 Communication (8; 53.3%)	1 Communication (8; 50%)	1 Communication (30; 63.8%)
2 Relationships (8; 30.8%)	2 Relationships (17; 40.5%)	2 Relationships (7; 46.7%)	2 Supervision (7; 43.8%)	2 Relationships (19; 40.4%)
3 Organization (6; 23.1%)	3 Supervision (15; 35.7%)	3 Research Methods; Physical Condition; Organization (4; 26.7%)	3 Manual Dexterity; Task Completion (6; 37.5%)	3 Research Methods (16; 34%)
4 Task Completion; Analysis (4; 15.4%)	4 Research Methods (7; 16.7%)	4 Travel; Organization (4; 36.7%)	4 Relationships; Micrographics (4; 25%)	4 Supervision (14; 29.8%)
5 Clerical; Supervision; Physical Condi-	5 Analysis; Organization (5; 11.9%)	5 n/a	5 Chemical Testing (2; 12.5%)	5 Statistics (12; 25.5%)
Total = 26	Total = 42	Total = 15	Total = 16	Total = 47

relationships and the organization of materials are next most frequently mentioned. Beyond these, a variety of skills and attitudes are reflected in these descriptions, including the ability to complete tasks, do analytical work, supervise, perform typing and other clerical-related responsibilities, lift boxes of a certain weight, and travel. Obviously, entry-level archivists can expect to be called upon to do a variety of tasks.

Educational and experiential requirements for the entry-level positions have less uniformity in description and are more difficult to characterize. Among the different entry-level positions that included specifications for educational requirements are many different requirement configurations, ranging from a high school diploma and two years archival experience, to a masters in history or library science and two years experience. Breaking the various educational requirements into basic components provides greater insight into the manner in which state archives view entry-level archivist positions (Table 2.5). All this reveals that a bachelor's degree requirement is most prevalent, history is favored as a subject matter, and while archival experience is preferred, archival course work is mentioned in only a few instances. The lack of emphasis on formal archival course work is an indication that in-service training may be viewed as a more important factor for these positions.

Mid-Level Archivist Positions

The nature of responsibilities for the mid-level positions reveal nothing surprising (refer to Table 2.2 again). About a third state that people hired for these positions will either work in a specific function in the state archives or administer a unit, section, or division of the institution. Nearly the same number simply describe the archival work to be carried-out to be of a "more complex level"; the general impression being conveyed is that these positions will serve as a conduit of internal promotion as well as recruitment for more experienced professional archivists (although the focus on arrangement, description, and reference in the entry-level positions is confusing unless these activities are somehow viewed as basic experience necessary for more sophisticated work). A small number indicate that individuals in these positions will be responsible for tasks involving planning, supervision, and other general administrative duties. One position description mentions internal training as a responsibility.

A greater difference is present in the knowledge requirements of entry-level and mid-level positions in state archives (refer to Table 2.3). A knowledge of archival administration together with state and local history remain, by far, the most often cited requirements. Research methods and records management are also frequently cited in both levels. The mid-level positions more often identify preservation administration, general management, and state and local government as important knowledge areas. The list for mid-level positions is more complex–with other fields of knowledge, legal issues, and security considered as necessary–demonstrating that these are somewhat more specialized as well as more administrative slots in the state archives.

Examining the skills and attitudes requirements of mid-level positions reveals a striking similarity to those for the lower archival levels (refer to Table 2.4). Communication and relationships are at the top of the list in frequency. The main divergence seems to be the inclusion of supervisory abilities and planning as a skill, indicating the increased load of administrative responsibility for these positions. Research is present as a skill, mainly because these individuals (in at least some of the state archives) are required to conduct research for their institutions; research is not limited to aiding researchers or analyzing archival materials. Analytical and organizational skills, physical condition, task completion and travel abilities all also appear (although inconsistently), suggesting that individuals in these positions will be less prone to perform a broad variety of tasks.

The educational requirements for these more advanced positions reveal a similar wide range to the lower-level positions (see Table 2.5), with some slight differences. Masters degrees take on more importance, not surprising since these are advanced positions. There is a slightly more pronounced emphasis on archival graduate study, but this is unimportant when compared to the continued stress on any level study in history or library science. The one major difference is the greater range of experience (from one to seven years) for these positions. Again, this may reflect that these positions are not only designed for more experienced archivists but also

TABLE 2.5. Breakdown of Educational and Experience Requirements in State Archives Positions

n = 146

	ENTRY	MIDDLE	SPECIALIZED	PRESERVATION	RECORDS MANAGEMENT
High School	1 (3.8%)	3 (7.1%)		10 (62.5%)	6 (12.8%)
2 Yrs. College				3 (18.8%)	
<u>Bachelor's</u>					
History	10 (38.5%)	22 (52.4%)	3 (20%)		2 (4.3%)
Pol. Sci.	4 (15.4%)	10 (23.9%)			5 (10.6%)
Government	1 (3.8%)	4 (9.5%)			
Business/ Public Admin.		1 (2.4%)			12 (25.5%)
Photography			1 (6.7%)		
Recs. Mgt.					8 (17%)
Inform. Sym.					5 (10.6%)
Unspecified	3 (11.5%)	3 (7.1%)		2 (12.5%)	16 (34%)
<u>Masters</u>					
History	6 (23.1%)	19 (45.2%)	5 (33.3%)		
Lib. Sci.	4 (15.9%)	11 (26.2%)	4 (26.7%)		1 (2.1%)

Archives/ Recs. Mgt.		2 (4.8%)	4 (26.7%)		2 (4.3%)
Other Subj. Deg.			2 (13.3%)		2 (4.3%)
Pol. Sci.		2 (4.8%)	2 (13.3%)		8 (17%)
Public Adm.					1 (2.1%)
Inform. Sci.					1 (2.1%)
<u>Doctorate</u>					
History		1 (2.4%)			
<u>Experience</u>					
1 year	5 (19.2%)	9 (21.4%)		6 (37.5%)	6 (12.8%)
2 years	6 (23.1%)	12 (28.6%)	4 (26.7%)	3 (18.8%)	9 (19.1%)
3 years		10 (23.8%)		5 (31.3%)	8 (17%)
4 years		3 (7.1%)		2 (12.5%)	2 (4.3%)
5+ years		7 (16.7%)		2 (12.5%)	3 (6.4%)
<u>Archival Course Work</u>	4 (15.9%)	8 (19%)	1 (6.7%)		
<u>Total Positions</u>	26	42	15	16	47

serve as internal promotion opportunities. Some of these differences may also be attributable to the differences in the development status of the various state archival programs reviewed here.

Specialized Positions

Archivists concentrating their activities on special records formats and topical areas have a somewhat different set of responsibilities but a very similar group of knowledge, skills and attitudes, and educational and experiential requirements when compared to their entry and mid-level counterparts. The archival responsibilities of these positions show a different mix, with appraisal moving to the fore but also revealing a clustering of the other basic archival functions of reference, arrangement and description, public outreach, and preservation (refer again to Table 2.2). The greater emphasis on appraisal and public outreach duties probably reflects that these positions are often fieldwork or collecting positions, responsible for filling in perceived documentation gaps or for concentrating on identified priority areas. These positions also have more supervisory and planning responsibilities than the entry and mid-level archivists, perhaps indicating that these individuals are also mid-level or higher positions responsible for administrating specialized units and programs within the state archives. These positions also have more miscellaneous responsibilities (such as records management, photographing events, writing grants, implementing automated systems, and security) thus demonstrating their more specialized responsibilities within the state archives.

The knowledge, skills and attitudes, and educational and experiential requirements of these positions indicate less divergence than the other archival positions. While state and local history and archival administration continue to be priority knowledge requirements, knowledge of automated information systems and historical photographs are new additions to the litany of requirements (refer again to Table 2.3). Skills and attitudes continue to remain virtually unchanged, with communication, relationships, and research still ranking high on the position descriptions (refer again to Table 2.4). The educational and experiential requirements of these positions show a marked difference from the other archival positions (refer again to Table 2.5). Undergraduate and graduate degrees in history and library science continue to predominate in importance, but there is more diversity in subject study and less emphasis on experience. Acquiring subject specialists may be more important than hiring those individuals who have significant archival experience, or these positions also may be less supervisory in nature than the mid-level positions.

Examining the *records management positions* in the context of archival administration poses some additional interesting problems. In one sense they are specialized archival positions. In another sense they are positions of a related discipline.[11] In this study they have been considered as a group for purposes of comparison. To facilitate this comparison, records management positions of all levels have been viewed together even though this skews the more subtle distinctions between the various levels within this sub-group. Titles of this group reflect much diversity: Archivist II, III and IV, Records Center Clerk, Records Management Technician, Records Management Officer, Records Management Analyst, Management Analyst II, Management Analyst Supervisor I and II, Records Management Assistant Division Director, Records Management Division Director, Records Analyst I, II, III, IV, V, Records Storage Supervisor, Records Center Manager, Operations and Management Consultant I, and Systems Project Analyst. It should also be noted that only about half of the state archives examined in this study (including Georgia, Mississippi, Illinois, Indiana, South Carolina, New Jersey, and Florida) have specialized records management positions; other states have records management programs located in other agencies.

A comparison of the records management positions with the other state archives positions reveals the widest differences in all areas. Although appraisal (including records scheduling) is by far the main responsibility of the records management positions, matching well with the other positions, there is little other uniformity in responsibilities or requirements (see Table 2.2). New areas such as forms design, systems analysis, and micrographics emerge as explicit responsibilities, reflecting the nature of this discipline. The same can be seen in the knowledge requirements (see Table 2.3). Records management totally replaces archival administration, although given the records analysis and scheduling function it is surprising that there is a complete lack of overlap in these areas.

State and local government replaces state and local history as another requirement, indicating that these positions are focused on government records management rather than historical manuscripts and records. Law emerges as a more important area, as does other traditional records management knowledge areas–such as micrographics, information systems management, systems analysis and organization, computer systems, office management, and statistics.

The skills and attitudes areas are the most similar, with communication and relationships again heading the list (Table 2.4). Even here there is divergence–with new areas like statistical information, records center operations, and office management. Finally, educational requirements continue to show the fundamental assumptions of state archives concerning archivists and records managers (Table 2.5). The orientation is toward the Bachelor's degree, away from history and library science, to records management, business and public administration; this clearly parallels the nature of records management educational programs and the specifications promulgated by the Association of Records Managers and Administrators.[12]

The final specialized group, *preservation/conservation positions*, included descriptions from only five states (Georgia, Mississippi, Maryland, South Carolina, and Illinois), indicating a general lagging behind the new emphases on archival preservation management and preservation education. As one recent report on preservation in state archives noted, "even were money available, only a small number of people have been trained in archives preservation administration and archives conservation practices" (Lowell, 1986, p. 21).[13] Titles from this group included: Conservator, Principal Archival Records Technician, Archival Records Technical Services Supervisor, Archival Conservator I and II, Microfilm Quality Control Technician, Microfilm Technician Supervisor, Assistant Microfilm Services Supervisor, Microfilm Quality Control Supervisor, Document Restorer, Archival Records Clerk, and Senior Archival Records Technician. Not surprisingly, this group has a very different set of duties (Table 2.2) from the other positions. While the entry- and mid-level positions have general responsibilities for preservation, this group works mostly on specific conservation treatments and reformatting such as through the use of micrographics. This technical group also has a higher responsibility to provide training and advisory services.

The preservation/conservation positions also have very different knowledge and education requirements. Knowledge prerequisites are very different with an emphasis on micrographics and photography and preservation/conservation techniques and principles (Table 2.3). Educational requirements are oriented to bachelor's degrees and have less stress on chemistry and preservation course work and/or apprenticeships (Table 2.5). This situation might reflect the continuing problem with the lack of educational programs available to prepare individuals for work in archival preservation. There is even some variation here in the skills and abilities enumerated for these positions (Table 2.4). While areas like communication and relationships emerge again, other skills and abilities such as manual dexterity and chemical testing also appear–reflecting the very different nature of the work. It is clear that positions in this area are seen as technical in orientation, requiring less formal education and more experience.

Other State Archives Positions

These government institutions possess a number of other positions to support their operations that are not specifically related to the archival functions. These positions have not been included in the general analysis, but it is worth describing them in order to give some indication of the ongoing staffing of the state archives. There are librarians who work with newspaper collections and perform other library-like services in the state archives. Several states have responsibility for historic preservation and archaeological activities and have specialized positions for this work (Historian I). There are also grant managers and related administrative positions. Some states utilize standard, non-specific government classifications–such as General Service Employee, Division Director, Administrator IV, and so forth–for staffing purposes. At least one state archives (Florida) has computer-related positions (Computer Operator I and III, and Computer Operations Supervisor) that probably operate in internal state archives administration and to assist in records management work. There are also, of course, many clerical and other support staff positions. Apart from the support and clerical positions, the range of other positions is largely dependent on whether the state archives is administratively a part of a historical society or another state agency.

STATE ARCHIVES STAFFING: CONCLUSIONS

The research question considered in this part of the study (that state archives are not revealing significant specialization) appears to hold true. In general, while there are some states that have expanded to include some specialized positions, the specialized position descriptions remain predominantly clustered about records management, preservation, or topical slots. Records management, which has had a separate identity for more than thirty years, is now beginning to face some challenges–with some records managers arguing for a merger and integration of their field with information technology and resources management. Preservation positions (while much fewer in number) represent more traditional hands-on conservators and micrographics technicians than the preservation managers that the profession needs to be moving toward. The topical specialists mainly show only a divergence in a topical specialty and greater supervisory responsibilities–reflecting much the same stress on arrangement, description, and reference as the entry and mid-level positions. In fact, there is only a single state that includes positions across the five categories used in this study, and only six of the states have representation in four of the five (see Table 2.6). Answers to the more specific questions posed earlier tend to support the conclusion that at this time in the state archives there is little specialization. There is, instead, a continuing emphasis on general archival responsibilities, knowledge, and skills with only minor stress on formal archival education. This conclusion is further supported by the results of a study on archival job advertisements described in the next chapter of this study.

Work Examples and Traditional Archival Functions

It would be far too lengthy an exercise to list, even by basic categories, statements of work examples included in the position descriptions. The most frequent kinds of statements, relative to the basic archival functions, are as follows:

> Conducts inventories and surveys of records and recommends retention schedules for records.
>
> Arranges and describes historical records, including the appraisal of records for historical value.
>
> Consults with donors, state and local agency heads, and the public regarding the accession and use of records.
>
> Aids researchers in using archival and manuscript collections by advising and guiding research.
>
> Prepares simple displays and assists in the research for more complex exhibits of documents, maps, photographs, and other archival materials.

Some states have begun to provide more specific and modern work examples that reflect changes in both basic archival practice and the increasing amount of records in electronic and other special formats. Examples of these kinds of statements are as follows:

> Plans and implements application of automated electronic information storage and retrieval system.
>
> Coordinates the long range planning activities of the Bureau including the development and maintenance of standards for microfilm, Computer Output Microfilm (COM), optical storage, and automated systems.
>
> Analyzes and evaluates new or modified systems and directs development of retention scheduling of information in electronic form.
>
> Researches and reviews computer technical developments in hardware and software equipment to provide up-to-date information in this field.

TABLE 2.6. Array of Positions in State Archives by State

n = 146

State	Entry	Middle	Specialized	Preservation	Records Mgt.
Alabama	1 (3.8%)	3 (7.1%)	2 (13.3%)	0	3 (6.4%)
Florida	2 (7.7%)	5 (11.9%)	1 (6.7%)	0	14 (29.8%)
Georgia	2 (7.7%)	4 (9.5%)	0	5 (31.3%)	6 (12.8%)
Illinois	1 (3.8%)	3 (7.1%)	1 (6.7%)	2 (12.5%)	2 (4.3%)
Indiana	0	0	0	0	3 (6.4%)
Maryland	1 (3.8%)	4 (9.5%)	0	3 (18.8%)	0
Michigan	2 (7.7%)	3 (7.1%)	3 (20%)	0	0
Minnesota	2 (7.7%)	1 (2.4%)	0	0	0
Mississippi	1 (3.8%)	3 (7.1%)	0	1 (6.3%)	4 (8.5%)

Nebraska	2 (7.7%)	2 (4.8%)	0	0	0
North Dakota	1 (3.8%)	1 (2.4%)	3 (20%)	0	0
New Jersey	2 (7.7%)	2 (2.8%)	0	0	7 (14.9%)
Ohio	4 (15.4%)	1 (2.4%)	4 (26.7%)	0	0
Pennsylvania	1 (3.8%)	6 (14.3%)	1 (6.7%)	0	5 (10.6%)
South Carolina	1 (3.8%)	4 (9.5%)	0	5 (31.3%)	3 (6.4%)
South Dakota	2 (7.7%)	0	0	0	0
West Virginia	1 (3.8%)	0	0	0	0
Total Positions	26	42	15	16	47

These latter work examples are more frequently part of position descriptions for records analysts in the records management units of the state archives. Position descriptions in the state archives tend to have more general statements of work examples focused on appraisal, arrangement and description, preservation, and reference.

Knowledge, Abilities, and Skills and the State Archives Position Descriptions

There is evidence that the identification of knowledge, ability, and skill requisites have not changed very much through the years in state archives positions. Nearly thirty years ago, in the most important study of state archives ever undertaken, Ernst Posner described the ideal state archives professional as follows:

> The archivist's work is not simply that of a custodian of records. He cannot carry out his most important functions–those of selecting the records of permanent value, of providing access to them through arrangement and description, and of making them available to government, scholars, and other users–unless, in addition to practical experience, he has certain prerequisites that are acquired through academic study. These prerequisites include: a good knowledge of history, especially of the history of the United States, and of its sources; experience in the techniques of historical research; familiarity with the organization and workings of government on its various levels; and mastery of the theory and methods of archives administration and of the essentials of records management. (Posner, 1964, p. 317)

Posner's description captures the essence of the current state archives position descriptions. Yet, the state archives personnel must be contrasted to the way in which state governments are creating and using information. A recent major study of information resource management in state government noted that

> state service job titles indicate a growing emphasis on telecommunications, office automation and end user computing, data base administration, policy development, planning, geo-

> graphic information systems, information resources management, software development and support, and forms design. (Caudle, Marchand et al, 1989, p. xxv)[14]

This implies a need for very different sets of knowledge, skills, and abilities than those which archivists have traditionally possessed. Furthermore it implies a necessary need if their institutions hope to operate in this arena. The position descriptions' most common citation–stressing the ability to communicate and to maintain relationships with state government officials, employees, and clientele–obviously requires some reshuffling of the requisites for employment.

Archival Position Descriptions and State Archives' Administrative Placements

There is a notable difference in the position descriptions when viewed by the administrative placement of the state archives agencies. The greatest divergence in the position descriptions is the existence of specialized (by topical emphasis, preservation, and records management) positions, positions frequently occurring in the state archives that are part of larger state agencies (such as the secretary of state or the state library) or are independent. Only slightly less than half of the topically specialized positions are in state archives that are part of state historical societies; none of the preservation or records managements positions are in these latter state archives (Table 2.7). Administrative placement also affects size, and size obviously has some effect on the degree of specialization. The state archives that are part of larger state agencies or that are independent average twice the number of professional staff than those located in state historical societies (Table 2.7).

Archival Position Descriptions and Position Levels and Specializations

The relationship between archival position descriptions and position levels and specializations provides an opportunity for a convenient summary of many aspects of state archives position descriptions. The strictly archival positions maintain a focus on the basic

TABLE 2.7. Type of Position Description by State Archives Administrative Placement and Size

n = 146

STATE PLACEMENT AND SIZE	ENTRY	MIDDLE	SPECIALIZED	PRESERVATION	RECORDS MGT.	TOTAL
Part of Larger State Agency Avg. = 15.3	12 (46.2%)	27 (64.3%)	6 (40%)	10 (62.5%)	34 (72.3%)	89 (61%)
State Historical Society Avg. = 9.4	11 (42.3%)	5 (11.9%)	7 (46.7%)	0	0	23 (15.8%)
Independent State Agencies Avg. = 15.4	3 (11.5%)	10 (23.8%)	2 (13.3%)	6 (37.5%)	13 (27.7%)	34 (23.3%)
Totals	26	42	15	16	13	146

archival functions of appraisal, arrangement and description, and reference. As the positions gain administrative responsibility or specialization, there are changes in all aspects of the position requirements. Management responsibilities and skills increase along with the need for different educational requirements and experiences. The biggest differences were evident in the preservation positions with an apprenticeship or experiential bias and the records management positions that stressed records management knowledge, education, and experience instead of similar requirements in archives administration. The records management positions also included areas like systems analysis, information technology, and statistics. Interestingly, the preservation positions seemed to be the least likely to deal with modern information systems, while the records management positions seemed to be the most equipped to work with such systems.

IMPLICATIONS OF STATE ARCHIVES POSITIONS DESCRIPTIONS FOR THE ARCHIVAL MANAGEMENT OF ELECTRONIC RECORDS

With the increased use and importance of electronic information technology in the creation of transactional records in all organizations, it is surprising that state government archives' position descriptions seem still to reflect a very traditional set of responsibilities and activities that pre-date the pervasive use of computers. This is contrary to what has been found in other similar kinds of disciplines. Among librarians, the growth of electronic databases and the increasingly sophisticated knowledge of computers by researchers have brought tremendous changes. One commentator has noted that "in larger libraries we are seeing the influx of new categories of staff: both paraprofessionals and people at the professional level, but without formal training in librarianship: programmers and system analysts, telecommunication specialists, media technicians and specialists, and conservators and restorers" (Rosenthal, 1991, p. 15). While this may be occurring in state archives, their position descriptions indicate that for them to be better situated tremendous obstacles need to be surmounted.

One obstacle might be the radical re-casting of their position descriptions, requiring, in some cases, elaborate and time-consuming work with their respective civil service agencies. This is obviously a program for all government archives. In mid-1991 the National Archives' Center for Electronic Records posted a position description that carried that institution's standard qualifications for an archival slot while, in fact, the duties were directed solely to working with electronic records.[15] Some of this challenge is reflected in the results of a follow-up survey to the seventeen state archives included in this study. This survey, resulting in responses from twelve of the states, sought additional information about the relationships the state archives had with their civil service agencies and their own sense of the need for revision of their existing position descriptions.[16] Figure 2.1 reveals the results of the state archives evaluation of their work with their respective civil service agencies. On a scale of five (5) being "very satisfied" and one (1) being "very unsatisfied," none of the areas rated here were higher than a 3.5. The lowest ratings were given in response to the questions "Do you

FIGURE 2.1. State Archives Rating of State Personnel Process

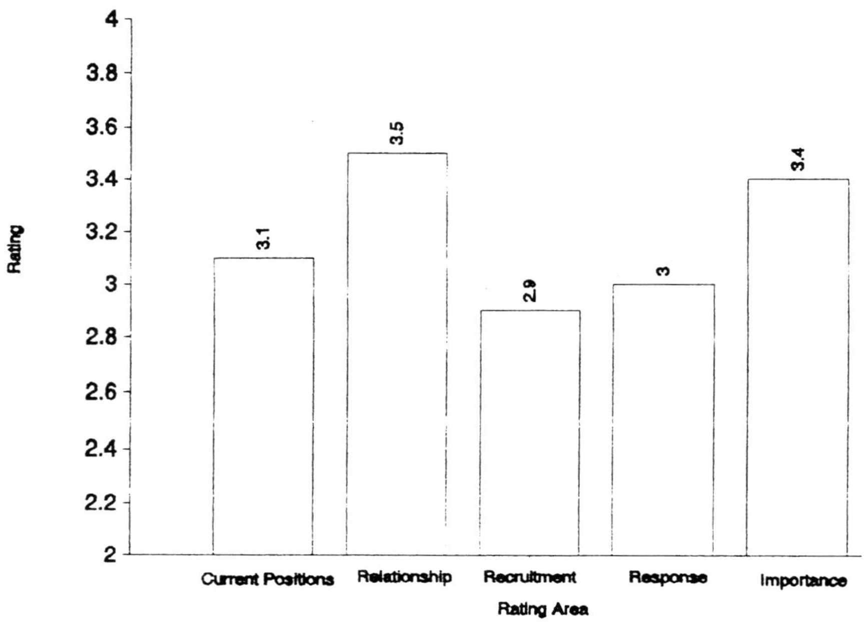

believe that you have been able to recruit and hire the kinds of professionals that you need with your present position descriptions?" (column three, "Recruitment"), "Are you satisfied with the response of the State government civil service to your needs for archival position descriptions?" (column four, "Response"), and "Are you generally satisfied with your present position descriptions?" (column one, "Current Positions"). The mid-range responses (2.9, 3.0, and 3.1 respectively) can be interpreted either as general satisfaction with the civil service process or, in contrast, a rather lukewarm reaction. The slightly higher rate of response (3.5) to the question "Do you believe that you have a satisfactory (that is, you are able to influence the development of position requirements) working relationship with the state personnel office?" (column two, "Relationship") is probably suggestive of a fairly good sense of satisfaction. This is also suggested by the response (3.4) to the question "Overall, how important do you believe position descriptions are for recruiting and hiring qualified archivists?" (column five, "Importance"). However, even though nine (9) of the twelve (12) state archives noted that their position descriptions can be revised upon request, the fact that most of the state archives possessed and used older sets of position descriptions suggested ongoing problems. Four (4) of these institutions had no major re-evaluations of their position descriptions in well over a decade. Only five (5) were in the process of working to correct the same situation.[17]

Another obstacle might be their own re-definition of what an archivist is and does. It is possible that the position descriptions reflect in-grained attitudes about archival work and the archival profession. A reflection of all this may be seen in the thirty year debate over the same issues regarding electronic records. This indecisiveness might be caused by a general lack of agreement about archival work, theory, practice, and related matters. It also might be a result of the archival profession's general comfort and security with traditional record formats. The study on state government information resource management noted that "archives are focusing their resources on processing their backlogs of material often from no earlier than 1900, and are not devoting the time needed to attend to the growing volume of records accumulating from the latter half of the twentieth century" (Caudle, Marchand et al, 1989,

p. 163). This clinging to traditional archival functions and practices might also be caused by a profession that is struggling with information technology (along with many other individuals and disciplines). Shoshana Zuboff noted that "computer-based technologies are not neutral; they embody essential characteristics that are bound to alter the nature of work within our factories and offices, and among workers, professionals, and managers" (Zuboff, 1988, p. 7).

The follow-up study with the state archives reflects some of these problems, but in an inconclusive manner. The ratings of the "most important attributes," asked for in the survey, for beginning and mid-level or advanced archivists in state archives shows that a knowledge of information technology is less important than other traditional archival areas such as arrangement and description–although it is higher than many of the other basic attributes that could be identified (see Table 2.8). However, when asked about the greatest needs for revision in the position descriptions, the state archives responded with a considerably higher rating in a "greater emphasis on technology" than in any other category (see Table 2.9). There is still, in these responses, a tendency to stress the "generalist" notion of the archivist. Seven of twelve preferred "position descriptions that favor general knowledge and skills" over "specializations," a characteristic certainly reflected in the actual state archives position descriptions described earlier in this chapter; and something that poses rather difficult issues, given the increasing need for archivists qualified to work with electronic records.

What else could explain state government archivists' inability (over a long period of time in which they recognized that electronic records were challenges to be met) to develop and fill positions focused on managing electronic records? A 1973 questionnaire sent out by the Society of American Archivists' Committee on Data Archives and Machine-Readable Records revealed that a sizeable portion of state agencies were producing electronic records–although few of the state government archives were able to work with them in any fashion. As this report suggested, "it is evident that more than half of the archives in the United States and Canada do not consider ADP media records and certainly do not plan to accession such media. . . . Although electronic computers have been in use since World War II and, importantly, since 1965, only a minor-

TABLE 2.8. Comparison of Desired Attributes for Beginning and Mid-Level/Advanced Archivists in State Archives

n = 17

ATTRIBUTE	BEGINNING LEVEL RATING	MID-LEVEL/ ADVANCED RATING
Archival Education Program	3.9	3.75
Appraisal Knowledge	3.3	4.3
Arrangement and Description Knowledge	3.9	4.5
Preservation Knowledge	3.0	3.8
Reference and Outreach Knowledge	3.2	4.3
Information Technology Knowledge	3.5	4.4
Archival Experience	2.5	4.6
General Management Knowledge	3.3	4.2

Note: The numerical ratings are based upon the scale 5 to 1 (Very important > Very Unimportant)

TABLE 2.9. Ratings of Need for Revisions in State Archives Position Descriptions

n = 17

Greater Emphasis on Technology	3.8
More Precise Management Abilities	3.3
More Precise Archival Specifications	3.3
Stronger Educational Requirements	3.25
Stronger Experience Requirements	3.25
More Precise Skills and Attitudes	3.25
More Precise Knowledge Requirements	3.2
More Precise Preservation Requirements	3.2

Note: The numerical ratings are based upon the scale 5 to 1 (Very Needed > Very Unnecessary).

ity of archivists have given much attention to the information revolution" (Fishbein, 1974, p. 10). A 1988/89 study on state government information resource management (encompassing archival operations) painted an only slightly different picture. One of the authors of this study noted that the "use of computers to carry out much of the business of state government has become the rule rather than the exception" (Fletcher, 1990, p. 31). Yet, as the author concluded, "what is noticeably lacking in most states is any explicit direction for the management of electronic records" (Fletcher, 1990, p. 27). Included in this is, of course, the state archives.

Even now state and other government archivists are still searching for adequate strategies to deal with electronic records. In 1991 the National Association of Government Archives and Records Administrators' Committee on Information Technology formulated a set of proposed projects that included the creation of a national center for electronic records "to provide leadership, promotion and coordination in public education, research, technical assistance and the development of materials and guidelines needed for the development of electronic records programs in government"; the development of a "program of Federal challenge grants to initiate electronic records programs" in the states and "major local governments";

the effort "to investigate the generally accepted automated information system design/redesign methodologies used in government and to explore the possibility of incorporating the archival/records management concerns of the identification, retention, conservation, and disposition of records in automated information systems into the system development life-cycle"; the analysis of the "effects of new information technologies on state records laws and to develop recommendations for new legislation"; and "to develop a layman's guide to those key information technology standards that archivists should be aware of as they develop archival electronic records programs."[18] Whatever the merit of these proposals, they nevertheless support the notion that the state government archivists have not progressed very far from the 1973 survey that showed them on the fringes of the information revolution. The proposal for a "layman's guide," as the NAGARA committee termed it, especially reflected this and a more serious problem. If state archives had done little to develop position descriptions that could support work with electronic records, and these institutions continued to look for non-technical solutions to technical issues, then how could effective programs be developed for electronic records?

Margaret Hedstrom, a pioneer in the archival profession in its work with electronic records, has carefully identified the elements of an ideal state archives electronic records program, stressing that such programs will reflect variations given their governmental and institutional environments and traditions. The four major elements that Hedstrom has identified are (1) "a coherent comprehensive state information policy"; (2) "a clear definition of electronic records"; (3) the possession of "authority in archival program to designate records as archival"; and (4) a "thorough knowledge of the 'information technology' environment." To these elements, Hedstrom has added the need for the state archives program to be able to render "useful" services in the electronic records area, have "sufficient staff with adequate training," be "acquainted with and . . . known to the user community," possess a "track record of successes," and have the ability to "adapt to new situations, take advantage of opportunities and innovate."[19] A comparison of Hedstrom's points to the NAGARA Committee on Information Technology's agenda reveals a wide gap. Even wider is the fact that, by the early 1990s, only *two* state archives had developed the first stages of effective electronic records programs.

Hedstrom also has made a preliminary effort to assess the degree of success that state archives have had in administering electronic records possessing archival value. First, she has noted that the state archives community should not be too quick to conclude that the state archives have failed with electronic records. Hedstrom suggested that the development of effective electronic records programs, slowed down by the fact the information technology environment is constantly changing and bringing more complexity, "will take years or even decades." If archivists look back on what they have accomplished, seeing expressions of interest in electronic records in the 1960s, discussions of whether these records fell under their jurisdiction into the 1970s, and the first efforts to manage these records not coming until the 1980s, then it is evident that this is correct. She also suggested "possible measures of success" for the improvement of efforts to administer electronic records. These measures include the following: (1) "ability to obtain resources for program based on strong case for anticipated benefits"; (2) "ability to mobilize a community of users/clients"; (3) "advice of archives/records staff is sought by creators/custodians of electronic records"; and (4) "change in outcomes attributable to electronic records programs," including improved access to electronic records, an enhanced accountability for working with electronic records, a better delivery of services to state agencies for electronic records management, and improved services for researchers needing access to these records.[20]

Hedstrom's long-range prognosis is certainly reflected in the state archives applications to the second installment of the Advanced Institute for Government Archives and Records Administrators held at the University of Pittsburgh School of Library and Information Science in June 1991 (and typical of the participants in the earlier institute). Of fifteen state archives only two (New York and Kentucky, discussed in more detail below) possessed viable electronic records programs, several more had established working committees to strengthen the state archives' roles in the information technology management environment, and one had established and filled a staff position of an Electronic Records Archivist.[21] States represented in the initial phase of this institute, held in June 1989 and 1990, also reflected a similar pattern of uneven success:

> Despite [the] diversity in institutional characteristics, the state archives shared a remarkable uniformity in problems in working with electronic records, or at least a notion of what these problems are . . . . Many states noted there is a basic problem in the definition of electronic records as records; task forces and other authorities responsible for coordinating or creating information policy do not include or are not influenced by the state archives; laws and regulations regarding electronic records are either non-existent or overlap and conflict; the legislature has minimal interest in information management issues; and standards for the review, design, and purchase of hardware and software is decentralized. Only a few state archives were developing programs to manage electronic records, and none of the institute participants believed that an adequate job was being done in administering these records (Cox, 1989, p. 4).

Out of this institute some of the states, such as Maine and Pennsylvania, have gone on to conduct internal strategic planning–building bridges with other state information technology and policy agencies and seeking the assistance of external funds to start electronic records programs.

New York and Kentucky have been the two most successful state archives in developing electronic records programs. New York, the youngest of the American state archives, has rapidly advanced to the forefront of these archival institutions in caring for archival records in electronic form. This advance has been crowned by the 1990 establishment of a Center for Electronic Records staffed by electronic records specialists and headed by Margaret Hedstrom. All this was the result of a long series of other developments going back at least six years. In the period 1985-1988 the New York State Archives ran a Special Media Records Project that, among a number of things, evaluated electronic records being created by seventeen state agencies. "The purpose of this . . . project was to assess the adequacy of State government policies and procedures for the management of computer-generated, machine-readable records, and to develop a program for the long-term preservation of selected, valuable machine-readable records at the State Archives" (New York State Archives and Records Administration, 1988, p. v). The result of this project was the state archives' gaining experience with electronic records, the acquisition of a nationally-known expert in electronic records, the training of other staff for working with electronic records, the building of increased credibility within state government for dealing with information technology issues, and the drafting of an important long-range plan for dealing with electronic records (New York State Archives and Records Administration, 1991; Hedstrom and Kowlowitz, 1988).

The Kentucky Public Records Division has followed a development pattern similar to that of New York. Recently, the Kentucky program established the Technology Analysis and Support Branch, the equivalent of New York's Center for Electronic Records. This too is the result of a long gestation. In 1985-88 Kentucky fostered a Machine-Readable Records Project, funded by the National Historical Publications and Records Commission, in order to do pilot efforts in the scheduling of electronic information systems and to work with the state's central data processing agency in the construction of a data dictionary that would provide information about all electronic systems maintained by Kentucky state government (Belding and Fortson, 1985). This project was the result of about five years of previous efforts, using existing staff, to administer state electronic records, starting with the inclusion of these records on state government records retention schedules. In mid-1983 the project moved on to the formation of a Machine-Readable Records Task Force in order "to study the problems associated with the identification, retention, preservation, and accessibility of MRR" (Belding and Fortson, 1985, pp. 60, 62). The preparation of qualified staff and the visibility of the state archives through the Machine-Readable Records Project enabled the state archives to gain a featured role in that state's information resources management plan (Kentucky Information Systems Commission, 1990) and an ability to work on projects such as the Public Records Management System, a "statewide locator" system to records (Robb, 1990).

What do these successful efforts suggest about electronic records and state archives? Hedstrom has identified four elements leading to success. Among the four elements is a long-term effort aimed at developing a program, finding and utilizing sufficient institutional resources in behalf of such a program, providing a strong focused or "dedicated" program for electronic records, and making a "commitment to solving problems rather than looking for models elsewhere."[22] What Hedstrom did not explicitly note, but which is implicit in all of these elements, is the acquisition of a staff interested in and knowledgeable about the electronic information technology. But, as the successful and unsuccessful programs, described above, indicate, this has obviously been a factor in the practical efforts accomplished.[23] The initial efforts to develop an electronic records program in the New York State Archives were slowed because "staff were not available to work on electronic records issues" (New York State Archives and Records Administration, 1991, p. 7). Hedstrom and Kowlowitz, reviewing the New York situation, have noted that "archivists need a solid background in archival theory and practice because most archival issues that arise when dealing with machine-readable records are similar to those that occur with traditional paper records" and, obviously, "computer literacy and fluency in EDP terminology are essential skills for archivists working with electronic records" (Hedstrom and Kowlowitz, 1988, p. 35).

Kentucky archival administrators have made similar statements about staffing:

> In the late 1970s, division staff began to include computer-related records on the records retention schedules of some of the larger agencies of state government. Because of a lack of in-house expertise and experience with these records, the appraisal and ultimate retention of these records was based largely on recommendations from agency EDP personnel, with less-than-usual regard for the archival principles used in appraising records in hard-copy form. It soon became apparent that this method of records management was unacceptable. (Belding and Fortson, 1985, p. 60)

This prompted the Kentucky state archives program to intensify efforts in preparing its staff for work with electronic records. This effort included gathering data about the state government use of electronic information technology, allowing its staff to gain "hands-on experience with the management of MRR through the development of automated systems to handle the Kentucky Guide Project data base and bibliographic control and indexing of Kentucky state publications," allowing staff to seek education on electronic records wherever there were opportunities for this, researching the legal admissibility of electronic records, and, finally, "sending and receiving data electronically, on a routing basis, to and from such agencies as the Finance and Administration Cabinet and DIS" (Belding and Fortson, 1985, pp. 61-62).

Perhaps the most dramatic evidence of the staffing portion of the state archives equation was the State Historical Society of Wisconsin's experience. A decade ago the Wisconsin state archives was the path-breaker in dealing with electronic records. Armed with two grants in 1979-1983, this work with the state government's electronic records provided the experience that enabled Margaret Hedstrom to write the major manual on electronic records in 1984 (Fox, 1984). In 1991, the newly-appointed Wisconsin state archivist wrote the following:

> A 1988 consultant's report on the status of Wisconsin's machine-readable records programs outlined some of the problems that led to its demise. One was the unanticipated events following the conclusion of the [grant-funded] projects: repeated rounds of budget reductions that deprived the State Archives of the resources required to extend the initial, grant-funded stages of work. Another was the departure of all the State Archives staff with training and experience in automated records. A more fundamental problem lay in beginning a program entirely on soft money instead of combining permanent and temporary staff positions. When the grant funds were spent, there was no program in place to continue, let alone expand the work that had begun.[24]

Wisconsin's experience stands as a stark monument to the efforts of state archivists to gain a federally-funded grant-in-aid program and to seek other sources of funding rather than building a solid, knowledgeable staff from within. The fact that Wisconsin's experience supported the New York State Archives' later work is also testimony to the fact that the archives profession is still plagued by a lack of experienced and technically-proficient electronic records archivists–a fact also reflected in the previous analysis of state archives position descriptions.

CONCLUSION AND NEEDS FOR ADDITIONAL RESEARCH

An analysis of the state archives position descriptions has suggested that state government archival programs are not thoroughly equipped to function in the modern information era. Although working with electronic records it is not likely, as David J. Murrah has suggested, that "because of the variety of demands placed upon an archivist, the broader the background, the better." Electronic records require individuals knowledgeable in archival practice and theory–and persons who have a specialized knowledge of computers and related technology. The position descriptions seem to answer the earlier-stated research question that state archives do not yet adequately reflect the trends in specialization and in responsibilities and requirements that would allow the state archival programs to operate effectively within the modern electronic information environment, especially with electronic records. As state agencies and individuals become more accustomed to using and interacting with new information technologies, the state archives staff look more like passive curators in information museums, rather than information professionals playing crucial roles in managing state government and serving the needs of its clientele. State government archives have clearly articulated a need for playing the broader role.

There are, of course, areas waiting for additional study, some which will only be mentioned here and then more fully discussed in the final chapter of this study. An examination of position descriptions alone is a very limited view of archivists' work with electronic records. State archivists need to be queried about how they are able to use their present positions to gather the diverse and specialized staffs that they need. Personal experience in two state archives indicated that individuals applying for entry and mid-level positions often exceed the qualifications specified in the position announcements. It is, of course, also possible that state archivists are often able to work around limitations in and problems with civil service developed and maintained position descriptions–the New York and Kentucky experiences being cases in point.

More importantly, a broader type of research regarding their staffs needs to be carried out in the state archives. The Position Analysis Questionnaire (PAQ) could be utilized to determine more specifically position requirements. The Critical Incident Technique (CIT) could be employed to identify actual behaviors on the job. The Job Element Method (JEM) is a tool that would allow more precise identification of attributes required for superior performance in specific positions. These and other techniques, like IJA mentioned earlier, being increasingly used by human resources managers and vocational or occupational psychologists, could help state archivists learn significantly more about their requirements for staffing (Ash, Levine, and Sistrunk, 1983). Comparisons also need to be made between the staffing of state archives, other archival institutions, and other information centers (e.g., libraries). A sophisticated analysis of advertisements for archival positions in state archives, universities and colleges, historical societies, corporations, and religious institutions could determine whether or not other archival institutions and programs have different patterns in requirements for archivists, and if the emphasis continues to be on general or very basic responsibilities, knowledge, and skills (Caudill, Caudill, and Singletary, 1987; Jackson, 1985). This kind of analysis is reported on in the next chapter. Similar comparisons (after this research is done for the archival profession) may then be made between archivists, librarians, and other information professionals.

ENDNOTES

1. In the early 1980s the Society of American Archivists sought to produce a concise definition of "archivist." Archivists were defined through their knowledge, values, and practice. Practice stipulated, according to this effort, that archivists appraised, arranged and described, provided access to, promoted the use of, and preserved archival records. See Society of American Archivists (1984a and b).

2. Murrah's article was based on secondary sources and the author's experiences; there was no survey of employers.

3. By "malformed," I only mean that what has passed for graduate archival education "programs" has usually consisted of only a few courses, at best, loosely tied to existing graduate degrees in other fields such as library science and history. The nature of graduate archival education in the United States will be more fully considered later in this study.

4. For an introduction to the debates and changes that have preoccupied archivists during the past decade, see Cox, 1990c.

5. While this will be examined in greater detail in subsequent chapters, some preliminary evidence can be mentioned at this point. An analysis of position advertisements in the *SAA Newsletter* for a two year period identified a "shift away from 'soft' requirements towards measurable ones." This was interpreted as a "move to increase the importance of formal and demonstrable competencies." On the other hand, the skills and formal qualifications portions of the advertisements suggested that archivists were still viewed somewhat generally. See Bearman, 1986, p. 9.

6. For explorations into the continuing use of position descriptions, a perusal of several recent issues of *Personnel Journal* or *Personnel* will reveal how human resources managers view these documents.

7. The state archives that Schulz studied were asked to send copies of full sets of their current position descriptions; of the twenty-four states included in the Schulz study, seventeen responded by sending copies of their position descriptions, providing a full range of the kinds of state archives that are typical to the profession.

8. Appendix One of my dissertation includes examples of each type of position description.

9. The author's experience in state government archives was also used as a guide in evaluating position descriptions. The author worked for five and one half years at two state archives, the first established state archives in Alabama (1901) and the most recently formed program in New York (1975). This experience, the position descriptions themselves, and the author's knowledge of archival programs led to the tri-partite division of the position descriptions. The segmentation is artificial in the sense that each state government archives will have slightly different variations in their structures, but this division does provide for some comparison and analysis.

10. This lag is especially noticeable when viewed against trends in archival job advertisements which show a decided swing to a knowledge of the US MARC Archives and Manuscripts Control format as a requirement for most entry-level and many specialized positions. The next chapter of this study provides more detail on this trend.

11. The records management field emerged from the archival profession in the 1950s. Since then, records managers have created their own professional associations, educational programs, journals, and the like. Records managers consider archival administration to be a function of records management, while many archivists view records management to be indispensable in fulfilling the archival mission. Numerous articles have appeared over the past thirty years examining the relationship between the two fields.

12. The vast majority of records management programs are in undergraduate business and office administration schools, while the archival programs are all located in graduate history departments and library and information science schools. See ARMA, 1990, for a directory of records management education programs; this directory is issued annually.

13. This reflects, despite the fundamental importance of preservation and conservation, the fact that only a small portion of state archives possess in-house programs in this area.

14. See especially chapter 8 on the state government records management and archives programs.

15. Vacancy announcement DEU 91-10. These standard archival qualifications are as follows: "Education/experience equivalent to a full 4 year course in an accredited college leading to a BA degree or higher that included 18 sem hrs in US history and/or American political science, public administration, or government, *plus* 12 sem hrs in history, American civilization, economics, political science, public administration, or government. . . . In addition, must have progressively responsible professional archival experience." A cover letter of July 23, 1991 from Thomas E. Brown did indicate, however, that another position was being developed "for an archives specialist whose position will not require academic course work in American history and related fields."

16. Appendix Two in my dissertation includes a copy of the survey instrument used to gather this data.

17. The breakdown of dates for major re-evaluations is as follows: 1976, 1; 1978, 3; 1982, 1; 1983, 1; 1984, 1; 1987, 1; and 1988, 1.

18. Larry J. Hackman to Members of NAGARA Committee on Information Technology, May 24, 1991, copy in author's possession.

19. These points were made by Hedstrom in a presentation to the Advanced Institute for Government Records and Archives Administrators in June 1991.

20. Hedstrom presentation to the Advanced Institute for Government Archives and Records Administrators, June 1991.

21. Based on the applications submitted in March and April 1991 and in the possession of the author.

22. Hedstrom presentation, June 1991.

23. This is not to suggest that there are not other issues, such as those formulated by the NAGARA Committee on Information Technology, besides staffing. There is certainly the need to re-examine the legal definitions of records, for example. But the problem with legal definitions may be well-overshadowed by the technical expertise of state archives staff needed to carry out any kind of electronic records program. As one review of Federal legislation indicated, "the legal provisions which relate to records and archives are 'media non-specific' in that the statutes relate to all record material regardless of media" and the problems relative to electronic records are more often because of "division of authority" in records management and archival responsibilities; Brown 1986, pp. 41-42. Such disagreements might be more frustrated by uneven balance of appropriate technical expertise among the various government agencies.

24. Peter Gottlieb to Richard J. Cox, March 28, 1991, copy in the NAGARA Institute Files, University of Pittsburgh, School of Library and Information Science.

Chapter Three

Archival Position Advertisements: Trends and Practices in the Information Age, 1976-1990

INTRODUCTION

Despite archivists having spent considerable time to consider the impact of electronic records on their mission, theory, and practice, it appears that state government archives–leaders in the archival profession and the institutions with the best opportunity to manage electronic records–have not done very well in establishing programs for such management. Technology seems to be driving *concerns* about archival practice and theory, but not the actual practice or development of theory. This part of the study proposes to show that state government archives are not the only ones with the problem in the American archival profession. In fact, the archival profession in the United States has not developed a sufficient number of positions requiring experience and expertise needed for administering archival records in electronic form–this is the primary research question being considered in this investigation. The archival profession also has not integrated fully into basic archival positions, such qualifications that would indicate how this discipline is com-

[Haworth co-indexing entry note]: "Archival Position Advertisements: Trends and Practices in the Information Age, 1976-1990." Cox, Richard J. Co-published simultaneously in: *Primary Sources & Original Works* (The Haworth Press, Inc.), Volume 3(3/4), 1994, pp. 97-130; and: *The First Generation of Electronic Records Archivists in the United States: A Study in Professionalization,* Richard J. Cox, The Haworth Press, Inc., 1994, pp. 97-130. Multiple copies of this article/chapter may be purchased from The Haworth Document Delivery Center [1-800-3-HAWORTH; 9:00 a.m. - 5:00 p.m. (EST)].

mitted to preserving and administering electronic records possessing archival value. Yet, archival literature suggests that electronic records are a primary focus of the profession (at least from the perspective of attention given to an issue).

The problem is exacerbated by the contrast of the archival profession's development against the expectations of the researchers it serves. Although user expectations are changing regarding their use of archival records, although this is a topic deserving fuller study than is possible here. Many researchers, however, are computer-literate and a portion of these are beginning to expect access to desired information through electronic means (Michelson and Rothenberg, 1992). A review of advertisements over the past fifteen years suggests, however, that little has changed as to how archivists view their responsibilities.[1] Most basic advertisements seem oriented to a static view of what an archivist does and how this professional fits into the institution and the broader society that the archivist serves. It may be that the archival institution is the last vestige of a profession to reflect change. This may be true also because most archival programs consist of small professional staffs and archivists, and therefore are expected to be generalists and carry-out a wide range of responsibilities.

Many of the professional problems initially identified in this study are clearly linked to what seems to be reflected in this role. The lack of an extensive *research* literature on archival records in electronic form seems to be connected logically to the fact that most of the job advertisements, in all types of archival programs, do not reflect any qualifications appropriate for the administration of modern electronic information systems. The relative under-emphasis on archival education and training seems to be a reflection of a serious problem in the American archival profession, i.e., the slowly emerging development of more comprehensive guidelines for education and training has certainly lagged behind the profession's need for expertise in electronic information systems.

ADVERTISED EVIDENCE

This part of the study is an effort to consider further how American archival institutions have endeavored to manage electronic records. Each job advertisement has been examined for some general characteristics about recent archival staffing patterns in the United States. The position advertisements have been examined to show patterns in educational, experiential, knowledge, and skill requirements. The position advertisements have also been broken down into repository types, positions by functions, and, finally, the changing patterns of the number of positions being advertised requiring automated techniques and electronic records knowledge and experience. This analysis is an effort to consider the question whether the archival profession in this country has not created an adequate number or variety of positions intended to be responsible for electronic records. Specifically, the following questions have been asked of the job advertisements:

1. Do the advertisements contain examples of work that extend beyond basic traditional archival functions (appraisal and accessioning, arrangement and description, preservation, reference, and public outreach) to take into account increasing uses of electronic information technology?
2. What knowledge, abilities, or skills are mentioned in the advertisements that reflect a requirement to know about electronic records?
3. Is there any growth in the number of archival positions requiring computer literacy?
4. Are there any patterns in archival job advertisements according to the type of archival repository (college and university, government, local, religious, or business)?
5. Are the patterns revealed in the archival job advertisements similar to the patterns revealed by the analysis of state archival position descriptions?

THE RESEARCH DESIGN

The research design (as that of the previous chapter on state archives position descriptions) is straightforward. Over fifteen hundred job advertisements from 1976 through 1990 were carefully examined to see what elements reflecting the increased use of electronic information technology were evident. The job advertisements were first grouped according to repository type, to determine whether they were typical of the panorama of archival repositories in the United States. Following this, each position advertisement was grouped according to main archival function, again to see whether any patterns emerge (if these advertisements were typical of the American archival profession's general predilections) and to determine whether these possible patterns relate to the changing use by society of electronic information technology. Then each position's requirements for education, experience, and other features were analyzed to determine whether there has been any noticeable change in the basic requirements over the past decade and a half. All of the above analyses have also been sketched out over time.

The main focus of the design is, of course, to identify every reference to computer technology and electronic records. These references have been related to the kinds of archival institutions, position responsibilities, and year to determine how the American archival profession has endeavored to cope with the electronic information technology. Emerging patterns have been related to the debate and discussion in the archival profession over the past quarter-century.

Unlike some of the semantic problems encountered in the state archives position descriptions in the use of knowledge, skills, and attitudes, the job advertisements are easier to characterize. Over the past fifteen years, the Society of American Archivists' *Newsletter*'s job advertisements have been remarkably consistent in format. Each advertisement has adhered generally to a pattern of responsibilities, qualifications, and salary and benefits. Salary and benefits have not been considered because these are outside the scope of this study and because these (of all the other elements of the advertisements) are the most inconsistently reported in detail sufficient to support evaluation. Government positions nearly always report salary. Other repositories are far less consistent in reporting salaries, preferring to use phrases such as "dependent upon qualifications and experience."

Some decisions were made to facilitate analysis of these job advertisements. Some advertisements were run in more than one newsletter issue, but for the purpose of this study they were analyzed only once. If a position's search was re-opened and the advertisement was repeated without any substantive change, it was also counted only once. If an announcement indicated that two or more positions were open meeting the qualifications, then the advertisement was counted that specific number of times. If an unspecified number of positions were open, then the advertisement was counted only once. Non-archival advertisements posted in the Society of American Archivists' *Newsletter* were not considered at all. Finally, an effort has been made to put the job advertisements within the context of research on such advertisements in other related information professions. Again, while there has been an insufficiency of such research, there is enough to suggest some comparisons.

A final comment needs to be made regarding the source of these advertisements, the SAA *Newsletter*. Publication of the *Newsletter* was started in the mid-1970s as the Society moved from a largely volunteer-run professional association to an association staffed by an executive director, other professionals, and support staff. The *Newsletter* has become the primary source for the posting of archival positions in the United States, in that it is the most complete and most regular for advertising such openings. Regional archival associations, such as the Mid-Atlantic Region Archives Conference (MARAC) and the Midwest Archives Conference (MAC), that publish newsletters also post job advertisements for their specific regions. Library journals, such as *American Libraries*, publish archival job advertisements for positions in libraries. Other topically-focused publications, such as *The Chronicle of Higher Education* and the newsletter of the American Institute of Physics (AIP) Center for the History of Physics, publish advertisements for archival jobs in the types of institutions related to their readerships; *The Chronicle of Higher Education* carries advertisements for archival positions in colleges and universities and the AIP publication will often mention positions in the area of science and technology archives. Only the SAA *Newsletter*, however, covers a broad range of archival programs and is nearly comprehensive in scope; it is the closest to a job listing of record for the archival profession in the United States.

Some archival positions may not be carried in the *Newsletter*. For example, over the past decade, the Society of American Archivists has published a *Job Employment Bulletin*, issued in the intervening months of the *Newsletter* (the *Newsletter* is published in January,

March, May, July, September, and October each year, with some occasional variation in the time span analyzed) and available for separate subscription. Because of the special subscription arrangement, the complete *Job Employment Bulletin* was not readily available to the author; a cursory glance at some issues of this publication suggests however that many of the advertisements are carried in both *Newsletter* and *Bulletin*. There are other factors, based on the author's experience in private and government archives, that work against publication of archival job openings in the SAA *Newsletter*. Some archival programs choose from time to time not to publish advertisements at all; they rely on personal contacts for recruitment. Government archival programs (such as in state and local government) face deadlines that sometimes require them to recruit outside the SAA *Newsletter*. Finally, some smaller programs, such as local historical societies or museums, elect not to publish archival advertisements because of low salaries or part-time and related characteristics of the positions. Still, the advertisements published in the *Newsletter* are representative of the types of positions and nature of archival programs in the American archival profession. This can be confirmed later by comparison of the job advertisement with other surveys and profiles of the American archival profession.

THE FINDINGS

The findings have been described below from a general nature to more specific issues about archival positions directly concerned with information technology. First, there is an analysis of the archival position advertisements by repository type, main archival function, and primary requirements (such as education, experience, and knowledge). This analysis provides a general profile of the archival position advertisements over the past decade and a half. Second, there is an analysis of the advertisements for what they suggest about requirements and needs for archivists working with electronic records and using information technology for other purposes (such as automated descriptive systems). In this segment of the analysis, the pattern of advertisements for specialized positions in both electronic records and automated techniques has been identified. Examples of such advertisements have been included. Finally, there is an analysis of wording indicating knowledge of electronic information technology for archivists.

General Patterns in the Job Advertisements

The archival job advertisements clearly reflect the general nature of archival programs in the United States. Consistently, through the years 1976-1990, job advertisements for academic institutions (colleges and universities) and for state and local government remain the highest portion of the total advertisements. Table 3.1 shows the actual number of positions advertised, revealing that federal government, business, religious, subject (such as those programs focusing on the documentation of specific population groups), and museum programs are consistently in the minor portions of the overall advertisements. As can be seen from the table, there are some general ebbs and flows in the number and types of positions in the specific repositories. Again, while there are some general shifts in the number of positions advertised (1983 represents a significant decline in job advertisements while 1988 shows a large increase) the academic and state and local government advertisements are clearly on the top end of the number of advertisements throughout the period analyzed.

The proportions of repository types appear to be consistent with other surveys of the American archival profession. Figure 3.1 is a graphical representation of the proportions of types of archival repositories placing job advertisements, with state and local government and academic institutions constituting 71 percent of the repositories advertising for positions in the SAA *Newsletter* (this representation has percentages rounded off and has combined federal and state government repositories and business, religious, and museum programs into the institutional category to make the diagram easier to view). Generally, these portions seem to be reflected in other analyses of the American archival profession. A 1990 survey of the Academy of Certified Archivists, a 1985 census of archival institutions, and a 1982 salary survey of SAA members, all reveal roughly similar breakdowns of the types of archival repositories (see Table 3.2 for comparison), although it must be remembered that none of these surveys were primarily conducted to determine the propor-

TABLE 3.1. Archival Position Advertisements by Repository Type

n = 1557

	1976	1977	1978	1979	1980	1981	1982	1983	1984	1985	1986	1987	1988	1989	1990	Total
Federal	1	3	1	0	1	2	0	3	2	1	1	11	20	9	4	59 *3.8%*
State	16	21	16	22	17	20	10	12	37	21	26	20	40	30	28	336 *21.6%*
Local	1	7	9	20	19	19	15	3	21	32	18	20	25	18	8	235 *15.1%*
Academic	16	25	39	29	28	31	32	20	39	47	42	50	45	42	49	534 *34.3%*
Business	4	4	2	5	1	1	1	1	2	9	2	10	6	9	4	61 *3.9%*
Religious	2	1	4	8	7	3	4	5	6	5	4	10	9	9	4	81 *5.2%*
Subject	3	15	9	14	29	12	6	5	13	11	10	11	20	11	17	98 *6.3%*
Museum	1	1	1	9	3	3	3	3	8	8	8	7	8	10	4	77 *4.9%*
Other	3	3	7	6	7	4	4	4	7	9	3	7	10	9	12	76 *4.9%*
Total	47 *3%*	80 *5.1%*	88 *5.7%*	113 *7.3%*	112 *7.2%*	95 *6.1%*	75 *4.8%*	56 *3.6%*	135 *8.7%*	143 *9.2%*	114 *7.3%*	146 *9.4%*	183 *11.8%*	147 *9.4%*	130 *8.3%*	1557

FIGURE 3.1. Archival Repositories in Job Advertisements, 1976-90

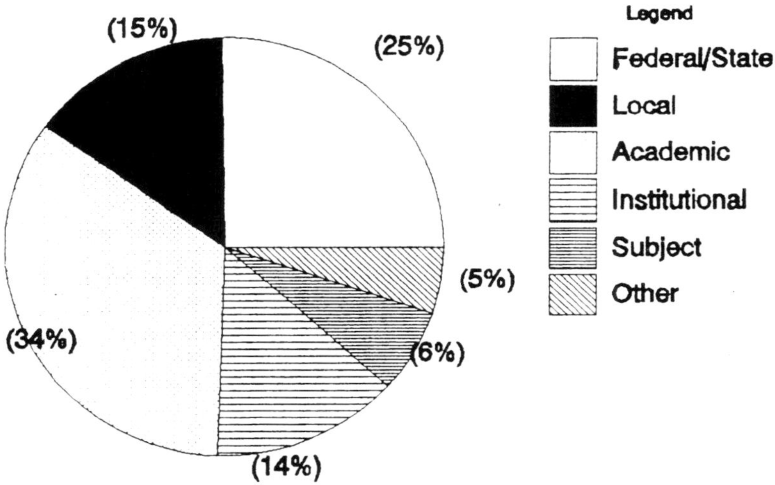

tions of repository types in the archival landscape.[2] Paul Conway's comments about the difficulties in characterizing archival repositories should also be kept in mind; he noted (1987, p. 78):

> the nature of the parent, holdings, and public did not, by themselves, necessarily define a repository, although sometimes one of these factors predominated. There was no perfect composition of any grouping, but the process of typecasting was a key to identifying patterns of resources underlying apparent institutional uniqueness.

The same difficulties also related to the identification of repository types using job advertisements. But the process of striving to identify the repository types confirms that the SAA *Newsletter* advertisements are typical of the American archival profession.

The next area of analysis of the job advertisements is the breakdown of these advertisements by primary archival function. Archivists generally characterize their work as constituting appraisal (identification and selection), arrangement and description, reference, preservation, and public outreach (cf., Bradsher, 1989; McCarthy, 1989;

TABLE 3.2. Comparison of Repository Types in Various Archival Surveys, 1982-91

	This Study n = 1557	1990 ACA Survey n = n/a	1985 Census n = 549	1982 SAA Survey n = 1717
Federal	3.8%	13.3%	5%	9.7%
State	21.6%	13.8%	11%	9.8%
Local	15.1%	N/A	5%	6.5%
Academic	34.3%	37.8%	38%	35%
Business	3.9%	N/A	6%	N/A
Religious	5.2%	6.5%	19%	13%
Special Subject	6.3%	N/A	13%	N/A
Museum	4.9%	N/A	3%	6%
Other	4.9%	28.6%	N/A	N/A

O'Toole, 1990, chapter 4). A position specialized in a particular archival function looks like the below job advertisement example:

> *Archival Specialist for Reference and Outreach.* Oregon State University Corvallis, Oregon. RESPONSIBILITIES: The Archival Specialist is one of two line positions involved in the daily operation of both the records management and the archival components of a major university records program. The Archival Specialist will perform appraisal, accessioning, arrangement, description, and preservation of the historical records of the institution, as well as providing most reference service to those materials. Designing, preparing, and assembling displays and exhibits will be required occasionally. The position will also provide the staff of other departments with assistance and consultation in basic records and files management techniques, such as inventory, analysis, scheduling, transfer, and disposition of university records. Participates in as well as trains and directs student workers in accessioning, processing, microfilming, computer indexing, and providing reference service to university records. May make group pre-

> sentations and workshops on historical and records management topics, as well as work individually with researchers and departmental records officers. QUALIFICATIONS: Minimum qualifications, BA or BS in social science, history, political science, or related field and one to three years of closely related working experience. Preferred Qualifications, MA or MS in archival administration, library science, or above-described field. Also prefer knowledge of history of the Pacific Northwest, computers and data-base applications, USMARC AMC format, audio-visual materials and techniques, as well as micrographics. Successful candidate must be capable of lifting and carrying 15-35 lbs and working in an environment which requires occasional exposure to dust, pollen, and mildew . . . (SAA Newsletter, September 1990, p. 18)

An advertisement for a specialized position is as follows:

> *Manuscript Processor/Cataloger.* University of Southern Mississippi Hattiesburg, Mississippi. De Grumond Children's Literature Research Collection, University of Southern Mississippi. Two year NEH grant funded position. Reports to curator of Collection. RESPONSIBILITIES: Include coordination of the arrangement and description of children's literature manuscripts and illustrations, preparation of descriptive registers, cataloging collections using USMARC AMC, and supervise 1.5 full-time employees. QUALIFICATIONS: ALA-accredited MLS or equivalent; training and 2-3 years experience processing manuscript collections; knowledge of historical and contemporary children's literature; knowledge of USMARC AMC; good supervisory and management skills; good oral, written and interpersonal communication skills . . . (SAA Newsletter, September 1990, p. 17)

Given that a large number of archivists also work as one-person operations, "administrative" and "general" categories as archival function also seem to be needed in any kind of analysis such as this; these categories have been used in this study to assist in the analysis of the job descriptions. An example of this kind of advertisement is as follows:

> *Archivist.* Rush-Presbyterian St. Luke's Medical Center Chicago. RESPONSIBILITIES: Management of an established archives for a Medical Center, including a health sciences university, whose roots go back [to] 1837 with the founding of the Rush Medical College. The program of collection development and archival services, includes accessioning, appraisal, arrangement, description of incoming documents, preparation of finding aids, budget control, and reference services. The 1,000 linear feet of holdings consist of corporate history, personal papers, publications, photographs, slides, books, and artifacts pertaining to all components of the Medical Center. QUALIFICATIONS: MA in history or related field and/or certified archivist, 3-5 years experience in archival administration, good communication, organizational and supervisory skills, ability to work with staff, members of the professional community, students, and researchers. Health science background helpful . . . (SAA Newsletter, May 1990, p. 31)

A few positions are also oriented to specific forms of documentation, a category that will become more relevant in the later discussion on electronic records. Beyond electronic records, positions are often advertised for archivists specializing in formats such as still or motion pictures, maps and cartographic records.

As was seen with the repository type in archival job advertisements, there are also some noticeable patterns in the advertisements when these are examined by main archival function. Table 3.3 shows the trends in archival position advertisements by main archival function through the years 1976-1990. While there is a slight difference in the numerical totals between repository type (1557) and main archival function (1652) (because some particular advertisements are for more than one position and all have been counted), the same kinds of patterns appear. There is a decline in the number of positions in 1982-83, and an increase in the years 1987-88. More importantly, as is easily seen in Figures 3.2 and 3.3, administrative duties constitute nearly a third (31 percent) of the job advertisements, followed by arrangement and description positions (24.8%) and those positions with broadly defined general duties (20.2%).

TABLE 3.3. Archival Position Advertisements by Main Function, 1976-90

n = 1652

	1976	1977	1978	1979	1980	1981	1982	1983	1984	1985	1986	1987	1988	1989	1990	Total
Administrative	3	8	8	8	7	3	4	4	11	8	4	9	11	5	9	102 *6.2%*
Arrangement & Description	8	26	32	43	31	34	20	12	29	16	29	29	42	26	32	409 *24.8%*
Reference	0	0	2	0	2	4	2	0	1	5	3	5	7	4	7	42 *2.5%*
Preservation	0	3	5	2	1	3	2	3	6	6	6	13	8	7	5	70 *4.2%*
Outreach	1	0	0	4	0	6	1	1	6	7	5	5	12	1	6	55 *3.1%*
Administrative	21	16	17	11	23	25	32	21	48	67	41	49	54	40	47	512 *31%*
General	13	19	20	29	33	5	10	11	16	18	24	25	33	57	20	333 *20.2%*
Forms	0	3	0	2	6	5	1	3	11	8	2	4	6	3	1	55 *3.3%*
Other	1	6	3	6	4	10	3	0	7	8	2	7	10	4	3	74 *4.5%*
Total	47 *2.8%*	71 *4.3%*	77 *4.7%*	105 *6.4%*	107 *6.5%*	95 *5.8%*	75 *4.5%*	56 *3.4%*	135 *8.2%*	143 *8.7%*	114 *6.9%*	146 *8.8%*	183 *11.1%*	147 *8.9%*	130 *7.9%*	1652

FIGURE 3.2. Percentage of Archival Position Advertisements by Basic Function, 1976-90

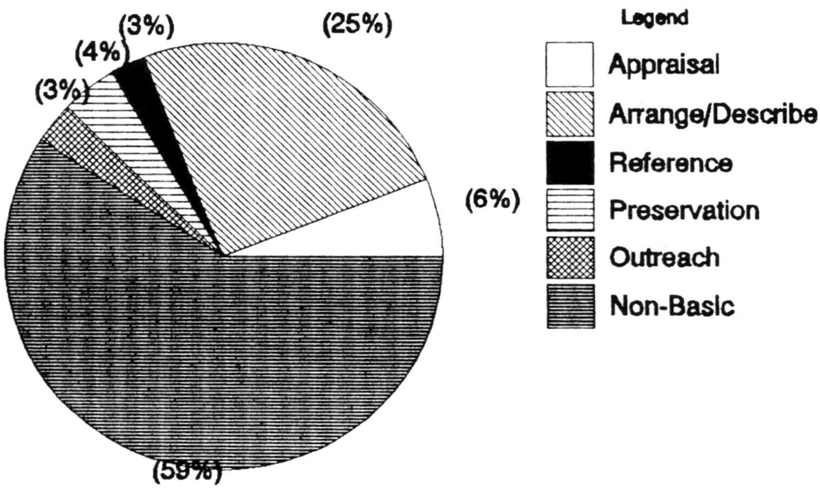

Figure 3.2 stresses the generally accepted "basic" archival functions, while Figure 3.3 emphasizes the non-basic functions such as administrative and generalized positions in which individuals are called upon to do the entire range of archival and non-archival work. More specialized archival functions, such as appraisal, reference, outreach, and preservation represent only a small proportion (no more than 6.2%) of the job advertisements. Positions concentrated about specific media or record forms also reflect the same pattern (3.3%).

These patterns–reflecting administrative, general, and arrangement and description responsibilities–exhibit a general orientation in the American archival profession. This can be seen, again, in a comparison with the only other recent survey in the American archival community that considered archival functions (see Table 3.4). The comparison with the 1982 SAA membership survey generally reveals the same proclivities to general, administrative, and arrangement and description functions. The reports on this survey "confirm a trend toward specialization" (Bearman, 1983, p. 236), but no such trend seems to be reflected in the present analysis of job advertisements. The 1989 survey of SAA members, which has had

FIGURE 3.3. Percentage of Archival Position Descriptions by Non-Basic Function, 1976-90

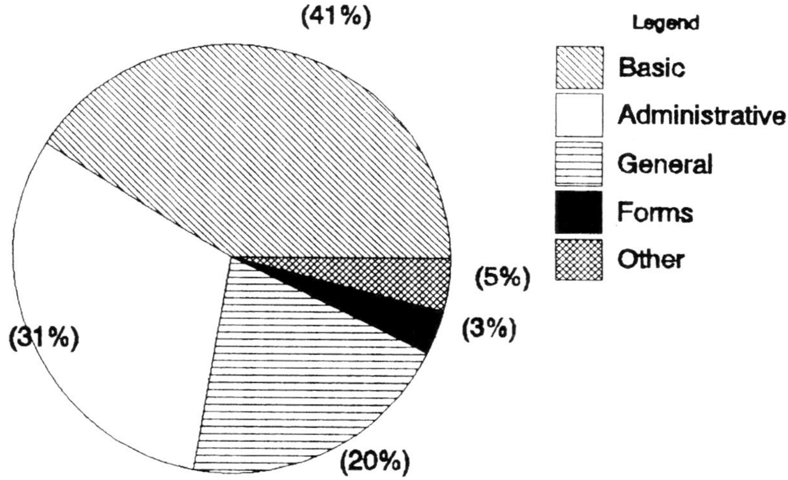

only a summary report, suggested that specialization was on the increase, but this survey also indicated that this trend should be taken cautiously: "Administration and management as a specialty is on the rise . . . With the exception of a 35 percent increase in reference specialists, there is virtually no change in the relative proportion of archivists who claim to specialize in particular archival functions" (Conway, 1992, p. 3). This has some implications (which will be examined later) as to just how American archivists are considering managing electronic records.

The next general aspect of the analysis of archival job advertisements is the development of trends in primary requirements for these positions. Table 3.5 displays these requirements, showing that the vast majority of archival positions require a graduate degree (76.0%) and archival experience (66.4%). The range of graduate degrees is quite broad and for the purpose of this study was not broken down. Most advertisements now list requirements for a masters or first professional degree in either history or library science, although there appears to be a general orientation to any variety of graduate degrees as long as relevant experiences and other requirements are met (this trend is seen in some of the exam-

TABLE 3.4. Comparison of Archival Functions in Various Archival Surveys, 1982 and 1991

	This Survey	1982 SAA Survey
	n = 1652	n = 1771
Appraisal	6.2%	"Handful"
Arrange/Describe	24.8%	16.5%
Reference	2.5%	7.3%
Preservation	4.2%	"Handful"
Outreach	3.3%	N/A
Administrative	31.0%	23%
General	20.2%	37%
Forms	3.3%	15%
Other	4.5%	N/A

ples of advertisements reproduced in this chapter). Typical statements now appearing in archival job advertisements read: "requires a masters degree in librarianship or other relevant field," "Masters of Arts degree in history or a related field," or "MA in library science or archives management" (SAA *Newsletter*, March 1990, pp. 20-21).

The requirements stipulated for formal archival education (36.4%) may appear to be quite low, but this may be offset by two other characteristics. Many of the positions advertised in the SAA *Newsletter* are obviously entry-level jobs or are in institutions where there continues to be an emphasis on in-service training. There is an increasing frequency of references to formal archival education as there is for archival experience and a graduate degree. Table 3.6 shows these three key requirements as percentages of requirements for all advertisements for selected years, revealing a significant increase in formal archival education requirements– while the other requirements of experience and graduate degrees have actually remained stable through the years. The portion of archival positions advertised with only undergraduate degrees as entry requirements continues to be quite low (Table 3.5), while foreign languages and subject knowledge remain fairly constant and of lesser importance through the years.

The fact that the overall proportion of advertisements listing

TABLE 3.5. Archival Position Advertisements by Primary Requirements, 1976-90

	1976	1977	1978	1979	1980	1981	1982	1983	1984	1985	1986	1987	1988	1989	1990	Total
Undergraduate Degree	3	8	15	16	17	16	8	11	14	19	16	23	40	18	22	236 *5.6%*
Graduate Degree	40	60	65	80	92	69	59	35	106	108	90	110	126	117	99	1256 *29.6%*
Archival Education	5	26	38	31	36	29	25	16	48	51	50	69	67	57	54	655 *15.2%*
Archival Experience	37	50	64	65	80	67	54	32	89	96	82	97	121	88	75	1167 *27.5%*
Foreign Language	4	3	9	12	9	3	9	7	10	10	13	9	9	7	16	329 *7.8%*
Subject Knowledge	11	29	35	46	40	27	31	18	42	46	36	48	31	32	36	605 *14.3%*
Total	100 *2.4%*	176 *4.2%*	226 *5.3%*	250 *5.9%*	274 *6.5%*	211 *5%*	186 *4.4%*	119 *2.8%*	309 *7.3%*	330 *7.8%*	287 *6.8%*	356 *8.4%*	394 *9.3%*	319 *7.5%*	302 *7.1%*	4237

TABLE 3.6. Percentages of Requirements for Formal Archival Education, Experience, Graduate Degree, and Subject Knowledge for Selected Years, 1976-90

	Education	Experience	Graduate Degree	Subject Knowledge
1976	10.6%	78.7%	85.1%	23.4%
1981	30.5%	70.5%	72.6%	28.4%
1983	28.6%	57.1%	62.5%	32.1%
1986	34.2%	71.9%	78.9%	31.6%
1990	41.5%	57.7%	76.2%	27.7%

requirements of formal archival education and subject knowledge (36.4 to 30.8%) is not as high as might be expected may suggest something about how American archivists view their own knowledge base. Although it was not considered in detail, the proportion of positions requiring subject knowledge remained fairly constant as formal archival education grew in importance (see Table 3.6). Although it was also not analyzed, subject knowledge was generally reserved for historical knowledge of geographic regions or certain kinds of disciplines (medicine or some scientific field) or organizations (state and local government). This kind of subject knowledge will be considered again when specific information technology knowledge and skills are examined. The change in formal archival education may be a reflection of the growth in graduate archival education programs and the improvement in continuing education workshops and institutes.

There was a large variety of other requirements mentioned in the archival job advertisements, many of these appearing according to a specific position mandating mention of them or, perhaps, as a factor of the length of the advertisement itself. These other requirements include writing and verbal skills, supervisory and management experience, oral history experience, knowledge of publications production or research, records management, preservation and conservation experience and training, outreach and public relations experience, and the ability to relate to people. Some of these statements appear in the job advertisements reproduced earlier in this chapter. These specific requirements all appear much less frequently than the others such as education and experience, although they may be an indication of what candidates should be aware of when applying for certain kinds of positions. The degree to which knowledge of computers and other forms of information technology is a requirement relates to this area.

The Advertisements and Electronic Records

The most notable finding was that there were few positions directly dealing with electronic information technology. Table 3.7 reveals only nineteen job advertisements for positions specializing in the administration of electronic records; contrasted as in Figure 3.4 with positions requiring knowledge of automated techniques and the archival profession's slow movement to deal with electronic records is quite evident.

One of the exceptions was the 1990 advertisement run by the New York State Archives and Records Administration to fill four positions in its Bureau of Records Analysis and Disposition. The advertisement stated, in part, the following:

> The Bureau of Records Analysis and Disposition provides records management advice to New York state government agencies, reviews records disposition schedules, and appraises records for archival value. We are recruiting public records analysts and archivists to fill four vacancies. These positions will provide an opportunity for professional growth and development, outreach and work with other professionals, and service in a dynamic, innovative program with special emphasis on archival records, complex information systems, and modern information technology in state government. (SAA *Newsletter*, May 1990, p. 28)

In fact, the sudden growth in electronic records positions is due to advertisements run by one institution, the New York State Archives and Records Administration, accounting for eight of nine of the positions in 1990 (and, this has continued to be the case in the subsequent few years). Another recent exception was Pennsylvania State University advertisement for a "Data Archivist":

TABLE 3.7. Number of Advertisements Relating to Automated Techniques and Electronic Records, 1976-90

Year	Total	Automated Techniques	Electronic Records
1976	47	0	0
1977	71	1 (1.4%)	0
1978	77	2 (2.6%)	0
1979	105	4 (3.8%)	0
1980	107	2 (1.9%)	0
1981	95	6 (6.3%)	0
1982	75	6 (8%)	0
1983	56	7 (12.5%)	0
1984	135	18 (13.3%)	1 (0.7%)
1985	143	32 (22.4%)	1 (0.7%)
1986	114	33 (28.9%)	0
1987	146	44 (30.1%)	4 (2.7%)
1988	183	54 (29.6%)	3 (1.6%)
1989	147	59 (40.1%)	1 (0.7%)
1990	130	54 (41.5%)	9 (6.9%)
1991	1652	322 (19.5%)	19 (1.2%)

This twenty-four month NHPRC-funded faculty position will play a key role in the appraisal of archived computer datafiles in the university's administrative computing center. RESPONSIBILITIES: The data archivist will also conduct an extensive study of research use on confidential data, work with administrative computing staff in examining on-line database archival issues, and work closely with university departments whose datafiles are being evaluated. QUALIFICATIONS: Master's degree in history, social science, library or information science, or a related field required. Experience with main frame computers and tape use and/or extensive experience with microcomputer programming, system design, maintenance, or networking required. Experience in archival appraisal and/or records management preferred. Excellent oral and written communication skills required. (SAA *Newsletter*, p. 29)

FIGURE 3.4. Advertisements for Archivists in Automated Techniques and Electronic Records

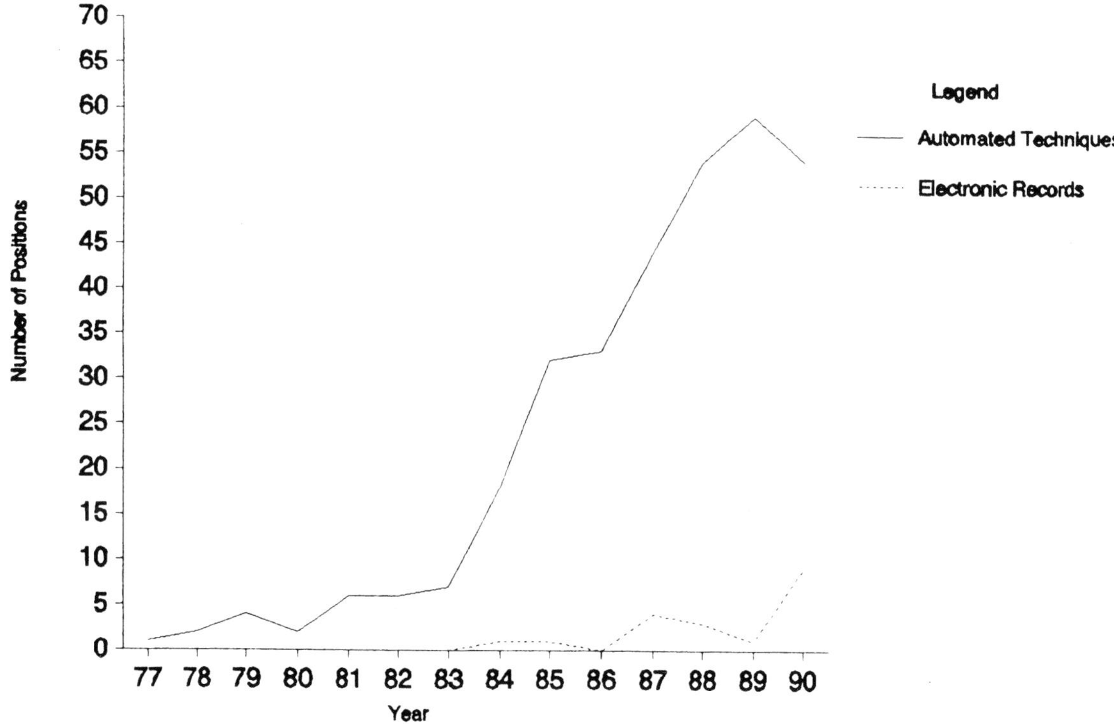

Of the nineteen job advertisements for electronic records positions (or with a concentration of focus on electronic records), the location and nature of these positions by type of repository is quite revealing about what is happening in the American archival profession concerning the practical management of electronic records. Most of these were advertised by one state government archives, New York, one of the few state archives with a successful electronic records program. The remainder of the advertisements came from the Society of American Archivists, an institution specializing in documenting the history of computing, another state archives, and the leading graduate North American archival education program located in Canada. The first advertisement, in 1984, is for a position "to direct a new state-funded program [in a state government archives], initially authorized for two years, for archival records in machine-readable, audio-visual, and micrographic formats" (SAA *Newsletter*, May 1984, p. 14); this is, again, the New York program. In 1985, the SAA itself sought a program officer "to implement all phases of a grant-funded automated archival information program, comprising research, education, and communications designed to foster the continued development and implementation of information systems within and among repositories" (SAA *Newsletter*, March 1985, p. 14).

The year 1987 brought with it the first major influx of advertisements for archivists to work with electronic records. An advertisement for a "records consultant trainee" in the Texas State Library Local Records Division sought an individual with "familiarity with more specific records management fields, including . . . records automation" (SAA *Newsletter*, January 1987, p. 19). The Charles Babbage Institute for the History of Information Processing opened a position, with National Historical Publications and Records Commission funding, for a project to document the Control Data Corporation; the advertisement asked for an individual "familiar with computers or the history of computing" (SAA *Newsletter*, March 1987, p. 24). When the New York State Archives assumed the records management responsibilities for state government, it ran an advertisement calling for applications from individuals "who have experience in . . . [the] design, management and evaluation of records and information systems including the application of modern technologies to such systems" (SAA *Newsletter*, May 1987, p. 28). Another university records manager advertisement sought an individual with "experience with . . . automated records keeping systems and equipment" (SAA *Newsletter*, May 1987, p. 29).

In the past few years, the number of advertisements with some specific orientation to electronic records has continued to increase. In early 1988 the SAA advertised a program officer for automation, seeking an individual with "thorough knowledge about applications of automation in archival settings, machine-readable records, the MARC/AMC format, and the other MARC-related projects currently underway" (SAA *Newsletter*, May 1988, p. 23). Later that year, the New York State Archives ran an advertisement seeking applicants for public records analysts. Two of these positions were intended to "assist State agencies with development of comprehensive records management programs, including retention and disposition scheduling, micrographics, files management, and use of modern information management technologies." Another, more senior, position was for the "development of a statewide information technology standards and technical assistance program" (SAA *Newsletter*, November 1988, p. 21). In 1989, the University of British Columbia School of Library, Archives, and Information Studies advertised for the *first* full time educator in the area of electronic records: "The school is seeking a candidate who will be able to plan and teach courses primarily in the area of applications of automation to the administration of archives, including the administration of programs for machine-readable records and archives" (SAA *Newsletter*, November 1989, p. 30). The following year the advertisements by the New York State Archives and Pennsylvania State University, quoted earlier, were published.

In the desired qualifications for archivists, there is, of course, reference to general knowledge of computers and electronic information technology beyond those specifically related to electronic records management. The earliest such reference is in the advertisement for a university records manager, seeking an individual possessing "familiarity with machine readable records" as one of many qualifications (SAA *Newsletter*, September 1981, p. 11). Three years later, an advertisement for a local government records specialist included, as a requirement, "experience in computer applications and systems conceptualization" (SAA *Newsletter*, March 1984, p. 14). Such references, apart from positions responsible for arrangement and description work or reference services, were extremely rare in the SAA *Newsletter*. Many other references, such as "familiarity with computer applications" for a university archivist (SAA *Newsletter*, p. 14) or "computer literate" for a historic site (SAA *Newsletter*, May 1987, p. 31) are cryptic in their meaning and implications. Still, there seems to be more specificity occurring in the job advertisements. A 1985 advertisement for a university records manager sought "familiarity with machine-readable records" as being "highly desirable" (SAA *Newsletter*, September 1985, p. 15). A 1988 advertisement for a director of historical resources position stated that "familiarity with telecommunications and computer systems [was] valuable" (SAA *Newsletter*, January 1988, p. 19).

The Job Advertisements and General Computer Literacy

One of the most notable characteristics of the job advertisements was the increasing attention given to automated archival techniques, providing quite a stark contrast to what was occurring with electronic records. Not only has there been an increasing number of archival positions requiring knowledge of or experience in archival automation, there has also been an appearance of archival positions that are entirely focused on automated techniques. Consider the position for "Retrospective Conversion Archivist" advertised by Duke University:

> RESPONSIBILITIES: Converting the manual catalog of manuscripts into machine-readable form; descriptive preparation; assignment of Library of Congress subject headings; coding of AMC format worksheets for entry into OCLC via PC-based Microenhancer software; supervision and revision of online data entry; and assisting the project director in training and supervising the Catalog Data Input Clerk and compiling monthly reports and project evaluations. QUALIFICATIONS: ALA-accredited MLS; knowledge of and experience with US-MARC formats, especially the AMC format; knowledge of and experience with archival processing and descriptive stan-

> dards, AACR2, and LC name and subject authority files; and familiarity with computer-based systems in libraries, in particular the OCLC system. (SAA *Newsletter*, September 1988, p. 23)

Or, in a more recent advertisement, Yale University's "Head of Technical Services" in its manuscripts and archives unit:

> RESPONSIBILITIES: Manages the functions of the technical services unit. QUALIFICATIONS: MA in American history or related field. MLS from an ALA-accredited library school preferred. Formal archival training or education. Two years of professional archival experience, including supervisory responsibilities and the processing of manuscript collections. Excellent oral and written communication skills. Strong management, organizational, and analytical skills. Demonstrated ability to work effectively with colleagues, administrators, staff, patrons, and donors. Demonstrated ability and commitment to work effectively in a group setting. Broad familiarity with automated bibliographic description (SAA, LC, AACR2). Experience with a system employing the USMARC AMC format. (SAA *Newsletter*, January 1990, p. 19)

In the positions concerned with automated techniques, there is a much greater frequency of reference to automation knowledge and experience (see Table 3.7). In a January 1977 advertisement for an assistant curator in a photographic archives located in a university library, a "knowledge of computerized cataloging methods" was listed as a requirement (SAA *Newsletter*, January 1977, p. 18). Such descriptive phrases accelerate (as seen in Table 3.7) and, more importantly, they become more specific in nature–a telling indication in the brief job advertisements listed in the SAA *Newsletter*. For the next several years references to automation knowledge remained general, such as "some knowledge of computer production of library aids would be helpful" (SAA *Newsletter*, July 1979, p. 25) and "experience with . . . automated systems desirable" (SAA *Newsletter*, July 1980, p. 14).

The first indication of a major change was the 1981 advertisement by the Society of American Archivists for the project manager for the National Information Systems Task Force (the group ultimately responsible for the move to the US MARC AMC format). This advertisement stated that candidates "should be acquainted . . . with the design of multi-institutional data bases and bibliographic utilities, with data communications standards and with current uses of automation within archives and manuscripts repositories" (SAA *Newsletter*, March 1981, p. 15). In the same year, advertisements, such as the advertisement for the directorship of a subject library/archives that sought an individual possessing "familiarity with OCLC automated cataloging system" (SAA *Newsletter*, July 1981, p. 22), began to appear that included references to specific national bibliographic utilities. The following year, 1982, advertisements appeared with references to SPINDEX (SAA *Newsletter*, January 1982, p. 11; July 1982, p. 19), AACR2 (SAA *Newsletter*, May 1982, p. 14), and, for the first time, to the anticipated "revised MARC format for archives and manuscripts" (SAA *Newsletter*, November 1982, p. 11). By 1984, advertisements with specific references to the MARC AMC format were appearing; five such advertisements appeared in this year (SAA *Newsletter*, January 1984, p. 11; March 1984, p. 15; July 1984, p. 17, 20; September 1984, p. 14). The next year, six advertisements required knowledge of the MARC AMC format (SAA *Newsletter*, May 1985, p. 17; July 1985, p. 13, 15; September 1985, p. 15; and November/December 1985, p. 18). In 1986, just two years after its official adoption as a standard, there were fully twenty-one advertisements with explicit reference to the format (SAA *Newsletter*, January 1986, p. 10, 11; May 1986, p. 19, 21, 23; July 1986, p. 12, 13, 14, 15; August 1986, p. 25, 26; November 1986, p. 10, 11). By 1990, 34 advertisements included reference to knowledge about the MARC AMC format (SAA *Newsletter*, January 1990, p. 19, 20, 23; March 1990, pp. 19-20, 21, 22; May 1990, pp. 30-31; July 1990, p. 23, 24, 25. 26, 27; September 1990, p. 18; November 1990, p. 26, 28). There was little doubt that the MARC AMC format had become a standard for archivists' knowledge and experience.

The trend in archival job advertisements with references to electronic records and automated techniques has been confirmed by other surveys. The 1982 survey of SAA members noted that archivists working with "specialties" such as "magnetic media" are "extremely small" (Bearman, 1983, p. 236). The analysis of state government archives reported earlier confirm that few of these archival programs have established electronic programs or are adequately staffed to support work with electronic records and the more sophisticated information technology. The archival literature on electronic records revealed some widely varying views towards electronic records that are, perhaps, reflected in the general lack of advertisements for electronic records archivists.

CONCLUSIONS OF THE ARCHIVAL JOB ADVERTISEMENTS PATTERNS, 1976-1990

This analysis of job advertisements published in the years 1976 through 1990 enables some unmistakable conclusions about the research questions posed in this part of the study. The research questions asked whether the advertisements would reflect any increasing mentions of work examples, knowledge, abilities, and skills specifically oriented to the changing nature of modern information technology, whether there would be discernible patterns in changes of information technology literacy or knowledge by type of archival repository, whether there would be any noticeable differences with the results of the examination of state archives position descriptions, and, finally, whether the job advertisements would reflect any increases in the basic number of archival positions requiring computer literacy. These research questions were linked to the broader question posed in chapter one: Do current archival position descriptions and job advertisements for new positions adequately reflect any trends in specialization about the responsibilities and requirements that would assist archival programs to operate effectively within an environment of more complex modern electronic information technology?

While the advertisements seem to reflect generally the nature of the types of archival positions and archival repositories in the United States, the advertisements also reveal a significant change in the required computer literacy that archivists are expected to possess. There is a dramatic increase of desired computer literacy in this area, and in related work examples, because of the growing acceptance through the years of automated bibliographic systems and standards, amenable to and propelled by automated techniques, such as the MARC AMC format. The computer is increasingly referred to in the job advertisements. But, as has been noted, this change is virtually limited to automated descriptive techniques–something that archivists have been working on since the late 1960s in very practical ways and more recently have been able to coordinate with their more experienced library colleagues.[3] These changes are also, of course, probably the result of the affordability and increased capability of personal computers and user-friendly PC software designed for archival applications. Nevertheless, stripped of these changes, the archivists sought in these advertisements would have needed very little (if any) information technology-oriented training or experience.

Another clear conclusion is that advertisements for electronic records positions are restricted to certain kinds of archival repositories. Most of the advertisements emanate from one successful state government archives (New York), but the remainder of the programs are nearly all institutional archives; the only major exceptions are advertisements published by a graduate archival education program and a discipline history center focused on the history and development of computing. This clearly reflects the fact that other than the National Archives in Washington, D.C., the New York State Archives and Records Administration has been the recent notable exception in the American archival profession. The temporary decline of the National Archives' influence in this area in the first part of the 1980s, after a promising start,[4] has made the New York program one of the few successful case studies that the profession can cite. This state government archives has also had a long commitment to publishing reports and articles about its work, a fact enhanced by this program's employment of one of the most prolific authors and experts (Margaret Hedstrom) on this topic. Moreover, the predominance of electronic records in institutional archives is probably the result of where the information technology has been most relevant–in the office place, and for archival programs concerned mostly about transactional records that are increasingly appearing in electronic forms (see, for example, United Nations, 1990).

The job advertisements certainly seem to suggest that the American archival profession is not oriented to managing electronic records. The extremely small fraction (less than one percent) of job advertisements oriented to electronic records is strong evidence in its own right, but this is more dramatically reflected in comparing these findings with those in the state government archives study (chapter two). While state government archives seem weak, they emerge as the stronger programs for electronic records work in the job advertisement analysis because one state archives (New York) has developed an aggressive program for working with electronic records. Overall, these programs now have few electronic records specialists and show no signs of shifting toward such specialization and creation of similar programs.

IMPLICATIONS OF THE JOB ADVERTISEMENT ANALYSIS

If the 1980s was dubbed as the "Age of Speed" because of remarkable advances in all aspects of technology, then the advertisements (especially coupled with the state government archives position description study) reflect nearly the exact opposite, except for the use of automation in descriptive practices. This seems strange, indeed, given that the archivist is mostly concerned with documentation produced by natural information transactions which are increasingly appearing in electronic form. Archivists have not naturally oriented themselves to facing modern information technology. The long gestation periods of the successful New York and Kentucky state archives electronic records programs perhaps reflect specific problems that archivists must overcome in order to manage electronic records, including a general predilection toward caution and slowness of adaptation in this technological "Age of Speed."

A possible factor in the American archival profession's response to such transforming information technology might be the matter of how the diffusion of ideas and innovation works in this discipline. Everett Rogers has defined diffusion as the "process by which an innovation is communicated through certain channels over time among the members of a social system" (Rogers, 1983, p. 5). Innovation is "an idea, practice, or object that is perceived as new by an individual or other unit of adoption" (Rogers, 1983, p. 11). In considering the diffusion of innovation, Rogers notes that "more effective communication occurs when two individuals are homophilous"–homophily being the "degree to which pairs of individuals who interact are similar in certain attributes" (Rogers, 1983, pp. 18-19). The communication that needs to occur between archivists, information scientists, and technical specialists is not a homophilous relationship. But it is also true that the process of diffusion of innovation for the archival profession is still in an early stage. Rogers laid out five stages to the "innovation-decision process": knowledge, persuasion, decision, implementation, and confirmation (Rogers, 1983, pp. 20-21). It may be that the archivists' work with electronic records of the past thirty years have all been contained within the first stage or two–with clear agenda, consensus, and stronger working relationships with information managers and technicians just beginning to emerge by the end of the 1980s.

There are lessons to learn in other related professions that have had analyses of changing patterns of their job advertisements. A study of the development of preservation librarian positions as revealed in job advertisements from 1975 through 1987 chronicled a sharp increase in such positions from the mid-1970s, the initial peaking of awareness about the need for such specialized positions and the immensity of the preservation challenge facing libraries, to the middle of the next decade. But this study also pointed out that the "preservation programs have been centered in large university and independent research libraries" (57 percent of these positions were Association of Research Libraries members) and that "there seems to be little consensus among library hiring committees about what qualifications preservation librarians should have" (Cloonan and Norcott, 1989, pp. 652, 654). The conclusion of this study was that the trends in advertisements for such positions represented very early stages for the entrenchment of the preservation function in the libraries. A similar case seems to have occurred with the patterns of job advertisements for electronic records archivists or, at the least, computer-literate archivists. These latter positions are in the largest state government archives, and the paucity of such advertisements (coupled with what was seen in the states archives position descriptions and reflected in the archival literature) do not suggest any consensus about qualifications.

More telling, for comparison purposes, may be the study on automation's impact on library catalogers–again using an analysis of job advertisements from 1970 through 1989. The author of this study (Furuta, 1990, p. 251) sees that the "introduction and spread of the utilities [requiring automated cataloguing skills] was very rapid." This is, of course, similar to what was seen with the development of advertisements requiring knowledge of automated descriptive techniques in the archival profession. The assistance of vendors, development of software packages assisting such work, and the use of standards may all be factors encouraging more attention because of the greater degree of specificity and larger support base for working in this arena.[5] The rapidly changing world of electronic information technology, driven by marketplace and other demands, requires different strategies and skills. The use of automated utilities is a far different area from that of endeavoring to influence the creation of technological information systems designers to incorporate the means to preserve information of archival value. Here archivists are in the realm of converging information professions. As one study suggested,

> an examination of the literature–from related areas of information management, information technology and business–demonstrates that information management is demanding that traditional job barriers be broken down and that traditional job descriptions need to be rewritten. There is a convergence of skills and attitudes and, at the senior level in organizations, where the 'hybrid managers' are now in evidence, a convergence of professions. (Herring, 1991, p. 147)

Archivists are just beginning to consider the re-writing of job descriptions to accommodate such matters, a development akin to the pattern of diffusion of innovation alluded to earlier.

The apparent bleakness of the job advertisement study for the ability of archivists to manage electronic records may be counterbalanced by the trend toward automated descriptive techniques and standards as basic knowledge for archivists. It is possible that as archivists become more comfortable with the computer and telecommunications, using them for their more familiar work with arrangement and description, they may branch into work with transactional records originally created as electronic forms. Or, in another possible scenario, computer-literate and experienced archivists may move into or be re-assigned to working in the realm of electronic records management. But, despite this possibility, these advertisements still seem to be in line with a 1969 archival assessment that the "archivist is not a technologist" (Fisher, 1969, p. 216). At best, archivists have not seen computer technology yet completely "weaved," as technologist Mark Weisner (1981, p. 94) suggested should be an objective, into their work.

CONCLUSION: NEEDS FOR ADDITIONAL RESEARCH

The first noticeable problem in conducting such job advertisement analysis is the lack of context of other studies on the archival profession. There are virtually no other such studies of archival job advertisements, nor are there many other surveys or profiles of the American archival profession that provide a basis for comparison with benchmarks for change and progress in general characteristics of the individual archivist and archival institutions. This present study may provide such a benchmark for subsequent research, but there are virtually no others by which to test its conclusions in assessing what has developed in the past generation of archivists. Furita's study (1990, p.250) of the impact of automation on library cataloguing noted that "although analyzing advertisements is a good way to follow trends in libraries, there are too many uncontrollable variables to support far-reaching conclusions."

There has been no major analysis of where archival institutions, successful in establishing electronic records programs, have recruited or re-educated individuals to staff such programs. Have these repositories taken advantage of continuing education workshops on electronic records administration offered by the Society of American Archivists and regional archival associations to re-train existing staff? A few articles in the archival literature suggest that while the continuing education efforts have been successful in raising the consciousness of individual archivists, the same efforts have not been successful in the creation of electronic records programs

(T. Brown, 1984). Have these repositories recruited non-archivists, individuals trained and experienced as data processors or information resource managers or in some other discipline, to staff these specialized programs? Lee Stout's comments (1990) relative to his own efforts as a university archivist to manage academic computing systems is typical of the problem:

> Lack of computing experience among many mid-career and senior archivists is a major obstacle to carrying forward electronic records programs in archives. Most computer-literate archivists tend to be young professionals, not yet in policy-setting roles with significant administrative responsibilities. Those few mid-career and senior archivists with computing experience beyond the recent microcomputer boom have gained it in highly varied and usually unsystematic ways and this is influencing the development of electronic records programs.

The question remains whether there is a sufficient number of computer-literate archivists to carry the profession forward into the end of the twentieth century.

It may be that American archivists have not really become as knowledgeable as they should be in understanding other kinds (pre-computer) of information technology. The study by American archivists of changing information systems has been extremely limited, remaining more in the province of the historical discipline than with archivists. Moreover, American archivists do not seem to be very familiar with studies produced by historians and information scientists in this area. It is difficult, at this point, to understand why this may have occurred. It may be that the lack of more traditional archival knowledge and studies, such as diplomatics and paleography, may have impaired such research and broader understanding. These more traditional areas are only now beginning through the publication of widely available writings in mainstream archival journals to become more familiar to American archivists (Cox, 1990a).

Finally, there have also been no studies of archivists' attitudes toward the computer. Sara Fine (1986, p. 88) has noted that resistance to technology "is not a function of personality nor of demographics but is rather related to the climate of the organization and the beliefs, abilities and values of the individual." M. T. Clanchy in an important study (1979, p.236) about medieval English record-keeping, noted that "documents did not immediately inspire trust. As with other innovations in technology, there was a long and complex period of evolution." Research into the attitudes of archivists about electronic records and modern information technology, through systematic surveys and other means, would be extremely helpful in assisting the profession understand why it has taken so long to respond in practical ways to managing the technology (e.g., Yoo, 1988). Understanding such attitudes is crucial to determining what should be taught in graduate and continuing archival education programs–a topic that is considered next in this study.

ENDNOTES

1. I had intended to update this study to include the last two years, but a review of recent position advertisements in the SAA *Newsletter* convinced me that so little had changed that there was no need to do this. In the 1992 *Newsletter*, for example, there were 119 advertisements for positions; only one, from the New York State Archives and Records Administration, solicited applications for individuals to work in an electronic records program (March 1992, p. 27). This simply reinforced the conclusion already reached, that the New York program has long been one of the few state archives developing adequate strategies and programs to deal with electronic information technology being utilized by state agencies.

2. These other surveys were reported in the *Academy of Certified Archivists Newsletter* 5 (November 1990): 2-3; cf., Conway, 1987; and Bearman, 1983.

3. The best and most recent evidence of this is in the "Report of the Working Group on Standards for Archival Description" and accompanying papers published as special issues of the *American Archivist* 52 (Fall 1989): 431-537 and 53 (Winter 1990): 22-108.

4. There have been no specific studies of the changes of the National Archives electronic records activities and efforts. My personal assessment derives from three sources: (1) Edie Hedlin's presentation to the Advanced Institute for Government Archivists at the University of Pittsburgh School of Library and Information Science on June 7, 1989 (reported in Cox, 1989, p. 5), (2) the report entitled *Taking A Byte Out of History*, 1990, by the U. S. House Committee on Government Operations that described the failures of the National Archives to get a handle on the growing use of the technology was another source for this statement; and (3) discussions and presentations at archival professional associations and meetings.

5. Kesner, Weber, and Wilson (1991) is a good example of where the archival profession has come and how it approaches (in a practical manner) this matter.

Chapter Four

Graduate Archival Education and Electronic Records: An Analysis of Current Approaches and Their Strengths and Weaknesses

INTRODUCTION AND REVIEW

In an assessment of information technology and library education during the mid-1980s, one commentator (Subramanyam, 1986, p. 172) stated that "computer literacy and skill in the use of computers are essential for survival in a society in which the computer's influence pervades every sphere of human endeavor." Harold Borko (1984, p. 191), also writing directly from the library and information science perspective, noted that "information professionals, in whatever environment they choose to work, will need to understand the processes of selection, acquisition, cataloging, reference, and the management of information systems. Graduates will also need to be familiar with advances in technology and their applications including the use of microcomputers, communication networks, microfilm storage and retrieval systems, bibliographic and numeric databases, interactive television, etc." The purpose of this chapter is to examine the American archival profession's cur-

[Haworth co-indexing entry note]: "Graduate Archival Education and Electronic Records: An Analysis of Current Approaches and Their Strengths and Weaknesses." Cox, Richard J. Co-published simultaneously in: *Primary Sources & Original Works* (The Haworth Press, Inc.), Volume 3(3/4), 1994, pp. 131-161; and: *The First Generation of Electronic Records Archivists in the United States: A Study in Professionalization*, Richard J. Cox, The Haworth Press, Inc., 1994, pp. 131-161. Multiple copies of this article/chapter may be purchased from The Haworth Document Delivery Center [1-800-3-HAWORTH; 9:00 a.m. - 5:00 p.m. (EST)].

rent attention to electronic records in graduate archival education programs and implications for the findings reported in the previous two chapters. If knowledge of information technology will remain essential for archivists working in the late twentieth century, this knowledge should be reflected in current graduate education programs.

The analysis of the state government archives position descriptions and archival job advertisements suggested that the American archival profession is struggling to make the transition from a paper to an electronic age, in much the same manner as many earlier occupations worked to make the transition from a scribal age to that of printing (Eisenstein, 1979). Survival of the archival profession and/or its mission in modern society, as some information professionals characterize their need to manage information technology, may not be an appropriate concern.

First, bear in mind when considering the roles of educational programs in preparing archivists to function in the modern information age, that an apparent change of broad proportions (albeit partial) has occurred within just the past few decades, in the expectations of employers for archivists to be knowledgeable about automated techniques. Earlier requirements (in the late 1970s) for a knowledge of automated techniques were simple by comparison: "some knowledge of computer production of library aids would be helpful"; "background in information science with hands-on computer experience"; "knowledge or experience in computer data programming"; and "knowledge of computer information systems preferred" (SAA *Newsletter*, July 1979, pp. 25, 27; September 1979, p. 15; and November 1979, p. 15).

A decade later, considerable change can be detected in the position advertisements. Not only had the numbers of these advertisements calling for computer literacy significantly increased, but the advertisements were more explicit in requiring a knowledge of automated techniques. It is also possible to detect in these advertisements a much greater sophistication in these requirements, at least for automated archival applications. While some position advertisements are still somewhat vague in their criteria (noting such specifications as "knowledge of computer systems" or "computer literacy"), the majority are far more precise: "special skills such as knowledge of automation (including MARC), experience with LCSH, and/or authority work preferred"; "knowledge of MARC/AMC format and familiarity with production of computer-generated inventories and indexes preferred"; "familiarity with archival processing, computer systems and MARC/AMC format are essential"; "be familiar with automated bibliographical and collections management systems, particularly OCLC or RLIN"; and "knowledge of word processing, especially WordPerfect [and] experience with RLIN/AMC and the USMARC Archives and Manuscript Control format" (SAA *Newsletter*, January 1989, pp. 21, 22; March 1989, p. 21; and May 1989, p. 17).

The somewhat surprising revelation from an examination of these position advertisements, however, is that only *one* made any reference to a required knowledge about electronic records. This solitary example was for a faculty position at the University of British Columbia graduate archival education program (SAA *Newsletter*, November 1989, p. 30). While it is encouraging that a graduate archival education program has advanced to have a faculty member specializing in these areas, it is sobering that archival repositories do not seem to be aggressively seeking individuals with expertise in electronic records. Is this because they are convinced they will not find suitable candidates in the present pool of archivists, or, perhaps, because these programs are finding candidates outside of the profession? Or, are there other problems preventing such employment, including availability of resources and the size and mission of archival programs? These reasons must certainly must be grappled by this profession's educators This issue will be discussed below.

The examination of the position advertisements also suggests that the archival profession in the United States has re-oriented itself to applying automation to the basic archival function of description, but that it has not fared as well in working with electronic records being produced by the increasingly sophisticated information technology. The constant reference to the US MARC AMC format is evidence that the creation of this format in 1983 and subsequent efforts to develop related standards essential to automated techniques, have had a profound effect on the elemental work of the archivist. This conclusion seems to be confirmed in other ways as well, especially when probing more deeply into the structures of archival institutions and reading the basic archival literature.

A more detailed analysis of position descriptions in a selected group of state government archives in the United States has found partial corroboration for what seems to be reflected in the employers' advertisements. While the position descriptions used by the state archives actually reveal substantially less of a requirement for knowledge about the US MARC AMC format than the published advertisements, they confirm an emphasis on arrangement and description and a general neglect of work with electronic records. In general, for both introductory level and advanced or specialized jobs, the state archives position descriptions stress the traditional skills and basic archival functions of the archival profession. Noticeably absent, however, are any indications that knowledge of and experience with automated techniques, electronic records, and new information technologies are important or desirable. The only references to automated techniques are in the considerably smaller number of positions with specializations in function or media. The only references to knowledge requirements in automated information systems are in state archives which have records management operations; these latter position descriptions seem to be more specific with such statements as "plans and implements application of automated electronic information storage and retrieval system" and "coordinates the long range planning activities of the Bureau including the development and maintenance of standards for microfilm, Computer Output Microfilm (COM), optical storage, and automated systems."[1]

These position descriptions, formed as they are by the respective state civil services and only stating desired characteristics, are obviously limited in what they suggest about the responsibilities, knowledge requirements, and skills and attitudes sought by archival employers. However, they also seem to reflect a similar neglect of electronic records, except perhaps for the records management positions and a general predilection for very broad definitions of work, knowledge, and skills characterizing the archivist (Murrah, 1990). This poses a number of interesting problems regarding graduate education, since the majority of records management education is offered apart from course work on archives administration.

Is there a cause and effect relationship between archival job advertisements or position descriptions and the way that archival knowledge is being taught in graduate and continuing archival education programs? The reason for posing this question is that the archival literature and curricula of education programs also reveal some essential characteristics about the profession's view of automated techniques and electronic records which need to be considered before exploring the potential roles of education programs in these areas.

An examination of the archival literature revealed a number of significant characteristics about the profession's interest in and response to automated techniques and electronic records that have implications for graduate education. First, there was little interest in either topic before 1960. This should not be surprising, given the impact of computer technology on institutions to that point and the relative lack of adoption of the technology by other information or historical disciplines. In fact, it was only during the 1960s that the concept of information science emerged and was defined (Rayward, 1985).

Another noteworthy characteristic is that during new interest by the profession in these topics, developed during the 1960s but this interest did not emerge fully until the end of the decade. The April 1967 *American Archivist* special issue on "Automation in Archives and Manuscript Collections" is a clear demarcation point for substantial new attention by the profession in automated techniques. This journal issue also featured Frank G. Burke's essay on "The Application of Automated Techniques in the Management and Control of Source Materials," a milestone in the literature on automated archival techniques.

Third, the archival profession's concern with electronic records visibly emerged in the 1970s as reflected by the literature, but remained both an occasional issue for discussion until the end of that decade and a matter nearly exclusively discussed by government archivists and records managers. The special *American Archivist* issue of April 1979 on "Archivists, Archives, and Computers: A Starting Point," the only special issue on these topics in this decade, revealed a continuing predilection by the profession to concentrate on automated techniques. Before then there were only sporadic appearances of essays on appraisal and inventorying topics, or bibliographical reviews of recent publications, that might assist the archivist with these matters. This literature certainly did not provide complete coverage of such topics, and the articles and reports were probably viewed more as curiosities by the majority of archivists in North America who regularly read this journal.

Finally, the past decade has seen a steadier stream of studies and opinions on automated techniques and electronic records, but these studies have represented extremely diverse perspectives on these topics so that, as a result, they pose special challenges to archival educators as well as archival administrators and the broader profession. The articles on archival automated techniques show a consensus building in the profession, at least among the larger repositories and the archival leaders. From the work of the National Information Systems Task Force in the first part of the decade to that of the Working Group on Descriptive Standards at the end of the decade, there is a move from a proposed descriptive framework to systems and standards that support this framework–all in a remarkably brief period of time. This phenomenon is also dramatically reflected in the changes in position advertisements in just a decade.

The articles on electronic records may reflect something completely different. These articles and studies range from archivists contending that electronic records fundamentally transform archival work and principles, to contentions that electronic records change nothing. In fact, there is no real profession-wide consensus evident in these articles, perhaps partly explaining the lack of position advertisements for working with electronic records and the state archives' lack of adequate specialization with such information systems. It appears that the profession simply has not made up its collective mind on this important matter.[2] The nature of these articles certainly poses, at the least, some difficult questions for archival educators responsible for teaching about such areas.

It is necessary to keep in mind that the archival literature may not only reflect changing perceptions by the American archival profession towards electronic records and automated techniques, but also the continuing change in and status of graduate archival education in this country. A brief description of graduate archival education will set the scene for a more specific analysis of how this education has treated the management of electronic records.[3]

Professional archivists emerged slowly as a distinct discipline in the first third of the twentieth century in the United States. The first modern public archives were established in the South, with Alabama taking the lead in 1901, and slowly spreading northward and through the rest of the country. The administrators and staff of these archival programs formed the Conference of Archivists in 1909, seeking a focused forum by which to exchange information, share ideas, and discuss and develop solutions to professional challenges that they faced. Until 1936, the Conference met under the auspices of the American Historical Association. In that year a completely independent Society of American Archivists was established.

The transition from the Conference of Archivists under professional historians to the independent Society of American Archivists captured the essence of the concern for the education of archivists. Most professional archivists were professionally-trained and educated as historians, and no formal archival education emerged for nearly the first four decades of the twentieth century. This changed in the late 1930s, partly as a result of the establishment of the Society, but also because of the newly-created National Archives and the emergence of the Historical Records Survey. All three put an emphasis on archival work, gaining an understanding of European archival principles and practices, experimentation with new archival techniques, and other similar activities. The Modern Archives Institute, first offered by the National Archives in 1938, was typical of the start of an effort to provide some form of specialized archival education. This brief institute was replicated by other institutes and remained the chief form of archival education until well into the 1960s.

As part of a continuing discussion on whether archivists should be educated in history departments or library schools, graduate archival courses began to appear in both history departments and library schools after the Second World War. While this debate on the place of graduate archival education has continued until the present, this has not been the main aspect of the development of graduate archival education of the United States over the past several decades. The number of courses constituting such programs has continued to change. For a long while, most programs–if they could be called programs–consisted of an introductory course and a field study or practicum. By 1977 things had improved enough that specific graduate archival education guidelines that endorsed a three course sequence–introduction, advanced, and practicum–in either history departments or library schools were adopted by the SAA.[4] Most of these courses were taught by practicing archivists, and this represented the second major change in graduate education for this profession. In the late 1970s the first full-time archival educator was appointed at the University of Maryland and the 1980s saw a steady growth in the numbers of such educators, although the total number is minuscule in comparison with these of other disciplines. Another significant development partly reflecting the arrival of archival educators as regular faculty members has been an expansion of the size of the educational programs far beyond the three course sequence. In Canada this change has brought forth the Masters in Archival Studies degree, a degree that SAA's Committee on Education and Professional Development recommended SAA to endorse in 1993.[5]

Especially in recent years there has been definite and significant growth in American graduate archival education. It is worth noting that the expansion of graduate archival education began at about the same time that archivists started to discuss automated techniques and electronic records. The significance of this relationship will be discussed later in the findings and the remaining sections of this chapter.

THE CURRENT SCENE

This chapter examines the American archival profession's current attention to electronic records in graduate archival education programs and its implications for the findings reported in the previous two chapters. The research question being posed here is as follows: Are graduate archival education programs providing opportunities for preparing prospective archivists to work in the modern electronic information technology environment and with electronic records? This chapter is an examination of what archival educators have tried to do in the realm of electronic records, what they have been teaching, their attitudes toward the topic, and what the profession has similarly agreed upon relative to curriculum content. Given that so little research has been done regarding graduate archival education, this is, at best, a preliminary examination of this issue (Cox, 1990c, chapter six).

On the surface, it would appear that North American archival educators are committed to teaching about electronic records. The guidelines for graduate archival education programs adopted by the Society of American Archivists (SAA) in 1986 and the Association of Canadian Archivists (ACA) in 1988 both strongly endorse the importance of automated techniques and electronic records as part of required knowledge for the graduates of these programs. The SAA guidelines state that graduates of the education programs should possess an "understanding of information and its recorded forms," the "development of written, oral, and other forms of communications," and the "changing nature of records." These guidelines also explicitly state that "students should . . . be introduced to the new automated descriptive formats and standards" and have "special attention . . . given to the impact of new technologies and storage media on archival theory and practice." Finally, these guidelines state that "students should have access to data processing equipment in order to gain experience in automated control of archives and to become familiar with the nature of automated records" (SAA 1988, pp. 382, 384-86, 388). The ACA guidelines (1989, p. 16) also stress automated techniques and electronic records with a strong statement on the importance of automation:

> Archivists are involved with automation in two different ways: through its application to the archival work and through the acquisition of machine-readable records. While machine-readable records should be treated in the course(s) of archival science with all other types of records, the purely technical aspects of their formation and treatment can be best analyzed in a course on automation. However, the main purpose of such a study is to provide archivists with a common grounding in the terminology, concepts and use of computer hardware and software, to enable them to understand and evaluate the pro-

> fessional literature dealing with automation, to use automation in their daily work, and to make judgments about the suitability of specific items of hardware or software for specific archival tasks.

Theoretically, at least, the North American archival profession has recognized the importance of these topics in its basic graduate educational programs. Unfortunately, upon closer examination, this appears not to be the case at all. If anything, archival educators have neglected teaching in these areas, perhaps answering the earlier question about how these individuals have resolved some of the profession's lack of consensus.

THE RESEARCH DESIGN

This chapter reports on an effort to analyze the degree to which American archival educators have addressed teaching on electronic records. Several research techniques have been employed to determine patterns in such teaching, emphasizing the degree to which these programs reflect any concentration of courses that concern the management of electronic records (see Figure 4.1). First, the SAA directories of archival education for 1990 and 1991-92 have been examined systematically to determine which courses relevant to educating archivists for working with electronic information technology are presently being taught in North America. These directories list every gradute school with archival courses, providing the name of the school, graduate school, contact person, and the title of every course being offered. While some of the course titles are somewhat cryptic, such analysis still provides a sense of what archivists seem to believe is important enough to be offered to their prospective colleagues.

Second, a brief survey was sent to members of the SAA Archival Educators Round Table (AERT) to determine more exactly what was being offered in graduate archival education programs on electronic records management and the attitudes of archival instructors about this topic. It sought responses as to whether students were being taught this topic, how such instruction was being offered, what textbooks and curriculum materials were being used, whether

FIGURE 4.1. Areas of Analysis of Graduate Archival Education and Electronic Records

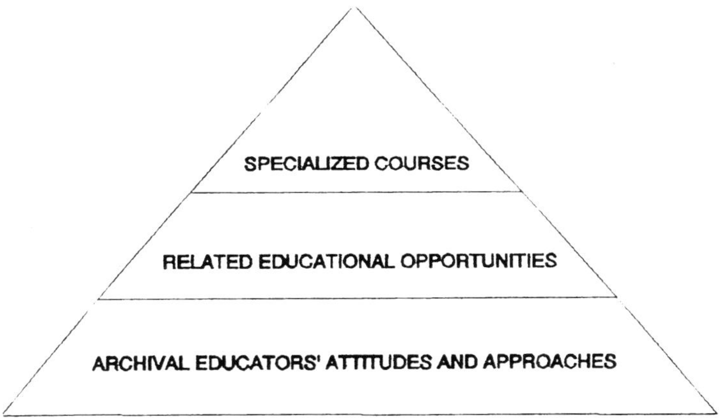

students were being asked to do fieldwork in electronic records management, how important archival instructors thought this topic was in comparison to other matters, and the general nature of their archival education programs. While this survey was conducted by the author for another purpose, it nevertheless provides enough additional insights into the nature of graduate archival education and the management of electronic records to merit its inclusion in this larger study.

Two other brief analyses were conducted to provide some contrast to the findings in specific graduate archival education offerings. A comparative study of the courses being taught in undergraduate and graduate records management programs was carried out; some of these programs include archival courses and many graduate archival programs likewise include records management courses. It is likely that many individuals graduating from the records management programs will find employment in government and institutional archives that are also responsible for records management. The question arises, then, whether these individuals might be better trained in electronic records management and could be seen as potential sources for hiring by archival operations to work with electronic records. This analysis was done by using the 1992

Association of Records Managers and Administrators education directory, a publication that provides similar information to that found in the SAA directories.

The preliminary work of the SAA Committee on Automated Records and Techniques (CART), whose intention was to propose a curriculum for the education of archivists to work with electronic records and automation in general, was also briefly examined. Five background papers on this topic were presented at an early 1991 conference on this topic, and these have been reviewed in the course of preparing this chapter.[6] More importantly, the meeting led to a proposal of a curriculum outline. This outline was compared with the courses already offered at the University of Pittsburgh School of Library and Information Science, generally considered the largest school of its kind in North America and one of the pioneering programs in information science, as a way of considering what prospective archivists should be encouraged to take in the way of graduate courses to prepare them to work better in the modern information technology.

FINDINGS

The analysis of the graduate archival education course work, using the SAA education directories, suggests that there is little commitment to introducing archival automation or the management of electronic records to graduate archival students. Initially this can be seen by examining whether, as suggested by the ACA guidelines, there are specialized courses on these subjects. Of 227 courses being offered in North America in 1990, as part of graduate programs, there were only four on automated techniques and two on electronic records–hardly an endorsement of the SAA or ACA guidelines (see Table 4.1). A year later, the number of courses remained stable. The University of Louisville history department lists a course entitled "Automation in Archives" (SAA, 1991, p. 6). The University of Maryland's dual program in history and library science offers a workshop in "Archival Automation," taught by one of the profession's pioneers in this area, Frank Burke (SAA, 1991, pp. 6-7). The University of Michigan offers a course entitled "Introduction to Machine Readable Records," taught by one of the

TABLE 4.1. Nature of Course Work in Graduate Archival Education Programs in the United States and Canada, 1990/91 and 1991/92

Nature of Course	1990/91	1991/92
Introductory Archives Courses	53	39
Practica/Internships	42	33
Advanced Archives Courses (Unspecified Topic)	18	14
Basic Functions		
Appraisal	3	2
Arrangement/Description	2	2
Preservation	21	23
Reference/Access	3	5
Public Programs	0	0
Total	29	32
Other Specialized Archival Courses		
Archival Automation	4	4
Others	10	13
Total	14	17
Special Media Courses		
Electronic Records	2	2
Others	4	3
Total	6	5
Courses on Archival Institution Types	6	5
Courses from Related Fields		
History	41	42
Library/Information Science	49	35
Museology	5	4
Total	95	91
Total Courses	227	236
Total Graduate Programs	50	36

Sources: SAA, *Education Directory 1990-91* and *1991-92.*

leading social science data archivists, Carolyn Geda (SAA, 1991, p. 7). New York University's Program in Archival Management, Historical Society Administration, and Historical Editing includes a course entitled "Computers and Archival Administration" (SAA, 1991, p. 8). And the University of British Columbia offers courses on both "Automation" and "Electronic Records" (SAA, 1991, p. 10). In fact, the vast majority of the courses in graduate programs are introductory in nature, practica or internships, or in related fields: history, library and information science, and museology (see Table 4.1).

That graduate students' orientation to these topics must be largely accomplished as part of basic or introductory courses does not bode well for enabling archival institutions to hire entry-level archivists who are competent in these areas or even aware of the majority of issues that these topics have for basic archival work. The fact that most of these programs (even counting internships) include no more than four courses in archives and preservation indicates the challenge that educators would have in introducing students to all the dimensions of archives work *and* such related issues as information technology and its impact on archival administration (see Table 4.2).

Nevertheless, there are a number of courses listed by the various graduate programs that are information technology oriented. Courses such as "Database Management," "File and Database Management Software," "Computer Based Management of Image Collections," "Planning and Managing Computer Based Information Systems," "History of Information Organization and Technologies," "Design of Information Systems," and "Image Management" are all listed by archival educators as being part of their programs in 1991-92 (SAA, 1991, pp. 6, 8, 9, 10). How important these courses are, how much archival principles and practices are included in them, and whether they are required are not known, but the general paucity of such courses (together with those specifically described as being focused on archival automation and electronic records management) makes such concerns almost superfluous.

This potential difficulty can be seen by examining the survey on how archival educators are actually introducing their students to topics such as information technology. This survey was sent to all

TABLE 4.2. Concentration of Courses in Archival Administration in North American Graduate Archival Programs, 1991/92

Number of Courses	Number of Programs	Number of Archives Courses
1	0	0
2	4	5
3	5	6
4	5	9
5	8	15
6	5	11
7	1	4
8	2	2
9	1	3
10	0	0
11	1	2
12	2	10
13	1	3
14	0	0
15	1	7
Total	36	77

Source: SAA *Education Directory 1991/92*

individuals on the AERT mailing list (as part of the July 1990 issue of this group's newsletter with the findings briefly summarized in the February 1991 number; Cox, 1991), including the representatives of the 36 graduate archival education programs as listed in the 1991/92 SAA education directory. Thirteen of these programs (36.1%) returned responses, not an impressive number, but these responses included most of the larger educational programs (in terms of course numbers and inclusion of an archival educator as a regular faculty member).[7] These results should be interpreted, then, as an indicator of the attitudes of the educators of the most comprehensive education programs in the profession.

This brief survey of graduate archival educators, and how they were teaching about electronic records, indicated that the respondents believed that electronic records represented a crucial concern. All thirteen educators responded positively to the question: "Are you introducing your students to electronic records management issues and concerns?" However, the manner in which they were fulfilling this interest and commitment was extremely diverse. Of the thirteen graduate educator respondents, the majority (9) noted that they were integrating material on electronic records and automation in their introductory archives courses, while only a small number (3) stated that they were planning to have separate, specialized courses on this topic. Three of the educators offered more than one lecture (but less than a full course), two stated that they did one separate lecture, and one noted that they had a guest lecturer on the topic.

What should be troubling about these responses, however, is the reliance on an introductory course already filled with other topics and issues. This was implied by the previous discussion of the kinds of courses listed in the SAA education directories, but others such as Timothy Ericson's examinations (1988, 1993) of the syllabi of introductory courses have corroborated similar problems by looking at different sources. Ericson noted a reliance on introductory courses which provided only cursory treatment of many basic and essential archival functions and the tendency to complete the curriculum of these programs with courses that often have only tangential relationship to archival administration. The reason for this is, of course, the relatively small number of courses that comprise graduate archival education programs in North America and the small number of full-time faculty who can influence curriculum. Of the respondents to this survey, the mean and median numbers of courses were 3.4 and 3 respectively, with as little as one course and as many as five courses. Of the thirteen respondents to this survey, only five identified themselves as full-time faculty; this certainly suggests that the respondents represent the larger, more comprehensive graduate archival education programs.

There are more troubling signs as well. Over half (7) of the educators have students read in information science journals and related texts, while most (10) still rely on the archival literature which is less than comprehensive or coherent; the continued reliance on Margaret Hedstrom's 1984 SAA manual on electronic records (9 educators continue to use it), a publication that is now more an historic document than guiding text, is indicative of the limitations reflected in these programs. Hedstrom herself noted (1984, p. 60) that the manual was limited to "numeric data files stored on magnetic tape and accessed sequentially," not an especially important challenge in today's information technology landscape. Only a small portion (4) of the educators have students complete field work in electronic records management, symptomatic perhaps of the few archival institutions with electronic records programs, and disappointing in the sense that such practical applied fieldwork could compensate for some of the classroom and curriculum deficiencies.

The few opportunities available for graduate work in the archival administration of electronic records is in direct contrast to the importance that the thirteen archival educators assign to this topic. Using a scale of 1 to 5 (5 being "very important" and 1 being "unimportant") to answer the question of how important are electronic records management issues and concerns for archival principles and practices, graduate archival educators gave this a mean score of 3.8 and a median score of 4; none gave it less than 2. Using the same scale and responding to the question of how important is a knowledge of electronic records management issues and concerns for a basic graduate archival education, graduate archival educators responded with a higher rating, giving this a mean score of 4.2 and a median score of 4; none rated this less than 3.

These two analyses suggest that although graduate educators themselves certainly recognize the importance of their students being introduced to this topic, there are, at present, few specialized courses on electronic records in graduate archival education programs. This poses related questions about whether graduate archival students are taking other information technology courses taught by non-archivists (and without the archival perspective) in the schools where their educational programs are located or whether students may be taking related courses in other educational programs or taking none at all. Two additional investigations were completed to look at these questions and to provide a broad profile of graduate archival education and the management of electronic records.

The SAA CART Curriculum Conference, held in March 1991, focused on the needs for educating archivists in both automated techniques in archival administration and the management of electronic records possessing archival value. At this conference Margaret Hedstrom presented (1991 discussion a curriculum outline for providing such education. She sketched a curriculum consisting of four major sections–archives and information technology, basic concepts and terminology, electronic records, and automated techniques–and numerous subsections providing a greater level of specificity to the broader areas.

This curriculum proposal has merit for several reasons. First, it is the product of an archival expert in information technology, an individual who already cited in this study and whose career spans two decades with experience in two of the state archives which have established electronic records programs. Second, her curriculum outline turned out to be the main basis for discussion about curriculum development in this area by the attendees at the CART conference. And third, no matter how flawed or rough this proposal is (Hedstrom herself commented that the speed of the technology's development could not allow any curriculum to be unchanged for very long), it still provides a useful point for discussing the prospects for what additional kinds of information technology courses graduate archival students could take in their programs. Given that 18 of 36 graduate archival education programs listed in the 1991/92 SAA education directory are connected to library and information science programs and an additional six are combined history-library/information science programs, such prospects would appear to be excellent. This returns us to the kind of integration of history/humanities and library and information science topics that Lawrence McCrank argued for fifteen years ago (McCrank) (1978) and that formed the basis for the current graduate archival education program at the University of Maryland.

To consider such prospects, a case study analysis–using the Hedstrom curriculum–of the courses in the University of Pittsburgh's School of Library and Information Science was conducted. The reasons for the selection of this school are straightforward. First, this school is one of the pioneers in information science education, as well as one of the largest schools of its kind in the world. It supports an undergraduate program in information science and graduate programs in both library and information science. The school offers a wide array of courses, over sixty graduate courses in both library and information science, many of which have a strong focus on information technology. Second, this school has also been developing a graduate program, as part of the Masters of Library Science degree, in archives and records management. It now provides six courses on this topic, along with a number of related courses in rare books, special collections, and other areas. As such, the prospect of graduate archival students taking information technology courses is real. For these two reasons, a comparison of the Hedstrom curriculum proposal with the school's broad array of graduate courses would suggest a strong opportunity for graduate archival students to seek other venues for gaining an orientation to information technology.

As it turned out, such a possibility is fraught with challenges (see Table 4.3). This comparison identified a total of twenty-nine graduate courses (Twenty-one from Information Science and eight from Library Science), not counting the courses on archives and records management topics, that had some bearing on the Hedstrom curriculum outline. Obviously there are *too many* courses for any individual's graduate program, whether at the Masters or Doctoral level. Even a selection of a few appropriate courses would prove to be a problem. Of thirty-seven topics and sub-topics included in the Hedstrom curriculum proposal, only eighteen have existing courses that are specifically focused on these areas. While it is difficult to make direct matches without more careful analyses of specific course content, it is nevertheless obvious that there may be some gaps or omissions in such courses. Topics such as the four aspects of "information systems concepts and design"–components, processes, systems design life cycles, and networks–are, for example, covered in the course with a systems design component. A more specific course analysis is not the point, however, since the overwhelming array of sources still poses a challenge. This clearly suggests that the logical approach, in such a school, would be to develop courses specifically designed to be graduate-level introductory courses on

TABLE 4.3. Comparison of Hedstrom Electronic Records Curriculum Proposal with Existing Courses in the University of Pittsburgh School of Library and Information Science

	Number of Courses		
	Inform. Sci.	Lib. Sci.	Total
I. <u>Archives and Information Technology</u>			
Legal Issues	1	1	2
Information Policy Overview	0	1	1
Impact of Information Technology on the Mission and Organization of Archives	0	0	0
Relationship of Archival Science to Other Information Service-Based Disciplines	0	0	0
Users and User Services in a Modern Technology Environment	0	0	0
II. <u>Basic Concepts and Terminology</u>			
Information System Components			
Data and Data Structures	1	0	1
Hardware	1	0	1
Software/Processing	2	0	2
Logical Organization of Data	0	1	1
Physical Organization of Data	0	0	0
Information Systems Concepts and Design			
Components	0	0	0
Processes	2	1	3
Systems Design Life Cycle	0	0	0
Networks	5	1	6
Overview of Information Technology Applications			
Numeric Data Files	0	0	0
Databases	2	0	2
Text Files/Office Systems	0	1	1
Geographic Information Systems	0	0	0
Imaging Systems	1	1	2
Computer Assisted Design	0	0	0
Bibliographic Retrieval Systems	0	1	1
Expert Systems	2	0	2

	Number of Courses		
	Inform. Sci.	Lib. Sci.	Total
III. Electronic Records			
Impact of Automation on Individual and Organizational Record Keeping Practices	2	0	2
Primary and Secondary Uses for Electronic Records	0	0	0
Documentation and Description Requirements in Automated Systems	0	0	0
Identification of User Committees and User Requirements for Electronic Records	0	0	0
Physical Preservation of Magnetic and Optical Media	0	0	0
Information Technology Standards, Compatibility, and Migration	1	0	1
IV. Automated Techniques			
Overview of Automated Applications for Archival Institutions			
Word Processing/Office Systems	0	0	0
Database Management Systems	0	1	1
Spreadsheets	0	0	0
Methods for Analysis of Current Procedures	0	0	0
Needs Assessment and Development of Functional Specifications	0	0	0
Decision-Making Techniques for Software Purchase/Development Paths	0	1	1
Implementing Automated Systems	0	0	0
Standards and Their Significance	0	0	0
Systems Assessment, Expansion, and Redesign	0	1	1

Source: University of Pittsburgh School of Library and Information Science *Bulletin 1991-93*

the matter of the archival management of electronic records systems. Yet, as has been seen, only a few such graduate archival education programs have moved in this direction, despite a decade of relatively rapid expansion in graduate archival education.

This examination suggests the possibility that graduate archival education students and their employers could seek other sources for education in the management of electronic records programs. It is clear, of course, that through institutes, workshops, and other forms of continuing education offerings the American archival profession has attempted to compensate for these kinds of deficiencies in their graduate archival education programs. In the area of automated techniques, the use of continuing education-which has been going for some time-seems to have been successful, as reflected by the increasing number of advertisements requiring that entry and intermediate level archivists have a knowledge of and experience in automated techniques and the US MARC AMC format (Weber, 1988). This issue will be looked at in greater detail in the next chapter. There is, of course, the distinct possibility that archivists could seek to take graduate courses in closely related disciplines that include courses in information technology. The most logical area to explore would seem to be the numerous education programs in records management education.

Records management can be dated back to ancient Greece and Rome, since its functions and purposes are closely intertwined with those of archival administration (Duranti, 1989). In the United States, modern records management primarily emanated from the efforts of the National Archives and other federal government staff to cope with the rapid growth of government records. Since that time, in many institutions and government agencies, records management and archives have been administratively, functionally and philosophically connected by many theorists and academicians in both fields (e.g., Evans, 1967). The life-cycle concept of records, espoused by both archivists and records managers, seems to be a unifying notion for the two fields and applied even to the management of electronic records (Couture and Rousseau, 1986; United Nations, 1990). The establishment of a professional association, the Association of Records Managers and Administrators (ARMA), in 1956, has also led to the development of many undergraduate and graduate educational programs for this discipline. Given that the definition of records management is a broad one–"the application of systematic and scientific control to records information required in the operation of an organization's business" (Robek, Brown, and Maedke, 1987, p. 569)–and one that is definitively related to the archivist's concerns, the records management education programs may be an additional source for addressing the education of archival administrators of electronic records.

An analysis of ARMA's current education directory reveals that information technology has a high profile in this discipline (ARMA International, 1992). Over sixty courses are clustered in the areas of office systems and information technologies or information systems and systems analysis (see Table 4.4). But other difficulties emerge. First, most of the programs are undergraduate; nearly two-thirds (63.1%) of the courses are taught in undergraduate programs, widely scattered about in business schools, community colleges, public administration, and other programs. Second, like the graduate archival programs, the greater majority of courses listed in this ARMA directory are single courses or part of very small programs. Over two-thirds (70%) of the courses are single courses; listings of three or fewer courses constitute the vast majority (86.3%) of programs described in this directory (see Table 4.5).

This profile is indicative of the fact that the records management field has itself struggled with how to deal with the rapidly changing information technology environment. Studies of the duties of professional records managers reveal activities that are still largely traditional and oriented to paper-based information systems (Wallace, 1981; Humphreys, 1984). Others have argued for more aggressive and comprehensive graduate education programs for records managers. Robert Williams (1987, p. 37) has stated that "formal records management education is dominated by the office administration/secretarial approach," and then argued that information resources management should be the primary focus of the educational programs . These weaknesses, plus others in the professional alliances between records managers and archivists, probably eliminate the possibility of archivists seeking any strong assistance for training in the management of electronic records. Although Robert Sanders (1989, p. 12) recently noted that the "records man-

TABLE 4.4. Nature of Course Work in Records Management Education Programs in the United States, 1992

Nature of Courses	Graduate	Undergrad.	Not Indicated
Introductory	25	174	21
Office Systems & Technology or Automation	1	23	1
Information Systems/ Systems Analysis	21	18	2
Filing Systems	0	5	4
Forms Management	0	10	2
Micrographics	5	9	2
Records Management by Type of Institution	0	6	3
Advanced Records Management	4	16	4
Other Records Management Courses	8	18	3
Archival Administration	58	3	1
Total	122	282	43

ager looks to the archivist to sanction the destruction of obsolete records, and the archivist relies upon the records manager to safeguard what merits preservation," another recent critic noted that archivists had allowed the historical function to take over their work, losing sight of "archives serving administrative needs" (Walker, 1989, p. 18). Such negative articles have predominated the discussion about the relationship between archivists and records managers for the past half-century.

CONCLUSIONS FROM THE GRADUATE ARCHIVAL EDUCATION PROGRAMS' ANALYSIS

The analysis of graduate courses in archival administration provides overwhelming, if only preliminary, evidence that the American archival profession has not yet developed a sufficient educa-

TABLE 4.5. Concentration of Courses in Records Management Education Programs in the United States, 1992

Number of Courses	Number of Programs
1	168
2	22
3	17
4	6
5	10
6	4
7	4
8	7
9	2
Total	240

tional framework for preparing archivists to work with electronic records. Graduate archival education programs certainly possess some orientation to electronic information technology, with a mixed array of courses that are technology-oriented, but there seem to be no consistent patterns to the nature of these courses. These courses seem to suggest more a listing of existing courses that archival students might wish to take. The analysis does not provide any reasons for this poor structural development, but it is nevertheless clear that the discussion and debate about electronic records over the past quarter of a century has not in turn led to efforts to educate archivists in this area at the graduate level.

The survey of graduate archival educators provided additional evidence about the nature of these educational programs and their treatment of electronic records. Electronic records were clearly identified as important, but the potpourri of approaches to introducing students to the management of these records is also indicative of the weak structural response to the education of entry-level archivists through such programs. Programs that include one or just a few lectures on the topic of electronic records can hardly be said to be providing good educational preparation to these students. The results of this survey indicated that the archival profession is still in a transition stage, seeking to become computer-literate and endeavoring to integrate electronic records into every basic and advanced archival science course.

This problem was highlighted, to some degree, by the comparison of the Hedstrom curriculum outline with the existing courses offered by one of the largest schools of library and information science, and by the analysis of the records management courses. The large number of courses and the possible gaps in content indicated a potential problem in how graduate archival students could take advantage of such an opportunity. Individual counseling between archival educator and archival student could work out some suitable approaches for individuals, based on their previous experience, education and career objectives, but this is hardly a major solution for the American archival profession. A present lack of knowledge about the number of graduate archival students, their background, career objectives, and ultimate placements make this a difficult aspect to evaluate. This brief profile of one model curriculum and its application to one school only points out the need for returning to more focused solutions such as full courses on the archival management of electronic records. The conclusion is bolstered by the profile of records management courses, which while revealing some concentration on electronic information technology did so at the undergraduate level and demonstrated that many of these programs were introductory at best. If anything, the education of records managers probably reveals a number of additional problems than those faced by archivists.

IMPLICATIONS

"The *raison d'etre* of any professional school," one British library educator (Grogan, 1985, p. 5) noted, "is that would-be practitioners can be more effectively and economically educated in the classroom than on the job." This guidance would seem to be untrue for archivists when it comes to electronic records. The lack of full courses on electronic records and the inclusion in other programs of a few lectures on electronic records may be more reflective of the continuing problems plaguing American archival education at the graduate level. Earlier, a brief review of the development of graduate archival education was provided. The slow movement from programs of a few courses to full graduate level programs with a larger number of specialized courses has long been one of the pre-eminent problems facing the archival profession. This larger problem has seemingly forced the handling of an area like electronic records through the offering of a few lectures. It may be that this handling of electronic records management has more to do with the nature of the archival profession and its educational foundations.

A decade ago Frank Burke (1981) wrote an important essay in which he argued that the lack of full-time archival educators and more formal graduate programs would weaken the development of archival theory (see also Conway, 1988). This article led to a lengthy set of responses about the nature of archival theory and even whether there were such a thing. The important matter of how a more comprehensive graduate archival education would contribute to the resolution of such matters as the administering of electronic records, however, has not been sufficiently explored, although there have been speculations about why such programs have not developed (Stielow, 1993). The cycle of poverty that was described a decade ago relative to the development of government archives could be expanded to what seems to exist here (Weber, ed., 1984, chapter 1). Few archival education programs led to a lack of research about electronic records. And the development of teaching materials and the lack of the research and other materials has led to a paucity of items that archival educators can utilize for teaching effectively in this area. One library educator has stated clearly the difference between education and training:

> Education is the process of conveying a broad range of ideas, concepts, relationships, and skills that may or may not be immediately needed by the student. It is concerned with foundations, principles, and basic knowledge in any field. Training, on the other hand, is concerned with imparting skills to accomplish specific tasks using appropriate tools and techniques. (Subramanam, 1986, p. 163)

How can archival educators impart such "foundations, principles, and basic knowledge" or even skills in the midst of an environment that has few electronic records programs, a literature that mainly describes case studies, and has failed to develop sufficiently the theory and principles of its subject?

What could break this cycle is a matter of conjecture. The long-standing three-course sequence in graduate archival education may no longer be suitable for preparing anyone but technicians and processors in archival institutions. Only providing several (or fewer) lectures on any of the basic archival functions, especially on matters such as electronic records, may be–because of the complexity of such systems–almost a fruitless exercise. Specialized courses on electronic records management seem to be a definite need. At the minimum, graduate archival students need to take an introductory information science course (see, for example, Healey, 1988). Archival educators need to explore using long-distance learning and developing software for self-paced instruction for presenting the basics of electronic records management (Fahey, 1989; Lee, 1989; Marchionini, 1989).

Current graduate archival education guidelines affirm that archival knowledge is interdisciplinary in nature. As the SAA guidelines state (1988, p. 382), "the adequate educational preparation of an archivist will continue to draw upon many related fields and disciplines while emphasizing the archivist's own knowledge, skills, and attitudes." Interestingly, the graduate archival education programs have been located in schools that stress such interdisciplinarity, but there appears to have been little effort to take advantage of this situation. The information professions have built their own education programs on interdisciplinarity, as William Paisley (1990, p. 6) more recently argued that "information science is part of a constellation of disciplines and interdisciplinary research areas that have a common focus: human communication." Yet the examination of the education directories gives an impression that education programs consist of a few specifically focused archives courses and a miscellany of other related courses. There is hardly a sense, except as stated in the education guidelines, of a coherent curriculum. The ACA guidelines (1988, p.10) state that "archival studies are part of the broader field of information studies, [and] therefore curriculum designers will have to establish some coordination with parallel programs in the field" (see also Stielow, 1993). That has not been done.

GRADUATE ARCHIVAL EDUCATION AND ELECTRONIC RECORDS: SUGGESTIONS FOR ADDITIONAL RESEARCH.

This analysis was intended only to (1) provide a profile of how graduate archival education has responded to the increasing use by organizations and individuals of new information technologies, and (2) to contrast this to how it may be related to what has occurred in state archives and, more broadly, to the profession's seeking electronic information technology literate individuals through published job advertisements. It is only a sketch, suggesting numerous other aspects that should be the topics for additional research.

It was mentioned in the findings section that the specific content of graduate courses in archival education programs was unknown. The Ericson studies (1988, 1993) of introductory archival courses (analyzing syllabi) indicates that this would be a fruitful additional way to assess the nature of graduate archival education programs. Using current syllabi would identify the number of course sessions on electronic records, the instructors used in these lectures, the specific nature of required readings, and the research and field work tasks that might be assigned. This would also open up the possibility of identifying successful approaches to educating individuals to work as archivists responsible for electronic records.

There also needs to be more research on the nature of students in the graduate archival education programs and their subsequent careers, that would provide the now missing context for understanding any dimension of this education. The American archival profession has not done any work in this area, even at the level of providing profiles of students in a single program. At the least, the archival profession needs to determine the level of computer literacy that these students bring to the graduate archival education programs. Such knowledge would assist in determining what information technology courses should be taken, as well as in the construction of specialized electronic records courses.

There could be some research about whether there is a sufficient corps of archivists with satisfactory training and experience in working with electronic records. The American archival profession has only sporadically done surveys of professional archivists, and none of surveys has identified any information that would give this profession a greater understanding of how it is presently prepared to work with modern information technology. Not only does this profession appear to be weak in position openings and educational opportunities, it lacks any certain knowledge of whether it has a sufficient corps of individuals who could work with electronic records.

There needs to be more research to define precisely the needs of archival employers for professional archivists to work with electronic records. There has been little in the way of coherent statements from the archival institutions about what they require from graduate programs; in fact, archival institutions have given the general impression of taking what they can get and (if there is a need for special knowledge in areas like automation) of being content to hire people with those backgrounds and experiences and then giving in-house training in basic archival principles, practices, and theories. Research to determine archival employers' needs would be helpful, as Alan Gabehart's recent work (1992) has suggested. Determination of what type of undergraduate programs best prepares individuals to be educated on the graduate level to work as archivists would be also of value. This would help the American archival profession to determine how many comprehensive graduate archival education programs are needed, and more specifically, how many full graduate courses in electronic records management are really needed.

Such research focused on graduate archival education would be especially helpful since the archival profession has primarily stressed solutions to this problem through the development of continuing archival education workshops, institutes, and other such offerings. But the lack of regular graduate courses on electronic information technology, the paucity of advertisements for electronic records archivists, and the few electronic records programs suggest that continuing education has not been as successful as the American archival profession would have liked. This will be explored, through a case study, in the next chapter.

ENDNOTES

1. For these and other examples of position descriptions see chapter three of this study.

2. It appears that this may be changing since 1990, at least as suggested by the work of the Society of American Archivists Committee on Automated Records and Techniques' Curriculum Project and the National Historical Publications and Records Commission's development of a research agenda and special call for project proposal submissions. Still, it is not hard to detect that the number of archivists working in these areas is small, has always been small, and that the vast majority of other archivists still do not reflect any clear sense of how to manage electronic records.

3. This brief outline is based on several more detailed discussions of graduate archival education (cf., Berner, 1981; Goggin, 1984; and Cox, 1990c, chapters five and six).

4. These guidelines, quite sketchy in nature, were published in the *American Archivist* 41 (January 1978): 105-06.

5. For a discussion of this recent proposal, see my "The Masters of Archival Studies and American Education Standards: An Argument for the Continued Development of Graduate Archival Education in the United States," *Archivaria* 36 (Autumn 1993): 221-31.

6. These papers, a report by CART, and other supplementary materials have been published in the Summer 1993 issue of the *American Archivist.*

7. Since most of the major graduate programs reported, there was no effort in follow-up. No such effort was made, as well, because the information captured in this survey was supplemental to the evidence of courses reported on in the education directories.

Chapter Five

The NAGARA Institute: An Evaluation of Its Effectiveness as a Form of Advanced Archival Education

INTRODUCTION

The purpose of this chapter is to describe and analyze the institute for state government archivists held at the University of Pittsburgh School of Library and Information Science for two two-week sessions in 1989 and 1990 and again in 1991 and 1992, as a case study of continuing archival education for the administration of electronic records.[1] Being a case study, this chapter is more descriptive than the previous three, but it concerns one of the most important recent efforts by archivists to grapple with the challenges of electronic records. The institute was also directed to state government archives, representing institutions that have not yet fully resolved approaches for developing knowledge, skills, and strategies for managing electronic records, yet which possess more resources and incentives for dealing with electronic records. Finally, the institute, as a case study, provides an excellent opportunity to consider educational efforts beyond the academy; as such, it should be read

[Haworth co-indexing entry note]: "The NAGARA Institute: An Evaluation of Its Effectiveness as a Form of Advanced Archival Education." Cox, Richard J. Co-published simultaneously in: *Primary Sources & Original Works* (The Haworth Press, Inc.), Volume 3(3/4), 1994, pp. 163-188; and: *The First Generation of Electronic Records Archivists in the United States: A Study in Professionalization,* Richard J. Cox, The Haworth Press, Inc., 1994, pp. 163-188. Multiple copies of this article/chapter may be purchased from The Haworth Document Delivery Center [1-800-3-HAWORTH; 9:00 a.m. - 5:00 p.m. (EST)].

in conjunction with the essays by Thomas Brown (1984-; and forthcoming) on the Society of American Archivists' decade-long efforts to provide continuing education in automation.

Given the generally weak graduate education on this topic and the problems facing state archives in their administration of electronic records, it is apparent that more continuing educational opportunities (such as this institute) are needed by archivists as they cope with the challenges caused by sophisticated information technologies, competing informational professionals, and limited resources and public profiles in the late twentieth century. A secondary purpose of this chapter is to consider what such advanced education is, and how it has been viewed (or should be viewed) in the archival profession. The description and analysis of the state archivists' institute is intended to amplify understanding about such archival education by considering its strengths, weaknesses and accomplishments. This secondary purpose is admittedly more subjective than the first aim of this chapter. It is also worth noting that this chapter represents a *preliminary* assessment, since the success of this particular institute can only be determined accurately over the long-term or as it has (or fails to have) an impact on the state archival institutions represented.

Considering the use of continuing education and other post-employment educational venues is important since the American archival profession has devoted more than a decade to this with, at best, mixed results. The Society of American Archivists, mainly through its Committee on Automated Records and Techniques and predecessors, began offering annual meeting sessions, workshops, and seminars on automated records and techniques in 1977, primarily with the aim of providing individuals the knowledge they needed for developing programs in their own institutions. In four years, the committee had developed a core curriculum, with levels of workshops supporting the continued enhancement of an individual's knowledge. A wide range of opinions and the difficulties of structuring the various levels of workshops and meeting sessions to support this curriculum, among other things, have weakened the ultimate impact of these continuing education efforts.

The obvious need to revise continuously the curriculum because of the rapid change of information technology has been another challenge for the Society of American Archivists. In 1991, Tom Brown, one of the leaders in these continuing education efforts, determined that reviewing "earlier SAA educational efforts raises some questions about whether a solid foundation has been laid" in the continued work to develop a comprehensive electronic records management curriculum (T. Brown, forthcoming study). A few years earlier, Lisa Weber (1984) described the array of current educational opportunities available for archivists in both automated techniques and electronic records management, but the sense of her evaluation was that the most important educational work remained to be done. More recently, Paul Conway (1993) has described the importance of continuing education for archivists, but he has also identified serious lapses in the evaluation of such programs. The advanced institute for government archivists developed in this milieu, driven by the awareness by state government archivists that their programs were not positioned to deal adequately with the increasingly complex electronic information technologies.

To accomplish an evaluation of this institute and to reflect on the roles of continuing education for electronic records management, this chapter is divided into four sections. The first is an effort to define what continuing archival education is, and how it has been seen to fit into other levels of archival education. This is a cursory treatment of a complex topic, but it is one that needs to be addressed at the outset. More thought, discussion, and research need to be directed by archivists to this topic to provide a workable definition. The second section is a description of the purposes and activities of the state archives institute. This provides a glimpse into what this institute was all about. The next part of the chapter is an assessment, based on formal evaluations completed by the institute participants, of the institute as a prototype of continuing archival education in the area of electronic records. The final portion of this chapter is an effort to suggest some conclusions and recommendations about continuing archival education, and how the archival profession needs to re-think some of its basic assumptions and attitudes about education in general; this part summarizes what this study has focused on and leads into the final chapter's recommendations for additional study.

DEFINITIONS: CONTINUING ARCHIVAL EDUCATION

The archivist's idea of continuing education does not appear to be very well-developed. There are, at least, several reasons for this. First, graduate archival education has only begun in the past decade to shift *from* one to three basic or introductory courses connected to a graduate program in history, public history, or library and information science *to* graduate programs that are more comprehensive in scope, requiring a more deliberate move toward both full-fledged masters degrees and full-time specialist faculty. It is difficult to consider what continuing or advanced education is if the basic graduate education has not been settled on or developed sufficiently. Continuing education is a relative term at best for the present archival community, dependent upon how archivists define their basic educational requirements and, as well, their notion of what an archivist is and does. Archival educator Luciana Duranti (1993, pp. 19-20) has criticized archivists in the United States for doing things backwards: "Most important . . . is that education necessarily precedes continuing education. . . why do American archivists spend so much energy, time, and money on emphasizing and creating continuing education programs, rather than on developing ideas about the substance of your professional education, and seeing that those ideas are translated into well supported degree programs?"

Second, and not unrelated to the first issue, archivists have tended to describe certain existing educational opportunities in fundamentally different ways. For instance, the Modern Archives Institute–a multi-week, intensive course offered by the National Archives with various co-sponsors for a half-century–is likely to be described by some archivists as basic continuing or even advanced archival education. For others, *any* sort of formal classroom education is an opportunity to participate in an educational process that is more advanced than the informal on-the-job training that has been their main source of education. With this range of views, it is difficult to pinpoint what continuing education for archivists should or could be; it is also easy to become confused or bogged down in semantics. Added to this are the continuing arguments about theory versus practice, the existence of archival theory, and even the scope of archival knowledge. A 1981 article by Frank Burke on the prerequisite of having full-time graduate archival educators for the development of archival theory led to a still ongoing debate in the American archival community about whether or not there is an archival theory (cf., Cappon, 1982; Kimball, 1985; Roberts, 1987 and 1990; and Stielow, 1991). Towards the end of that decade, Paul Conway (1988, p. 255) again addressed this need, stating: "Today's archival education system is a drag on the development of the archival profession, because it is tied too closely to the very practitioners it serves. Simply put, the archival profession needs a larger corps of full-time faculty committed to a career of teaching, research, and service." With a matter such as this still seemingly unresolved, it is difficult to develop curriculum for graduate, continuing, and advanced education or even inservice training.

Third, the archival profession has not ascertained its own educational needs in a very competent manner. There is little empirical research about what various archival practitioners require in the way of pre- or post-appointment education or on the actual effectiveness of existing educational opportunities (Conway, 1993). At this point, what archivists mostly possess are some very well-reasoned and articulate *opinions* (extending over a half-century) about how archivists should be educated, but these views need to be tested in a more careful manner than has been done. The practicum, for example, continues to be given high marks as a fundamental aspect of archival education without any real proof of its utility in equipping individuals to function as archivists. Neither does the archival profession have any studies on the placement of graduates of archival education programs in repositories, nor on how these graduates view the relevance of their education as they gain experience (Cox, 1990c, chapter six). Surely, such questions must loom large for archivists when they work to determine their educational programs.

Having expressed these reservations, it is important to suggest that archivists still have some basis for at least developing a coherent definition of continuing or advanced education and its relationship to other forms or levels of archival education. This definition is more theoretical than reflecting actual practice, but it provides a useful discussion point for the profession and its employers and educators. This degree of definition is now possible because of work that has been done by the Society of American

Archivists' (SAA) Education Office and, more recently, the Association of Canadian Archivists (ACA) Education Committee.

The main contribution–in terms of any articulation about the nature of archival education–of the SAA Education Office primarily has come through Timothy Ericson's 1988 article, "Professional Associations and Archival Education." In his essay, Ericson noted that archivists' failure to define precisely the distinctions between pre-appointment and post-appointment education has led him to opt for a pragmatic definition of "postappointment" as "education for archivists who are already on the job, regardless of their background or educational pedigree." The reasons for such pragmatism are that existing graduate (pre-appointment) programs presently reach only a small population, appointments to archival positions continue to be made with individuals who lack experience and formal education, new ideas and practices continue to emerge rapidly, and many graduate programs (due to the limitation of the number of courses) do not adequately cover basic archival functions. Ericson's effort to refocus archival education in content, not just the means of purveying the content, perhaps, has laid the foundation for some creative thinking about the levels of education matched to educational needs. His analytical work certainly helped to demonstrate that the importance of continuing education is not its providing first-time exposure on archival principles and practices to individuals, or to fill in the gaps of any one person's educational preparation and experience, but rather assisting the profession to meet its mandate of preserving and managing the documentary heritage. Advanced or continuing education, however it ultimately may be defined and carried out, is a vital part of the education needed to meet the archival mission.

The Association of Canadian Archivists (ACA) has more deliberately and purposely dealt with the matter of advanced education, providing a useful paradigm for advanced archival education. The ACA (1990-91) has recently adopted in principle "Guidelines for the Development of Post-Appointment and Continuing Education and Training Programs." The strength of these guidelines may be that they rest on the concept that "pre-appointment professional archival education is to be at the Masters level in a university context," while acknowledging that "many who call themselves archivists and are hired as such by their employers will continue to enter the profession without formal pre-appointment education in archival theory and practices." This readily matches the SAA's own educational presuppositions as reflected by the Ericson essay and other statements of this professional association.[2]

The ACA has developed definitions for three levels of archival education: fundamental, advanced, and specialized. The fundamental level leads to a "comprehension of basic archival principles and practices" and has a "focus . . . on those archival functions that must be understood before an individual is able to work effectively as an archivist." The advanced level "expands upon the knowledge gained at the fundamental level, allowing examination of specific aspects of archival concepts and functions, and drawing upon knowledge and techniques from related professions and disciplines." The specialized level "includes the same subjects as advanced level education, but permits focus on even more specific aspects . . . as required. It is envisioned that this type of educational activity would be used as a vehicle for in-depth study of specific issues in response to defined needs as they arise."[3]

The ACA's three-tiered definition of education provides the necessary starting-point for any discussion about a specific form of archival education, be it a graduate course, formal graduate program, or basic short-term workshops. As will be seen in the following description, the state archivists' institute held in 1989-1992 is an example of the variety of continuing or advanced archival education that has generally been lacking in the archival profession *if* such education is intended to be post-appointment (beyond the basics) and focused on specific concerns and functions.

THE STATE ARCHIVISTS' INSTITUTE: A DESCRIPTION

The purpose of this institute, entitled "Archival Administration in the Electronic Age: An Advanced Institute for Government Archivists," was to provide intensive instruction for state government archivists on the characteristics and projected future changes in modern information systems and the management tools needed for operating in this new environment. It was offered for experienced archivists in senior positions. This institute (first held in June 1989 and 1990 and supported with a grant from the Council on Library Resources and co-sponsored by the National Association of Government Archives and Records Administrators [NAGARA]–the professional association that initially articulated the need for such advanced institutes–and then again in 1991 and 1992 with NHPRC funding) grew out of the state assessment and reporting grants funded by the National Historical Publications and Records Commission in the early to mid 1980s. These reports and subsequent meetings and efforts, such as the 1985 report of the Committee on the Records of Government (Committee on the Records of Government, 1985), showed the traditionally humanities-trained state archivists the need for re-tooling themselves, their programs, and their staffs in order to be more involved in state and national information policy agencies and initiatives and to gain a better knowledge of the electronic records information technology. In other words, the institute was specifically designed to confront issues and concerns prompted by the new information technology and policies that had already resulted in considerable debate in the archival community and its literature. The challenges for the state archives were confirmed by other studies, such as the National Association for State Information Systems study on state government information resources management (Caudle and Marchand, 1989). Many of the problems and issues previously discussed in this study were in the minds of the designers of and participants in the institute.[4]

The specific purposes of the institute were, then, to address the management needs of state archives, improve the state archivists' capability to conduct strategic planning for better positioning their institutions to cope with matters such as electronic records, develop cooperative links among state archives and between the state institutions and the National Archives (two representatives of this latter institution participated in both phases of the institute for this reason), and aid state archivists coping with electronic records.

To accomplish these purposes two primary tracks were followed through the institute's two phases, one on general management and strategic planning and the other on electronic records. It was anticipated that by the end of the first institute, participants would achieve two things: a statement of vision for their particular state to meet archival needs that could be used with staff, governing boards, and the public, and an outline of a model strategic plan that provided a proactive, participatory role for the state archives in the management of electronic records. The goals for the second institute held in 1991/92 were similar except that the aim of developing a specific workable strategic plan was dropped based on the experiences of the first institute. The objectives of the second institute were to provide technical information about new trends in information technology, to offer an introduction to the value of strategic planning for working in the state information policy and technology environment, and to afford an opportunity for these administrators to share insights, solutions, and experiences gained from working in this environment.

The first track, on modern electronic information technology, exposed the institute participants to a variety of perspectives and technical content. The participants heard presentations by both information scientists (mostly faculty members of the University of Pittsburgh's School of Library and Information Science) and archivists working on the appraisal and management of electronic records, information processing standards, electronic data display and use, electronic data processing and retrieval, electronic data transmission and storage, and information systems design. During the second institute the same emphasis continued with a slight variation: speakers and emphases shifted from technical issues to information policy and related matters.

The other track, primarily presented by a professor from the Graduate School of Business at the University of Pittsburgh, introduced the concept of strategic planning and the various aspects of such planning. Buttressing both tracks were presentations targeted to assist the institute participants in focusing on the trends in state and federal and national information policy and practices and provided the participants with a fuller view of the environment in which their planning needed to occur. During the first phase, Edwin Levine (Staff Director of the Joint Committee on Information Technology Resources for the Florida Legislature) discussed state policy issues for archives in the changing information environment. At the close of the 1990 institute, participants were provided a more in-depth analysis of a recently released report on information resources management in state government (Caudle and Marchand,

1989) and a view of current state and national information policy issues and concerns given by Levine, J. Timothy Sprehe (then Senior Policy Analyst in the Office of the Management of the Budget's Office of Information and Regulatory Affairs) and Jerry Berman (then Director of the ACLU Project on Information Technology and Civil Liberties). Much of this latter discussion focused on the proposed amendments to the Paperwork Reduction Act then being considered by Congress. In the second 1991/92 institute, this emphasis was provided by Michael Hale (Executive Administrator, Florida State Information Resources Commission).

Throughout both phases, besides these two tracks, institute participants worked on individual and small group projects. Between the completion of the first phase and the start of the second, the various state archivists were asked to prepare planning documents for their state archives programs and (more specifically) on how they intended to work with electronic records in their governments. During the second phase, two working groups were established to prepare statements on national issues and initiatives supporting state archival affairs and on considerations and guidelines for state archival programs to manage electronic records. For the second institute similar small groups worked on state and national issues, and institute participants worked on individual state archives electronic records, statement and planning documents.

In providing a description of the institute, it is helpful to know who participated in the institute, the nature of their own educational backgrounds, and the variety of state archives that were represented. This data show that this was an advanced institute both in terms of a highly specialized topic and a form of educational objective directed to senior (both by education and experience) archivists.

During the first institute (1989-90) a remarkable homogeneity was evident in the sixteen persons representing state archives. Among these participants, twelve were primarily educated as historians. Eleven had additional training in management and ten in archives administration. The participants also were a very experienced group, all having more then ten years work as archivists, mainly in state archives. For 1990 participants (there was a slight change between the two phases with two state archivists declining to attend the second segment and being replaced by two other state archivists),[5] the average length of professional service was 15.1 years with a range from 3 years to 27 years. However, exactly half had been in their current position for less than two years; in fact, participants in the 1990 institute had a mean time of 6.3 years in their present position with a range of one to 24 years. The majority held very senior positions in their institutions, ten of the participants holding the position of state archivist or its equivalent.

The participants in the 1991/92 institute represented a slightly different mix, with both the directors and senior staff of the state archives in attendance. These participants had an average of 13.8 years experience in the archival profession, with just over three (3.4) years in their present position. Most of these individuals (15 of 22) had academic preparation in some field of history, with most of the remainder having some educational preparation in library science (4) and political science (3). Over half (14) had an advanced degree (10 had masters degrees and 4 held doctorates). Their profile was, then, extremely similar to that of the 1989/90 participants, certainly supporting the need for re-tooling in information science and technology which the planners of the institute perceived as a strong need. Frederick Stielow (1991, p. 19), in his recent assessment of the state of archival theory, has suggested that there has been a shift "toward an administrative and information science focus," but the profiles of the state archival administrators suggest that the educational backgrounds and experiences have not prepared them for such a transition. In the modern information arena in government, state archives may be largely staffed by historians and humanists with different outlooks than the technologists with whom they must work.

The diversity of institutions that characterizes state archives was evident at this institute. The oldest (Alabama) and newest (New York) state archives were present at both institutes. Independent state archives (part of cultural resources or affairs agencies, located in education departments, associated with historical societies and state libraries, placed under secretary of state departments, and operated as part of the legislative branch) were also present at the institute. Staff sizes (12 to 87 employees) and budgets ($200,000 to $3,000,000) ranged widely at the first institute. And while no funding data was collected for the 1991-92 institute, the staff size of the institutions represented revealed a similar range (an average of 27.8 professional staff). Half of the state archives had direct records management responsibility, while the remainder either only reviewed records retention schedules or had no authority in this function whatsoever.

A fact that enabled the institute to function in the first place was that despite the similarities in individual backgrounds and diversities in institutional settings, there was remarkable uniformity when it came to the concerns for the role of state archives in the modern information age. Nearly all of the state archivists came to the institute with some anxiety for re-educating themselves and re-forming their institutions for work with records in electronic form. One state archivist summarized it best when he noted that in dealing with electronic records, he and his staff were "barely more than uninformed amateurs."[6] Likewise, the variety of problems that state archives faced in working with such records were clustered about a limited number of major issues. Many states noted that there is a basic problem in the definition of electronic records as records. For example, task forces and other authorities responsible for coordinating or creating information policy do not include or are not influenced by the state archives; laws and regulations regarding electronic records are either non-existent or overlap and conflict; the legislature has minimal interest in information management issues; and standards for the review, design, and purchase of computer hardware and software is decentralized. Only a few state archives were developing programs to manage electronic records, and none of the participants believed that an adequate job was being done in their states in administering these records.[7]

EVALUATING THE INSTITUTE AS ADVANCED OR CONTINUING ARCHIVAL EDUCATION

There are three criteria by which this institute can be evaluated. One is to look at the actual products that resulted in light of what the institute planners had intended. Another is to consider the actual evaluations of the institute participants as gathered through a survey instrument, administered at the conclusion of both institute phases[8] and soliciting views on both the institute itself and the perception of the institute by its participants as a form of advanced education. The second form of evaluation is somewhat less subjective and is the better place to begin the institute's assessment as a form of advanced or continuing archival education. A third evaluation means was to consider what impact the institute has had on the specific institutions involved. However, this is problematic because much more time is needed to evaluate such programmatic effects.

Generally, participants gave the institute high marks. On a scale from one to five (with five being excellent and one being poor), the participants gave the first institute a mean score of 4.40 (with none giving it less than a four) and the second institute a mean of 4.24 (see Table 5.1). As one state archivist mentioned, the 1990 institute was "not perfect, but [it provided] the best public archival education available so far." Although the rating dropped a little for the first phase of the succeeding institute, the comments were also generally positive. These comments ranged from "one of the most worthwhile continuing education institutes that I have attended" to more balanced assessments such as "I thought it provided an excellent environment for studying and discussing the issues surrounding electronic records, [although] somewhat hectic and some lectures more useful than others, but that's to be expected."

Likewise, both institutes received superior evaluations in its other basic components (see Table 5.1). On the same scale, the content lectures on information technology and policy and strategic planning received a 4.0 rating for the first institute and a slightly higher rating of 4.1 for the 1991 institute. The major complaint (and for some the major weakness) expressed by the first institute participants was their perception of the non-archival speakers as not being

TABLE 5.1. General Evaluation of the Institutes

	1989/90	1991
General Rating	4.4	4.2
Lectures	4.0	4.1
SLIS	4.9	4.8
Groups	3.6	3.5

well-versed enough in archival practices and concerns. This concern was balanced by a number of the participants' comments that this forced them to communicate their concerns to non-archivists–which was, after all, one of the intended purposes of the institute. One state archivist captured this concern very well when he noted that the "strengths and weaknesses [of the lectures] derive from the same source: presenter's lack of understanding of public archives roles and goals. Frustrated participants were forced to seek new explanations of our purposes." Similar comments were made about the 1991 institute. One participant noted: "Excellent in strategic planning and standards. Technology needed more direct application to our [the archival] profession." Another stated: "Most of the lecturers had trouble relating to our field. It might be better to find someone closer to us, who could better answer our questions." While the 1991 institute participants were more critical of the non-archivists and their knowledge of archival work, the general ratings suggested the content was nevertheless valuable. As one participant observed: "Overall the content was high quality. Now I have to spend time analyzing information and constructing a plan suited to our environment."

The other areas of general ratings presented quite a contrast (see Table 5.1). SLIS' support of the institute–in its facilities, support staff, and ongoing assistance–also received a very high average mark in both institutes (4.9 and 4.8 respectively). The high marks accorded this aspect require little comment. The lowest rating (3.6 and 3.5) was allocated to the small group meetings in both phases. Some participants believed that these groups lacked sufficient focus or were unsure whether they were the base mechanism for advancing work on intended individual and institute products. While some of the participants enjoyed the lengthy interaction with their peers, others complained in the first institute that the groups were "often rambling and unfocused," requiring "improved facilitation to make use of [their] time more effectively." Nearly identical comments were made about the small groups in the 1991 institute, although there was more comment about lack of time to do the small group work. Again, some participants believed the groups, as constituted, were the greatest weakness of the institute. Nevertheless, as will be discussed, some of the immediate specific products of the institutes were mainly the result of these small groups.

Institute participants were also asked what had been the "most important" aspect of their summers, being given a choice to rank in order of importance the presentations and discussions on information technology, the sessions on strategic planning, the opportunity to interact with colleagues, time away from the office, and any other aspect they thought was important. Institute participants from the 1991 group were asked to provide a more specific ranking (see Table 5.2), but there is a sufficient basis for comparison. Here the value of the institute as an educational venture was underscored. During the 1989/90 institute, the sessions on strategic planning (1.60) and information technology (2.20) were ranked one and two in importance followed by time with colleagues (2.40) and, with a much lower ranking, time away from the office (4.00). Others noted that the handouts, readings and opportunity for reflection were very important. Indeed, a number of individuals noted that the greatest strength of the institute was, as one summarized it, the "appropriateness of [the] overall mix of lectures, content, group work, and planning" that led to building consensus, shared visions, and strategies for state archival institutions in the modern information age.

The 1991 institute brought strong ratings for time with colleagues (2.0), electronic records programs sessions (2.3), and strategic planning (2.4), with a significant gap in the perceived impor-

TABLE 5.2. Ranking of the "Most Important" Aspects of the Institute

1989/90	1991
Strategic planning (1.6)	Time with colleagues (2.0)
Information technology (2.2)	Electronic records programs (2.3)
Time with colleagues (2.4)	Strategic planning (2.4)
Time away from office (4.0)	Information resources management (4.8)
	Electronic records implications (4.9)
	Information technology (4.95)
	Time away from office (5.9)

tance of the other aspects of the institute. The greatest shift between the groups from the two institutes was the lower rating of sessions on information technology by the 1991 institute participants. No real explanation was offered for this. The one comment made in response to this question might be explanatory: "I think the most rewarding aspect was hashing some of these things out amongst the members." The 1991/92 participants seemed to place a greater emphasis on the value of peer interaction than what occurred in the 1989/90 institute. Corroborative comments were made by 1991 participants in response to a question about the greatest strength of the institute. These responses generally supported the value of the group interaction: "Addressing electronic records issues through the interaction of participants"; "Being able to network with people in the same profession and have more hours of intense training"; "Face to face communication among people who do similar work in isolation, *plus* directed readings of source material"; and "Interaction with peers."

The state archivists and state archives representatives were also asked to rate the institute as a form of advanced (or continuing) archival education using a scale of 5 (excellent or strongly agree) to 1 (poor or strongly disagree); Table 5.3 portrays the results from these two institutes. As a form of advanced education, participants from both institutes gave it a high rating (4.5 and 4.4 respectively). Participants from the first institute added comments such as the institute's "intensive, concentrated environment is the most efficient, productive format to address strategic planning and electronic records." A 1991 participant commented in a similar fashion: "I prefer these short intensives in the academic setting. They usually form a good platform for more reading and training."

Participants from both institutes were also asked whether the intensive two-week sessions had introduced them to any new information. First institute participants gave a 4.5 rating when asked to rate whether the institute had introduced them to new information, although this rating slipped somewhat to a 4.2 for the following institute. Some of the first institute participants commented that the value of the institute was also in allowing them to look at things in a "fresh way," or to rearrange old information. Participants in the 1991 institute made similar assessments: "A new (relatively) field/

TABLE 5.3. Evaluation of the Institutes as a Form of Advanced Education

	1989/90	1991
General Rating	4.5	4.4
New Information Sources	4.5	4.2
Replicate Institute	4.5	4.8
Add to Graduate Education	4.0	4.6
Staff Benefits	4.5	4.5

area, therefore new information" and "Helped me to synthesize and refine and reconsider idea."

When asked whether there should be additional institutes or whether their own staffs would benefit from such an institute, the ratings were even higher (4.5 in both cases in the first institute, and 4.8 and 4.5 in the 1991 institute). Some first institute participants suggested minor adjustments or even other topics, but there seemed to be strong consensus that this institute-format was "an effective way to focus on either a particular issue or to bring together an important group of leaders or others who need to provide leadership or develop a common agenda." The participants in the more recent institute also made suggestions, but they also confirmed the importance of continuing such educational work. One participant noted that "there ought to be some way to formalize electronic records training for archivists." Another suggested that "this is the kind of training opportunity that should be widely available to archivists at many levels of expertise and experience."

The first institute participants assigned their lowest rating (4.00) to the question of whether the institute "added to existing graduate archival education programs and continuing education workshops." There seemed, in hindsight, to be some misunderstanding about the intent of this question, with 1989/90 institute participants providing the widest range of written comments. They noted that there were no other alternatives, or that the institute represented an "important departure from most existing institutes and workshops," or that it wasn't necessary for the institute "to be attached to a formal graduate program." It is still possible to discern, however, that these experienced archivists detected that the kind of instruction that they were receiving was not available in the existing graduate programs. The 1991 institute participants provided a stronger response to this question, giving it a 4.6 score. Their written responses were, however, more critical about graduate education than what the first institute participants seemed to think. One respondent to the evaluation wrote: "How can you judge the value of this as opposed to graduate archival education? Preposterous! Graduate archival education is nebulous, at best." Another noted: "Graduate archival education is a waste of time! Continuing education is very much enhanced by this Institute." These responses may hint at one reason why graduate archival education programs have been as malformed as they seem; that is, the existence of a wide diversity of opinion by professional archivists regarding their value.

Finally, in the formal written evaluations, the institute archivists were asked to indicate the relative importance of other topics that could be handled through an institute format. The responses were very similar (see Table 5.4. Appraisal and public programs and advocacy ranked high on both lists. Reference and access, other special media (such as cartographic records or photographs), and arrangement and description were consistently ranked at the bottom. The second institute participants gave a very high rating to management as a potential institute topic, this was the only real discrepancy between the two groups of institute participants. That none of these topics dropped below a middle rating may indicate both that the institute format is successful and that advanced continuing education (in all of the archival basics) is a desirable goal. Individuals also suggested a variety of other topics as well, including marketing, personnel management, budgeting, and the legislative process.

The second criterion in which to evaluate the institute is to consider final products. Earlier in this chapter it was mentioned that the first institute participants hoped to achieve two things (or products) by the end of the institute: a statement of vision that could be used with staff, governing boards, and the public for their particular state to meet archival needs, and an outline of a model strategic plan that provided a proactive, participatory role for the state archives in the management of electronic records. Neither was achieved. However, some useful products were developed that indicate success for the

TABLE 5.4. Ranking of Other Topics for Institutes

1989/90	1991
Appraisal (4.5)	Management (4.7)
Public Programs and Advocacy (3.9)	Appraisal (4.4)
Preservation (3.7)	Public Programs and Advocacy (4.3)
Management (3.7)	Reference and Access (3.9)
Reference and Access (3.4)	Other Special Media (3.8)
Other Special Media (3.3)	Preservation (3.4)
Arrangement and Description (3.1)	Arrangement and Description (3.3)

institute in terms of its potential real impact on the state archival institutions coping with electronic records and in the increasingly complex modern electronic information age.

First, during the initial institute each of the states took steps to begin conducting strategic planning, thereby initiating an array of written products reflecting the fact that each of the states were at extremely different points in their institutional lives. The University of Pittsburgh business school faculty expert on strategic planning evaluated the products created up to the time of the second institute, indicating that while there were specific problems with the efforts all of the state archives had made significant progress from the year before and that the problems were typical of the early stages of strategic planning. This progress was evident in the brief statements prepared by each state on their intended future activities and appended to the final report of the institute. These statements indicated a number of initiatives already underway or to be started, led by starting or continuing strategic planning and working with state government information policy agencies (see Table 5.5). Other activities included experimenting with model or prototype pilot projects, changing legislation, issuing standards, educating and/or hiring new staff, gaining new resources, and establishing electronic records programs.

Second, the first institute participants issued several statements regarding electronic records meant to influence their future actions

TABLE 5.5. Future Activities of the First State Archives Institute: In Ranked Order

Start or Continue Strategic Planning	9
Work with State Information Policy Agencies	8
Pilot Projects on Electronic Records	3
Introduce or Revise Legislation	3
Issue Electronic Records Standards	3
Educate State Archives Staff	3
Hire New Specialized Staff	2
Create Electronic Records Program	2
Increase Budget for Electronic Records	2
Revise Mission Statement	1

(and those of the broader archival profession) regarding the management of archival records in electronic form. One of these documents was a set of proposed revisions to the Paperwork Reduction Act that would establish mechanisms to assess the financial impact of federal information policies and practices on state and local government, enable early records management and archival review of plans for federal information systems, allow the location of electronic information systems, influence government standards for information systems in order to identify and preserve the archival record, and provide for regular intergovernmental review of federal information systems. Another document was a draft statement (proposed to NAGARA for publication, modified and published in late 1990) on "electronic records, archives, and state governments" that provided basic guidelines on the "continued development of an overall coordinating body for the management of the state's information resources" and the recognition and strengthening of "programs to preserve electronic records of long-term value to the state and its citizens." The final document was a statement of "areas of national concern and recommended initiatives" regarding the management of electronic records.[9]

It is possible to see, then, that these final products, while different than initially perceived by the original institute planners, were important elements of a new vision of what government archives should be in the modern information age and statements of strategies for meeting this new vision.

The purposes of the second institute were modified. The main change was a de-emphasis on the production of a specific strategic plan for each state. The objectives of the second institute were to provide technical information about new trends in information technology, to provide an introduction to the value of strategic planning for working in the state information policy and technology environment, and to provide an opportunity for these administrators to share insights, solutions, and experiences gained from working in this environment. The participants' evaluations, as described above, suggest a positive result.

There were also other more immediate results. Small groups prepared drafts of statements on federal challenge grants to initiate electronic records programs, specific strategic issues which affect the development of electronic records programs, contributions which state government archivists and records administrators can make to state government information resources management, the matter of the viability of traditional archival and records management approaches with electronic records, and a proposal to study the adequacy of state records laws for the management of electronic records. Some of these statements have been revised and discussed by state government archivists and records administrators and others, but their impact at this early point is impossible to detect. If the first institute is any indication, one or more of these statements will be formalized as position papers or serve as a platform for additional work by the state archives and records communities.

The final results, and therefore the final evaluation, of the two institutes will likely be seen only through what actually happens in these state archives by the mid-1990s. Just as archivists can look back now and see the actual relative importance of the SAA's Committee on the Seventies or the NHPRC-sponsored state assessment and reporting projects of the early 1980s, the true importance of the institute can only be accurately measured at some future date.

I had hoped to complete a survey of the state archives institute participants to determine what level of activity had occurred in the development of electronic records programs in these institutions.

Two factors convinced me that such a survey should be postponed until much later. First, and already mentioned, the development of such programs must be tracked over a long period of time. Considering the slow response to the increasing development of electronic information technology over the past quarter-of-a century, as discussed in the other chapters in this study, it is unreasonable to expect that a period of just a few years will bring great changes. Frederick Stielow (1991b p. 6), an archival educator with a keen interest in the archivist's response to information technology, captured the nature of this response: "Archivists must realize we are buying into a process, not a product, and that automation demands careful planning. . . . Panaceas are unlikely and the new archival law is that 'with each new storage medium, archivists must reexamine their theory and can expect to meet new challenges in preservation'."

The second factor is the increasing difficulties with state government funding, which have plagued the initiation of any new state archives programs. Throughout the time of this institute, funding has become an increasing problem. What has occurred in several states reveals the nature of the problem. North Carolina, a participant in the first institute, had neither a program for electronic records nor any staff specifically trained to manage such a program. In early 1992, it did have a budget request for approximately $200,000 to provide seed money for such a program (for two new staff and equipment), but it had been fighting for such an appropriation for more than several years. The North Carolina state archivist (Olson, 1993) has stated that the institute has provided a catalyst for his organization's continued efforts in this regard, but that new ideas and approaches were hindered from being put in use by the bleak government budget.[10] Nevertheless, this same individual has described in a very positive manner the value of the institute to his institution. Maine offered an even more dramatic evidence of this dilemma. This state's chief archivist noted that the institute provided the basis of a planning document for creating an electronic records program, but there were no prospects for any new staff; in fact, the state archives had no staff even to answer the telephone. This state archivist suggested that the institute provided "emotional and intellectual resources," but that the devastating downturn in the economy and state government finances had undermined what real resources were available for staffing the needed program.[11] The real impact of the institute in developing electronic records programs must wait until more time has elapsed and the state archives have had opportunities to position themselves in better ways for working with the modern information technologies.

IMPLICATIONS OF THE INSTITUTE FOR ARCHIVAL EDUCATION

While awaiting the long-term final results of the institute, it is still possible to suggest some implications of the institute for archival education generally and advanced archival continuing education specially. Here are five observations that can be made about the institute and its place in archival education. Some of these relate to the need for additional research, a topic which will be more fully explored in the next and final chapter of this study.

1. *The institute needs to be carefully considered as a way of better defining what advanced archival education in the area of electronic records is and should be.* The state archivists' institute was a combination of both classroom learning and professional agenda-setting. If its success is attributed to this (as some of the participants suggested it should be), does this structuring represent a model for future advanced archival education? The SAA and NAGARA education committees need to consider this as they continue to define educational levels and initiatives. The continuing work of SAA's CART also needs to be re-examined because of its primary focus on continuing education. As Paul Conway has stated, archivists must first determine the goals of such training before they can be effectively evaluated (Conway, 1993).
2. *The topics that were the focus of the institute (electronic records, strategic planning [or management], information policies [or advocacy], and appraisal) need to be re-evaluated for what they indicate to the archival profession about existing graduate and continuing archival education programs.* There have been statements that such topics are not receiving ade-

quate attention in graduate programs limited to a few courses. On the other hand, electronic records has been the subject of numerous short-term workshops. The question needs to be considered, therefore, as to how such topics are being taught and the adequacy of the teaching. Again, both the SAA and NAGARA education committees should make this a priority. The relevancy of these topics for other archivists in colleges, universities, religious institutions, museums, historical societies, and corporations also need to be considered.

3. *The archival profession needs to conduct an employer evaluation of their educational needs for archivists in the area of electronic records management.* The state archivists attending this institute were clearly identifying gaps in their own educational backgrounds. These, and other, archival employers need to be surveyed and interviewed to determine what are the basic educational requirements for beginning, middle, and senior archivists. This should provide needed information to archival educators of how they need to plan for and direct the development of their educational programs. SAA (both its Committee on Education and Professional Development and the Archival Educators Round Table), NAGARA, and the newly formed Academy of Certified Archivists are all likely sponsors of such research.
4. *It is important that a national perspective on archival education in electronic records be maintained as new educational initiatives are planned and implemented.* Jerry Ham (1989, p. 88) recently wrote, in his assessment of the NHPRC state archival plans, that these reports had all focused locally on educational needs. He commented that the "real point is that graduate [and other] education is not a problem every state has to solve. Part of the remedy is national." Ham's observation was certainly borne out by this institute. Despite the diversity of state archival institutions represented at the institute, their interests, problems, and needs turned out to be very similar. Advanced education, such as this institute, can be formulated on the national level–provided needs and interests are known–with all the resources of the national associations and

other bodies in order to meet the educational needs of archivists in a diversity of repositories and institutional settings.

5. *Finally, at the advanced level archivists must be willing to listen to, interact with, and learn from non-archivists who are specialists in other information disciplines relevant to electronic records.* As was mentioned earlier in this chapter, the most consistent criticism by the institute participants was that many of the non-archivists were not sufficiently versed in archival terminology, theory, or practice. On the other hand, this institute was specifically designed to allow the participants to learn about new technical areas and to equip them to converse with other information professionals. To expect that these other specialists should understand the archival field, when archivists lack knowledge of the information disciplines, is contrary to the aims of such an institute. Archivists need to learn how to interact with other professionals in order to advance the archival mission.

ENDNOTES

1. The institute has been continued for 1993 and 1994 with funding by the National Historical Publications and Records Commission, but this chapter examines it for the years 1989 through 1992.

2. Specifically, this attitude is reflected in its 1988 guidelines for graduate education (Society of American Archivists, 1988).

3. Admittedly, this institute could be viewed as either advanced or specialized archival education.

4. Much of the background information on the origins of this institute derives from the presentations of Edwin C. Bridges to the institute participants and reported on in the three summary reports of the institute's activities published by the University of Pittsburgh School of Library and Information Science. These reports, entitled *Archival Administration in the Electronic Information Age: An Advanced Institute for Government Archivists*, were published annually in 1989, 1990, and 1991.

5. There was also a slight shift with one state having a change in its second representative from the first to second phase, and another state bringing a new staff person assigned to electronic records to the second phase.

6. These statements are from the applications to the Institute. The records of the Institute are housed in the University of Pittsburgh School of Library and Information Science archives maintained at the school.

7. This description was derived from the participants' statements in the two institutes prepared in advance. Copies of these documents are with the records of

the institute held at the University of Pittsburgh School of Library and Information Science.

8. A full copy of the evaluation form is included in Appendix Five of the original dissertation.

9. NAGARA used these products to publish in 1991 a brochure on state governments and electronic records.

10. Conversation with David Olson, March, 31 1992.

11. Conversation with James Henderson, March, 30 1992.

Chapter Six

Archivists, Archival Institutions, and Electronic Records: Problems, Challenges, Opportunities, and Needs for Additional Research

INTRODUCTION: SUMMARY OF FINDINGS AND GENERAL IMPLICATIONS

David Bearman, part of the small group of the American archival community who has worked extensively with electronic records, recently presented at a conference an interesting hypothetical case study of how government will be producing records in the not too distant future. Bearman's example (1991c) related to a state government attorney general's office work on a single legal case. In his example, a team of lawyers would create the legal brief using a "groupware" writing tool, search online databases into previous case law, look at census records and other demographic sources, communicate through telecommunications, and employ a variety of other electronic information systems. While Bearman used this example to argue for archivists' need to work with information technology standards, the case also demonstrates the importance, indeed the necessity, of archivists being able to manage electronic records from an archival perspective.

[Haworth co-indexing entry note]: "Archivists, Archival Institutions, and Electronic Records: Problems, Challenges, Opportunities, and Needs for Additional Research." Cox, Richard J. Co-published simultaneously in: *Primary Sources & Original Works* (The Haworth Press, Inc.), Volume 3(3/4), 1994, pp. 189-199; and: *The First Generation of Electronic Records Archivists in the United States: A Study in Professionalization*, Richard J. Cox, The Haworth Press, Inc., 1994, pp. 189-199. Multiple copies of this article/chapter may be purchased from The Haworth Document Delivery Center [1-800-3-HAWORTH; 9:00 a.m. - 5:00 p.m. (EST)].

The results of this study suggest, however, that the archival profession in the United States, despite long-term discussion of the challenges and opportunities posed by electronic records and the long-held definition of archival records existing in any medium, has not yet developed an appropriate structure (educational, programmatic, legislative, and so forth) for dealing with such records. Some individual archival institutions have made significant progress in working with electronic records, but these pale in contrast to the pervasiveness of the information technology and the archival profession's needs to manage the technology. There is little specialization in even larger archival institutions such as state government archives, a missing trend that does not provide a sufficient foundation for work with electronic information systems and their records. And, as this aspect of the study revealed, position descriptions within state government archives reflect responsibilities, activities, and requirements that seem to pre-date the pervasive use of computers.

The lack of specialization in state archives is revealed to be a larger professional problem through an examination of archival job advertisements. Only nineteen job advertisements directly concerned with electronic records over a sixteen-year time span is evidence that the archival profession has not developed electronic records programs. Moreover, most (twelve) of these advertisements were placed by one institution, the New York State Archives and Records Administration, with the remainder being placed by a professional association, an institution specializing in documenting the history of computing, another state archives, and the leading graduate North American archival education program located in Canada. This dearth of job advertisements hardly suggests the existence of an adequate structure for managing electronic records. The only positive aspect of this analysis is the increasing emphasis on computer literacy.

Whether there is any correlation between the dearth of job advertisements focused on electronic records positions or not is a question worth contemplating, but it is certainly true that at this time there has not been any strong catalyst offered in either graduate or continuing archival education. There are no consistent patterns of electronic records courses offered by graduate archival education programs, and the approaches to offering such education are extremely inconsistent as well. Whatever the long-range impact of the University of Pittsburgh's Institute, it is a rarity in the American archival community, and it too reflects some serious problems in attitudes, resources, and approaches brought to bear by archivists on the growing reliance on electronic information technology.

Many commentators on the influence on technology note that most technology (that which is innovative, useful, and successful) eventually is incorporated or co-opted by a society. Ralph Waldo Emerson, a century and a half ago, reflected on the fact that even in the midst of the onslaught of the Industrial Revolution, with all its curiosity and newness, there was a tendency to become numbed by the technological innovation. Emerson's concerns were far-reaching, but the reasons for the concerns were simply that society had learned, or was in the process of learning, how to harness the technology for its benefit (Kasson, 1976, chapter three). Technologist Mark Weisner (1991, p. 91), as cited in the initial chapter of this study, suggested that the "most profound technologies are those that disappear . . . into the fabric of everyday life." At this time, electronic records remain a special challenge for the archival profession and their institutions in the United States. This may suggest why American archivists have sometimes referred to electronic records as "special media." They are special *not* in that they represent unique or formidable records, but they are special in that they possess many characteristics different from the more commonplace paper-based records that archivists have worked with for centuries.

The integration by society of technological innovation is not an easy process nor devoid of problems and other difficulties. The concept of a dynamic society is a phenomenon that American archivists may have discovered is hard to manage, if we relate a society to a discipline. It is unlikely that this will change. William Saffady (1984, p. 5), reviewing office automation through the twentieth century, noted that "office automation has had one goal since its inception–the improved cost-effectiveness of office operations." This aim will remain, of course, but it does pose the issue of why archivists, dealing with this objective for so long, have found it so difficult to manage the technology. David Bearman (1992), once again, has suggested that the response of archivists will be greatly influenced by both their organizations and their own training.

But there are other issues as well. The technical and sociological challenges of electronic records may have been too immense for the generally humanistically-oriented archival profession to adapt to quickly enough. The conservator or custodial function of the American archivist is one that may have also led to a conservative or more slowly adapting mind-set not conducive to quick adaptation, innovation, or risk-taking. This kind of concern has been hinted at, but not really examined. In a seminar on archives and authority control, Richard Szary (1989, p. 41) noted, in passing, that he was "convinced that the major obstacles to improved description and retrieval of archival and other historical materials are cultural and psychological within our professions rather than technical." The long interest by the archivist in information technology still has been an interest largely focused on simpler technological systems, such as pen and paper and copying devices. Electronic records are the byproducts of technology that is more far-reaching in its impact, altering even the very concept of document or record as well as the manner in which individuals and institutions use information. This requires more serious efforts by the archivist to intervene in the records-creating process, a scenario that many archivists still object to because of allegiance to traditional archival theory, principles, and practices.

And, finally, there is the question of resources and authority, challenges dramatically pointed to in the recent report on the National Aeronautics and Space Agency's maintenance of its magnetic tapes. This report concluded that "hundreds of thousands of tapes containing space science data are stored under deplorable conditions. Furthermore, NASA needs to improve its management of tape archiving and storage activities" (Information Management and Technology Division, 1990, p. 2). The report also cited problems in resources, avoidance of Federal regulations, inadequate Federal regulations, and other similar problems.

The American archivist's lack of grappling head-on with the information technology of the past thirty years perhaps owes its origins at least partly to other internal problems in this profession. First, there is the continuing debate about the basis of professional practice and theory–history, library and information science, or something else–that dates back at least one half century and continues to emerge, for various reasons, in meetings and in the pages of professional journals and newsletters. This tension may be a factor in encouraging many archivists to ignore the information professions, reflected in a profession that seems to ignore the research of other disciplines doing work relevant to their mission. Second, there is the more recent debate about the existence of an archival theory. This reveals the absence of a strong consensus about professional theory and a knowledge base that weakens the archivist's ability to examine computer hardware and software and determine *archival* needs for such systems. Both of these problems undermine other concerns that archivists have in their work with electronic records. Bearman, in his comparison of how Americans and Europeans have approached electronic records, noted that there are two ways–technology and policy–that can be used in the archival administration of electronic records (Bearman, 1992). Both require, of course, that the archival profession has individuals knowledgeable about electronic information systems, as well as information policy.

It is also true that the pioneers and subsequent developers of computer technology have, in the interest of establishing their own discipline, established barriers that outsiders, even users of the technology, have found difficult to overcome. John A. Barry (1991, p. 7), in an interesting study of "technobabble," wrote the following:

> In part because of the military origin of computer development, technobabble was initially a kind of secret language developed by a special technological priesthood. But the cabalistic nature of technobabble was not strictly a result of the military foundations of computing. Early computers were as difficult to operate and as unreliable in service as early cars and aircraft. The unreliability of these early machines required a leap of faith to undertake their use. They demanded patience and expertise not available to anyone outside a small, discrete group. The very first computers and those that were developed in the early years of the computer industry were accessible only to a select few whose power and prestige derived from keeping their minions in thrall.

Archivists need to learn the appropriate language for communication, and, at the same time, be careful not to develop their own barriers to effective discussion.

Archivists may also have approached the issue of information technology in an inappropriate fashion, by making it an issue. Margaret Hedstrom (1989b, p. 17) has proposed that archivists should focus on information systems–the "set of rules and procedures for collecting, processing, maintaining, and distributing information in order to achieve predetermined results"–instead of the products of such systems. Hedstrom stated that archivists have been hesitant to move in this direction because "there has been a tendency to reduce fundamental changes in the organization and use of information that result from automated record keeping to the narrow issue of what to do about machine-readable records." Another reason is "that there is not always a neat fit between the structure of an information system and the structures of the organizations it serves" (Hedstrom, 1989b, p. 19). This present study suggests, perhaps, another reason: there is an insufficient corps of qualified archivists at present to focus on information systems, and there has not developed an effective mechanism to increase the size or quality of this corps.

The degree to which all this threatens either the American archival profession or the archival mission in American society is, of course, a matter of intense speculation. However, the archival profession is certainly part of the information professions and its mission–the identification, preservation, and management of information possessing continuing or enduring value–is especially important in the late twentieth century. Theodore Roszak (1986, p. 162) was correct when he wrote in the mid-1980s that "if anything, we suffer from a glut of unrefined, undigested information flowing in from every medium around us." The archivist plays a unique role in refining and digesting the information and, yet, it appears that the archival perspective has largely been blocked out of being able to deal with the major instruments in the creation and management of that information, the computer and computer software.

NEEDS FOR ADDITIONAL RESEARCH

Throughout this study, a number of specific research needs were described. The purpose of this concluding section of the final chapter is to summarize and identify some of the more important research needs. This list of research is tentative, at best, primarily because of the dearth of research conducted within and about archival work, institutions, and practitioners. The purpose of this brief research agenda is to consider other research which will enable the archival profession (and others interested in this and other information professions) to consider how and whether it can structure itself to manage more effectively electronic records.

One major area of research regarding the American archival profession and electronic records is the broader education and practical training of American archivists in the management of electronic records. The Society of American Archivists' general membership profiles provide some clues on this matter, but these profiles have no specific focus on how archivists have equipped themselves to work with electronic records. This study's analysis of job advertisements has revealed an increasing call for computer literacy, but there are many statements in the professional literature that suggest that such knowledge is not essential or even very important. There needs to be more analysis of what success the few graduate courses in North America have had in prompting the effective start and sustenance of electronic records programs. More specific assessments of the success of the continuing education workshops and institutes also need to be completed, both as a comparison with the graduate courses and for a measure of success in their own right. From such studies, new, more effective educational programs can be developed and tested.

There remains a dearth of information about employers' needs and expectations for archivists in electronic records management. The American archival profession's understanding of what employers need and expect for archivists in all areas is actually quite limited; at the least, there is a dearth of benchmark studies with which to compare the research results of this study. In the mid-1980s there was a study to determine employers' images of archivists (Levy and Robles, 1984). It remains one of only a few systematic efforts to gain an understanding of employers' expectations and needs (see Schulz, 1988 and Gabehart, 1992). All that remains are subjective statements of employers' needs.

This is quite a problem for strengthening the archival profession to work with electronic information systems. It limits the capability of graduate and continuing education programs to turn out individuals most suited to work in this area. It also provides little incentive for a stronger connection between such educational offerings and the main archival employers. The interests of the state government archivists led to the advanced educational offering at the University of Pittsburgh, but this same institute also failed (through 1992) to produce a coherent statement about such educational and employment needs. Such lost opportunities weaken the American archival profession's infrastructure, an infrastructure already damaged by a lack of consensus on archival theory and knowledge, approaches to education, credentials, and, in some areas, coherent strategies for practice. More rigorous analysis of position descriptions and job advertisements, expanding on what has been offered in this study, could significantly add to the profession's knowledge of employment needs, future directions for graduate and continuing education, and so forth. Without such data, how can the American archival profession project its needs for computer-literate archivists?

More information, systematically and carefully gathered, analyzed, and distributed, is needed to galvanize the American archival profession into action. But the need for such information is weakened by some negative attitudes about both basic and applied research. Margaret Hedstrom (1991a) has suggested that archivists have had a priori notions about what electronic records and computers mean for their work and the documentary heritage. This may explain why so little research has been done by archivists, although the general absence of research suggests other reasons such as the lack of graduate research programs and an absence of reward systems for those who conduct such research. In every other archival function–appraisal, arrangement and description, reference, and the like–careful research studies are rare. Most archivists continue to base their decisions on assumptions or intuition, a dangerous road to follow even if the decisions prove to be generally correct. It is even more dangerous where careful information is required, such as in developing information technology standards that will govern the identification and maintenance of archival records in electronic forms. Here intuition and "ballparking" are useful only to a point, needing to be set aside for precise definitions and technical standards.

Case studies about successful and failed electronic records programs could also provide very important information which the archival community currently lacks–what are the barriers to developing such programs and how can these barriers be overcome? The successful New York and Kentucky state archives programs could be usefully studied for this purpose. Their different settings (one in a state library, the other in a cultural education unit in a state education department) suggest an interesting basis for comparison, while their initial use of external funding to hire experts to develop such programs indicates the variety of catalysts required for developing these programs. While the archival profession has employed case study methodology, it has primarily been weak methodologically because it has been reported on by insiders with vested interests rather than studied by more objective observers.

Is all this undermined by archivists' attitudes about technology? This was suggested in numerous points in this study, but it is a topic for a more direct analysis. Basic attitudes held by archivists toward technology could be researched and the results used in the developing of new strategies for educating archivists in this area and in helping archival programs seek and find suitable candidates for electronic records positions. The lack of studies in this area may be more interesting as a way of determining the nature of the archival profession in the United States than it is in developing practical solutions to the effective management of electronic records. However, greater information on the personal and psychological barriers may improve the effectiveness of educational programs in this area. The discovery by consultants of the power of corporate culture in blocking logical and practical advice certainly has counterparts on a broader professional level. Only additional study will indicate to archivists the degree of importance of this matter in blocking electronic records program development.

As has been noted throughout this study, there have been successful electronic records programs, such as in the Kentucky and New York state archives. Margaret Hedstrom has presented in a number of places about lessons learned during her more than a decade of working with electronic records. A series of specific case studies of successful and failed electronic records programs could provide some powerful lessons for the archival profession in the United States. At this point, there is only a superficial understanding of why some programs have succeeded and others have failed. Success in the larger programs causes some to consider that resources are the most important factors in effective electronic records program. Others want to see models developed that can be applied to their situations. Still others see information policy environments and the profile of archival institutions in these environments as crucial nesting grounds for electronic records programs. But only objective, comprehensive studies will reveal the parameters or factors essential for successful electronic records programs. The factors might be discovered to be as basic as leadership and staff expertise.

There also needs to be critical study of the changing nature of archival work and impact on the profession. Roma Harris, in a recent study on the impact of computers on reference librarians and women in the profession, has made some chilling conclusions about the impact of technology:

> Despite the optimistic forecasts of high technology enthusiasts, it seems inevitable that the professional library work force will shrink and that the jobs remaining to librarians will be of a very different nature than those of the past. Many of the service roles played by librarians in the past will, in future, be taken over by paraprofessionals and clerical workers. (Harris, 1992, p. 14)

Will this hold true for the American archival profession? Already, archival arrangement and description work has been transformed from a subjective art to a technical skill by the adoption of a basic bibliographic form and corresponding standards required to support this bibliographic form. This has led to an impact on many other areas. For example, it is likely that the automated descriptive records will become more user-friendly online systems and that these systems will support enhanced access to full text electronic archival records. What will this mean for the archival repository and the basic skills and definition of the working archivist?

Since this is the conclusion of a research study, the litany of additional research was an appropriate exercise. Clifford Lynch's 1990 presentation on networked information systems provided another perspective that needed to be considered in this conclusion. Instead of research and development, Lynch urged research and innovation. "Research is the usual process of investigation and study and experimentation, often in unexplored directions and with results that are hard to predict. *Innovation* is the activity of applying advanced technology within an organizational or national setting to change the way the system operates."

What this is really suggesting is a new attitude towards problems or challenges or opportunities. Rollo May, in his recent book about myth, suggested that "myths precede discovery." In this vein May (1991, p. 91) suggests that the era of European discovery required such a change: "It took an *inner* change in Europe before the people could let themselves see and experience a new world." Perhaps American archivists require an inner change which will encourage a more innovative spirit in work in such areas as typified by electronic records. This is not a new suggestion, as David Bearman's brief examination (1989) of *Archival Methods* was a proposal for more energetic risk-taking. Such a spirit and outlook seems particularly important in the volatile, rapid world of modern information technology. Otherwise, archivists remain more onlookers than participants in the late twentieth century information age.

Works Cited

Abbott, A. (1988). *The Systems of Professions: An Essay on the Division of Expert Labor.* Chicago: University of Chicago Press.

Ahlgren, D. and J. McDonald (1981/82). The Archival Management of a Geographic Information System. *Archivaria, 13*, 59-66.

Ambacher, B. I. (1989). Managing Machine-Readable Archives. In J. G. Bradsher (Ed.) *Managing Archives and Archival Institutions*, (pp. 121-33). Chicago: University of Chicago Press.

American Records Management Association (ARMA) International (1990). *Directory of Collegiate Schools Offering Courses & Majors in Records & Information Management.* Prairie Village, Kansas: ARMA International.

_______. (1992). *Directory of Collegiate Schools Offering Courses & Majors in Records & Information Management.* Prairie Village, Kansas: ARMA International.

Anderson, M. (1985). The Preservation of Machine-Readable Data for Secondary Analysis. *Archives, 17*, 79-93.

Ash, R. A., E. L. Levine, and F. Sistrunk (1983). The Role of Jobs and Job-Based Methods in Personnel and Human Resources Management. In K. M. Rowland and G. R. Ferris (Eds.) *Research in Personnel and Human Resources Management: A Research Annual* Vol. 1, pp. 45-84. Greenwich, Connecticut: JAI Press.

Association of Canadian Archivists (ACA) (1987). *ACA 87; McMaster-Hamilton: Conference Proceedings.* Hamilton, Ont.: Association of Canadian Archivists.

_______. (1989). Guidelines for the Development of a Two-Year Curriculum for a Master of Archival Studies. *ACA Bulletin, 13*, 380-89.

_______. (1990-91). Guidelines for the Development of Post Appointment and Continuing Education and Training Programmes. *Archivaria, 31*, 60-90.

Augarten, S. (1984). *Bit by Bit: An Illustrated History of Computers.* Boston: Unwin Paperbacks.

Bailey, C. (1988). Archival Theory and Machine Readable Records: Some Problems and Issues. M.A.S., University of British Columbia.

_______. (1989-90). Archival Theory and Electronic Records. *Archivaria, 29*, 180-96.

Barry, J. A. (1991). *Technobabble.* Cambridge: The MIT Press.

Barry, R. E. (1989). UN Tackles Electronic Records Issues. *Archives and Museum Informatics, 3*, 4.

Bearman, D. (1983). 1982 Survey of the Archival Profession. *American Archivist, 46*, 233-41.

______. (1986). Recruitment of Archivists: 1985-1986. *SAA Newsletter* (November), p. 9

______. (1987). *Collecting Software: A New Challenge for Archives and Museums*, Archival Informatics Technical Report, vol. 1, no. 2. Pittsburgh: Archives and Museum Informatics.

______. (1989). *Archival Methods*. Technical Report, vol. 3, no. 1. Pittsburgh: Archives and Museum Informatics.

______. (1990a). Review. *Archives and Museum Informatics*, *4*, pp. 11-12.

______. (1990b). Review. *Archives and Museum Informatics*, *4*, p. 14.

______. (1990c). Electronic Office Records. *Archives & Museum Informatics*, *4*, pp. 12-15.

______. (1991a). Impact of Electronic Records on Archival Theory. *Archives and Museum Informatics*, *5*, pp. 6-8.

______. (1991b). An Indefensible Bastion: Archives as a Repository in the Electronic Age. *Archival Management of Electronic Records*, Archives and Museum Informatics Technical Report, no. 13. Pittsburgh: Archives & Museum Informatics, pp. 14-24.

______. (1991c). Information Technology Standards and Archives. Paper presented at the "Archives & Europe Without Boundaries" conference, Maastricht, The Netherlands, October 3.

______. (1992). Diplomatics, Weberian Bureaucracy and the Management of Electronic Records in Europe and America. *American Archivist*, *55*, 168-80.

Belding, R. N. and L. G. Fortson (1985). Kentucky's Machine-Readable Challenge. *Provenance*, *3*, 58-69.

Berner, R. C. (1981). Archival Education and Training in the United States, 1937 to Present. *Journal of Education for Librarianship*, *22*, 3-19.

Bolter, J. D. (1991). *Writing Space: The Computer, Hypertext, and the History of Writing*. Hillsdale, NJ: Lawrence Erlbaum Associates.

Borko, H. (1984). Trends in Library and Information Science Education. *Journal of the American Society for Information Science*, *35*, 185-93.

Bradsher, J. G. (ed.). (1989). *Managing Archives and Archival Institutions*. Chicago: University of Chicago Press.

Brown, R. (1976). *Modernization: The Transformation of American Life 1600-1865*. New York: Hill and Wang, 1976.

Brown, T. E. (1984). The Society of American Archivists Confronts the Computer. *American Archivist*, *47*, 366-82.

______. (1986). Archives Law and Machine-Readable Data Files: A Look at the United States. *ADPA*, *5*, pp. 37-42.

______. (1987). The Evolution of an Appraisal Theory for Automated Records. *Archives & Museum Informatics*, *1*, pp. 49-51.

______. (1989). Review. *Archives & Museum Informatics*, *3*, pp. 5-7.

______. (forthcoming). A Decade of Development: The Educational Programs for Automated Records and Techniques Within the Society of American Archivists. *American Archivist*.

Brown, T. E. and W. A. Reader (1987). The Archival Management of Machine-Readable Records from Database Management Systems: A Technical Leaflet. *Archival Informatics Newsletter, 1*, pp. 9-12.

Burke, F. G. (1981). The Future Course of Archival Theory. *American Archivist, 44*, 40-46.

Cameron, R. (1983). Appraisal Strategies for Machine-Readable Case Files. *Provenance, 1*, 49-55.

Cappon, L. J. (1982). What, Then, Is There to Theorize About? *American Archivist, 45*, 19-25.

Caudill, S., E. Caudill, and M. W. Singletary (1987). 'Journalist Wanted': Trade-Journal Ads As Indicators of Professional Values. *Journalism Quarterly, 64*, pp. 576-80, 633.

Caudle, S. L., D. A. Marchand, *et al.* (1989) *Managing Information Resources: New Directions in State Government.* Syracuse: Syracuse University School of Information Studies.

Chandler, A. D., Jr. (1977). *The Visible Hand: The Managerial Revolution in American Business.* Cambridge: Belknap Press of Harvard University Press.

Clanchy, M. T. (1979). *From Memory to Written Record: England, 1066-1307.* Cambridge: Harvard University Press.

Cloonan, M. V. and P. C. Norcott (1989). Evolution of Preservation Librarianship As Reflected in Job Descriptions from 1975 through 1987. *College & Research Libraries, 50*, 646-56.

Cloppinger, J. N. and B. R. Konsynski (1989). Information Refineries: Electronically Distilling Business' Raw Material to Make It More Useable. *Computerworld, 23.*

Committee on the Records of Government (1985). *Committee on the Records of Government: Report.* Washington, DC: The Committee.

Conway, P. (1987). Perspectives on Archival Resources: The 1985 Census of Archival Institutions. *American Archivist, 50*, 174-91.

______. (1988). Archival Education and the Need for Full-time Faculty. *American Archivist, 51*, 254-65.

______. (1992). G.A.P. Track: Membership Survey Results. SAA *Newsletter* (January).

______. (1993). Effective Continuing Education for Training the Archivist. *Journal of Education for Library and Information Science, 34*, 38-47.

Cook, M., (Ed.). (1987). *Computer Generated Records*, Approaches to Problems in Records Management, no. 2. England: Society of Archivists.

Cook, T. (1984-85). From Information to Knowledge: An Intellectual Paradigm for Archives. *Archivaria, 19*, 28-49.

______. (1991). Appraisal in the Information Age: A Canadian Commentary. *Archival Management of Electronic Records*, Archives and Museum Informatics Technical Report. (no. 13, pp. 50-56) Pittsburgh: Archives & Museum Informatics.

______. (1991-92). Easy To Byte, Harder To Chew: The Second Generation of Electronic Records Archives. *Archivaria*, pp. 202-16.

Couture, C. and J. Y. Rousseau (1986). *The Life of a Document: A Global Approach to Archives and Records Management*. Montreal: Vehicule Press.

Cox, R. J. (1989). *Archival Administration in the Electronic Information Age: An Advanced Institute for Government Archivists*. Pittsburgh: School of Library and Information Science, University of Pittsburgh.

______. (1990a). The History of Primary Sources in Graduate Education: An Archival Perspective. *Special Collections, 4*, 39-78.

______. (1990b). RAMP Studies and Related UNESCO Publications: An International Source for Archival Administration. *American Archivist, 53*, 488-95.

______. (1990c). *American Archival Analysis: The Recent Development of the Archival Profession in the United States*. Metuchen, NJ: Scarecrow Press.

______. (1990d). Archivists and Professionalism in the United States Revisited: A Review Essay. *Midwestern Archivist, 15*, 5-15.

______. (1991). Graduate Archival Education and Electronic Records: A Brief Report on the AERT Survey. *AERT Newsletter, 2*, pp. 4-5.

______. (1992a). *Archivists, Electronic Records, and the Modern Information Age: Re-Examining Archival Institutions and Education in the United States, With Special Attention to State Archives and State Archivists*. PhD dissertation. University of Pittsburgh School of Library and Information Science.

______. (1992b). *Managing Institutional Archives: Foundational Principles and Practices*. New York: Greenwood Press.

______. (forthcoming). Readings in Archives and Electronic Records: A Preliminary Annotated Bibliography and Analysis of the Literature. *Archives and Museum Informatics Technical Report* (Pittsburgh: Archives and Museum Informatics).

Cunliffe, W. and M. Miller (1989). Writing a General Records Schedule for Electronic Records. *American Archivist, 52*, pp. 350-56.

Dearstyne, B. (1993). *The Archival Enterprise: Modern Archival Principles, Practices, and Management Techniques*. Chicago: American Library Association.

Diebold, J., J. Duffy, and J. Levy (1987). Trends and Forecasts: OA and the Next Five Years. *Administrative Management, 48*, 18-23.

Dollar, C. (1978). Appraising Machine-Readable Records. *American Archivist, 41*, 423-30.

______. (1986). Trends in New Computer Technology. *ADPA, 5*, 25-36.

______. (1992). *Archival Theory and Information Technologies: The Impact of Information Technologies on Archival Principles and Methods*. Macerata, Italy: University of Macerata Press.

Duranti, L. (1989). The Odyssey of Records Managers. *Records Management Quarterly, 23*, pp. 3-6, 8-11.

______. (1993). The Archival Body of Knowledge: Archival Theory, Principles and Practice and Graduate and Continuing Education. *Journal of Education for Library and Information Science, 34*, 8-24.

Durrance, C. (Ed.). (1989). *Management of Recorded Information: Converging Discipline*. New York: K. G. Saur Verlag.

Eastwood, T. (1993). Nailing a Little Jelly to the Wall of Archival Studies. *Archivaria, 35*, 232-52.

Eisenstein, Elizabeth (1979). *The Printing Press as an Agent of Change: Communication and Cultural Transformation in Early Modern Europe*. Cambridge: Cambridge University Press.

Ellis, J. (Ed.). (1993). *Keeping Archives* (2nd ed.). Port Melbourne, Australia: Thorpe in association with the Australian Society of Archivists, Inc.

Ericson, T. L. (1988). Professional Associations and Archival Education: A Different Role, or a Different Theater? *American Archivist, 51*, 298-311.

______. (1993). 'Abolish the Recent': The Progress of Archival Education. *Journal of Education for Library and Information Science, 34*, 25-37.

Evans, F. B. (1967). Archivists and Records Managers: Variations on a Theme. *American Archivist, 30*, 45-58.

_____. etal. (1974). A Basic Glossary for Archivists, Manuscript Curators, and Records Managers. *American Archivist, 37*, 415-32.

Fahey, M. (1989). Long-Distance Learning. *Network World, 6*, pp. 39-42, 49-50.

Fine, S. (1986). Technological Innovation, Diffusion and Resistance: An Historical Perspective. *Journal of Library Administration, 7*, 83-108.

Fischer, G. (1984). Human-Computer Communication and Knowledge-based Systems. In H. J. Otway and M. Peltu (Eds.), *The Managerial Challenge of New Office Technology* (pp. 54-79). London: Butterworths.

Fishbein, M. (1970). A Viewpoint on Appraisal of National Records. *American Archivist, 33*, 175-87.

______. (1972). Appraising Information in Machine Language Form. *American Archivist, 35*, 35-43.

______. (1974). Report of the Committee on Data Archives and Machine Readable Records–Fiscal Year 1973. *ADPA, 1*, pp. 5-10.

______. (1975). ADP and Archives: Selected Publications on Automatic Data Processing. *American Archivist, 38*, 31-42.

______. (1985). *A Model Curriculum for the Education and Training of Archivists in Automation: A RAMP Study*. Paris: General Information Programme and UNISIST, UNESCO.

Fisher, B. (1969). Byproducts of Computer Processing. *American Archivist, 32*, 215-23.

Fletcher, P. T. (1990). Electronic Records Management in State Government: Planning for the Information Age. *Records Management Quarterly, 24*, 26-32.

Forester, T. (1988). *High-Tech Society: The Story of the Information Technology Revolution*. Cambridge: MIT Press.

Fox, M. J. (1984). Wisconsin Machine-Readable Records Project. *American Archivist, 47*, 429-31.

Furuta, K. (1990). The Impact of Automation on Professional Catalogers. *Information Technology and Libraries, 9*, pp. 242-52.

Gabehart. A. D. (1992). Qualifications Desired by Employers for Entry-Level Archivists in the United States. *American Archivist, 55*, 420-39.

Gavrel, S. (1986). Preserving Machine-Readable Archival Records: A Reply to John Mallinson. *Archivaria, 22*, 153-55.

______. (1988). The National Archives of Canada: Machine-Readable Records Program. *Reference Services Review, 16*, 25-29.

Geda, C. L. (1979). Social Science Data Archives. *American Archivist, 42*, 158-66.

Geda, C. L., E. W. Austin, and F. X. Blouin, Jr. (Eds.). (1980). *Archivists and Machine-Readable Records*. Chicago: Society of American Archivists.

Gilliland-Swetland, L. J. (1991). The Provenance of a Profession: The Permanence of the Public Archives and Historical Manuscripts Traditions in American Archival History. *American Archivist, 54*, 160-75.

Goggin, J. (1984). 'That We Shall Truly Deserve the Title of Profession': The Training and Education of Archivists, 1930-1960. *American Archivist, 47*, 243-54.

Grant, P. (1988a). Why Job Descriptions Don't Work. *Personnel Journal, 67*, pp. 52-59.

______. (1988b). What Use is a Job Description? *Personnel Journal, 67*, pp. 45-53.

Griffiths, J. M. and D. W. King (1986). *New Directions in Library and Information Science Education*. White Plains, New York: Knowledge Industry Publications, Inc. for the American Society for Information Science.

Grogan, D. J. (1983). Education for Librarianship: Some Persistent Issues. *Education for Information, 1*, 3-23.

Gurnsey, J. (1985). *The Information Professions in the Electronic Age*. London: Clive Bingley.

Ham, F. G. (1989). Documenting America: Observations on Implementation. *Midwestern Archivist, 14*, 83-92.

Harris, R. (1992). Information Technology and the De-Skilling of Librarians; Or, The Erosion of a Woman's Profession. *Computers in Libraries, 12*, 8-16.

Harrison, D. F. (1986). An Archivist's Challenges: Adapting to Changing Technology and Management Techniques. *IASSIST Quarterly, 10*, 8-13.

______. (1987). Computers, Electronic Data, and the Vietnam War. *Archivaria, 26*, 18-32.

______. (1989). Machine-Readable Sources for the Study of the War in Vietnam. In L.J. McCrank (Ed.), *Databases in the Humanities and Social Sciences 4* (pp. 279-91). Medford, NJ: Learned Information, Inc.

Harrison, D. F. and W. J. Hedesheimer (1987). Downloading for PC Users, Pt. 1: The U. S. Government Experience. *IASSIST Quarterly, 11*, pp. 3-10.

Hays, S. P. (1965). Archival Sources for American Political History. *American Archivist, 28*, 17-30.

Healey, J. S. (1988). The Electronic Library: An Alternative Approach in Library Education. *Technical Service Quarterly, 6*, 17-26.

Hedlin, E. and D. F. Harrison (1988).The National Archives and Electronic Data. *Reference Services Review, 16*, 13-16.

Hedstrom, M. (1984). *Archives & Manuscripts: Machine-Readable Records*, Basic Manual Series. Chicago: Society of American Archivists.

______. 1988). Optical Disks: Are Archivists Repeating the Mistakes of the Past? *Archival Informatics Newsletter, 2*, pp. 52-53.

______. (1989a). Is Data Redundancy the Price Archivists Will Pay for Adequate Documentation? *IASSIST Quarterly, 13*, pp. 24-30.

______. (1989b). New Appraisal Techniques: The Effect of Theory on Practice. *Provenance, 7*, pp. 1-21.

______. (1991a). Understanding Electronic Incunabula: A Framework for Research on Electronic Records. *American Archivist, 54*, pp. 334-54.

______. (1991b). Teaching Archivists About Electronic Records and Automated Techniques: A Needs Assessment. Paper presented to the SAA CART Curriculum Conference, March 17, Washington, DC.

Hedstrom, M. L. and A. Kowlowitz (1988). Meeting the Challenge of Machine-Readable Records: A State Archives Perspective. *Reference Services Review, 16*, 31-40.

Hernon, P. and C. McClure (1987). *Federal Information Policies in the 1980's: Conflicts and Issues*. Norwood, NJ: Ablex Publishing Corporation.

Herring, J. E. (1991). Information Management–The Convergence of Professions. *International Journal of Information Management, 11*, 144-55.

Humphreys, A. C. (1984). Records Managers as Professionals: A Sociological Perspective. *Records Management Quarterly, 18*, 16-20, 29.

Information Management and Technology Division, General Accounting Office (1990). *Preserving Valuable Space Data*. Washington, DC: General Accounting Office.

Jackson, J. A. (1985). A Documentation and Analysis of Status and Employment Variabilities in Job Descriptions Among Academic Librarians. PhD dissertation, George Peabody College for Teachers of Vanderbilt University.

Jacobson, R. (1989). *An "Open" Approach to Information Policy Making: A Case Study of the Moore Universal Telephone Service Act*. Norwood, NJ: Ablex Publishing Corporation.

Jenkinson, H. (1980). *Selected Writings of Sir Hilary Jenkinson*. Gloucester, England: Alan Sutton.

Jimerson, R. C. (1989). Redefining Archival Identity: Meeting User Needs in the Information Society. *American Archivist, 52*, 332-40.

Kasson, J. F. (1976). *Civilizing the Machine: Technology and Republican Values in America 1776-1900*. New York: Bantam Books.

Kenney, A. R. and L. K. Personius (1992). *Joint Study in Digital Preservation; Report: Phase I (January 1990-December 1991); Digital Capture, Paper Facsimiles, and Network Access*. Washington, DC: Cornell/Xerox/Commission on Preservation and Access.

Kentucky Information Systems Commission (1990). *Managing Information Re-*

sources for Kentucky; Volume 1: Strategies for the Future 1990-1992. Frankfort: Kentucky Information Systems Commission.

Kesner, R. (1981). Computers, Archival Administration, and the Challenges of the 1980s. *Georgia Archive*, *9*, 1-18.

______. (1983). *Information Management, Machine-Readable Records, and Administration: An Annotated Bibliography*. Chicago: Society of American Archivists.

______. (1984/85). Automated Information Management: Is There a Role for the Archivist in the Office of the Future? *Archivaria*, *19*, pp. 162-72.

______. (1985). Whither Archivy?: Some Personal Observations Addressed to Those Who Would Fiddle While Rome Burns. *Archivaria*, *20*, pp. 142-48.

Kesner, R., L. B. Weber, and R. Wilson (1991). *Automating the Archives: A Beginner's Guide*. Chicago: Society of American Archivists.

Kimball, G. D. (1985). The Burke-Cappon Debate: Some Further Criticisms and Considerations for Archival Theory. *American Archivist*, *48*, 369-76.

Kowlowitz, A. (1988). *Archival Appraisal of Online Information Systems*. Pittsburgh: Archival and Museum Informatics.

______. (1991). Appraising in a Vacuum: Electronic Records Appraisal Issues–A View from the Trenches. *Archival Management of Electronic Records*, Archives and Museum Informatics Technical Report (no. 13, pp. 31-37). Pittsburgh: Archives & Museum Informatics.

Law, M. and B. K. Rosen (1989). *Framework and Policy Recommendations for the Exchange and Preservation of Electronic Records: A Report to NARA*. Washington, DC: National Institute for Standards and Technology.

Lee, C. (1989). All Hands on DEC. *Training*, *26*, 34-38.

Levy, S. J. and A. G. Robles (1984). *The Image of Archivists: Resource Allocators' Perceptions*. Chicago: Society of American Archivists.

Lowell, H. (1986). *Preservation Needs in State Archives*. Albany, New York: National Association of Government Archives and Records Administrators.

Lynch, C. (1990). Achieving the Promise: A Proposed Strategic Agenda for Libraries and Networked Information Resources in the 1990s. Paper presented at the Networks for Networkers II Pre-Conference, Chantilly, VA, December 17-19.

McCarthy, P. (1988). The Management of Archives: A Research Agenda. *American Archivist*, *51*, 52-69.

______. (Ed.). (1989). *Archives Assessment and Planning Workbook*. Chicago: Society of American Archivists.

McCrank, L. J. (1979). Prospects for Integrating Historical and Information Studies in Archival Education. *American Archivist*, *42*, 443-55.

______. (1981). Conservation and Collection Management: Educational Problems and Opportunities. *Journal of Education for Librarianship*, *22*, 20-43.

______. (1983). Review of Carolyn L. Geda *et al.*, eds., *Archivists and Machine-Readable Records*. *Midwestern Archivist*, *8*, 47-50.

______. (1985). Public Historians in the Information Professions: Problems in Education and Credentials. *Public Historian*, *7*, 7-22.

______. (1987). Recycling Databases: Turning Databases into Archives. In T. E. Moberg (Ed.), *Databases in the Humanities and Social Sciences 1985* (pp. 268-75). Osprey, FL: Paradigm Press, Inc.

McDonald, J. (1985). An Approach to the Identification and Scheduling of EDP Data. *ADPA*, *5*, pp. 51-68.

Mallinson, J. C. (1986). Preserving Machine-Readable Archival Records for the Millenia. *Archivaria*, *22*, pp. 147-52.

Marchionini, G. (1989). Electronic Problem Scenarios: Integrating Computers Into Instruction. *Journal of Education for Library and Information Science*, *29*, 165-76.

May, R. (1991). *The Cry for Myth*. New York: W. W. Norton and Co.

Michelson, A. and J. Rothenberg (1992). Scholarly Communication and Information Technology: Exploring the Impact of Change in the Research Process on Archives. *American Archivist*, *55*, 236-315.

Miller, M. (1991). Is the Past Prologue? Appraisal and the New Technologies. *Archival Management of Electronic Records*, Archives and Museum Informatics Technical Report (no. 13, pp. 38-49). Pittsburgh: Archives & Museum Informatics.

Mitchell, T. W. (1970). New Viewpoints on Establishing Permanent Values of State Archives. *American Archivist*, *33*, 163-74.

Mosco, V. (1989). *The Pay-per Society: Computers and Communication in the Information Age; Essays in Critical Theory and Public Policy*. Norwood, NJ: Ablex Publishing Corporation.

Mosco, V. and J. Wasko. (Eds.) (1988). *The Political Economy of Information*. Madison: University of Wisconsin Press.

Murrah, D. J. (1990). Employer Expectations for Archivists: A Review of a 'Hybrid Profession.' *Journal of Library Administration*, *11*, 165-74.

National Archives and Records Administration (NARA) (1990a). *Managing Electronic Records*, Instructional Guide Series. Washington, DC: National Archives and Records Administration.

______. Archival Research and Evaluation Staff (1990b). *A National Archives Strategy for the Development and Implementation of Standards for the Creation, Transfer, Access and Long-term Storage of Electronic Records of the Federal Government*, National Archives Technical Information Paper 8. Washington, DC: National Archives and Records Administration.

National Historical Publications and Records Commission (NHPRC) (1990). *Electronic Records Issues: A Report to the Commission*, Commission Reports and Papers, no. 4. Washington, DC: National Historical Publications and Records Commission.

______. (1991). *Report of the Working Meeting on Research Issues in Electronic Records*. Washington, DC: National Historical Publications and Records Commission.

Naugler, H. (1984). *The Archival Appraisal of Machine-Readable Records: A RAMP Study with Guidelines*. Paris: General Information Programme and UNISIST, UNESCO.

New York State Archives and Records Administration (1988). *A Strategic Plan for Managing and Preserving Electronic Records in New York State Government: Final Report of the Special Media Records Project*. Albany: New York State Archives and Records Administration.

______. (1991). SARA Tackles Challenge of Electronic Records. *For The Record, 9*, pp. 6-7.

Nisbet, R. (1980). *History of the Idea of Progress*. New York: Basic Books.

O'Toole, J. (1990). *Understanding Archives and Manuscripts*, SAA Archival Fundamental Series. Chicago: Society of American Archivists.

Pacey, A. (1983). *The Culture of Technology*. Cambridge: MIT Press.

Paisley, W. (1990). Information Science as a Multidiscipline. In J. M. Pemberton and A. E. Prentice (Eds.). *Information Science: The Interdisciplinarity Context* (pp. 3-24). New York: Neal-Schuman Publishers, Inc.

Peterson, T. H. (1984). Archival Principles and Records of the New Technology. *American Archivist, 47*, 383-93.

Posner, E. (1964). *American State Archives*. Chicago: University of Chicago Press.

Radding, A. (1989). Supporting the Flatter Organization. *Computerworld, 23*, pp. 59-64.

Rayward, W. B. (1985). Library and Information Science: An Historical Perspective. *Journal of Library History, 20*, 120-36.

Richardson, Jr., J. and P. Hernon (1981). Theory vs. Practice: Student Preferences. *Journal of Education for Librarianship, 21*, 287-300.

Rieger, M. (1966). Archives and Automation. *American Archivist, 29*, 109-111,

Robb, C. (1990). Networking Metadata in Kentucky. Paper presented to the National Association of Government Archives and Records Administrators, Boston.

Robek, M. F. G. F. Brown, and W. O. Maedke (1987). *Information and Records Management*, 3rd. ed. Encino, CA: Glencoe Publishing Co.

Roberts, J. W. (1987). Archival Theory: Much Ado About Shelving. *American Archivist, 50*, 66-74.

______. (1990). Archival Theory: Myth or Banality. *American Archivist, 53*, 110-20.

Rogers, E. M. (1983). *Diffusion of Innovations* (3rd ed). New York: Free Press.

Roper, M. (1980). The Changing Face of the File: Machine-Readable Records and the Archivist. *Archives, 14*, 145-50.

Rosenthal, J. A. (1991) Crumbling Walls: The Impact of the Electronic Age on Libraries and Their Clienteles. *Journal of Library Administration, 14*, 9-17.

Roszak, T. (1986). *The Cult of Information: The Folklore of Computers and the True Art of Thinking*. New York: Pantheon Books.

Saffady, W. (1984). *The Automated Office: An Introduction to the Technology*. Silver Spring: National Micrographics Association.

Sanders, R. (1989). Archivists and Records Managers: Another Marriage in Trouble? *Records Management Quarterly, 23*, pp. 12-14, 16-18, 20.

Schlereth, T. J. (1989). The World and Workers of the Paper Empire. In *Cultural*

History and Material Culture: Everyday Life, Landscapes, Museums (pp. 145-78). Ann Arbor: UMI Research Press.

Schulz, C. (1988). Analysis of the Marketplace for Educated Archivists: State Archives as a Case Study. *American Archivist, 51*, 320-25.

Smith, E. (1990). *The Librarian, the Scholar, and the Future of the Research Library*, Contributions in Librarianship and Information Science, no. 66. New York: Greenwood Press.

Smith, Wilfred (1974). Broad Horizons: Opportunities for Archivists. *American Archivist, 37*, 3-14.

Society of American Archivists (SAA) (1982). The Ideal Archivist: What Employers Look For. *SAA Newsletter* (January), p. 2.

______. (1984a) Archivist: A Definition. *SAA Newsletter* (January), pp. 4-5.

______. (1984b). Commentary on 'Archivist: A Definition.' *SAA Newsletter* (March), pp. 3-4.

______. (1984c). *The Image of Archivists: Resource Allocators' Perceptions.* Chicago: Social Research, Inc. for the Society of American Archivists.

______. (1985). The Status of Virtue: Resource Allocators' Perceptions of Archives. *SAA Newsletter* (August), pp. 5-7.

______. (1988). Society of American Archivists Guidelines for Graduate Archival Education Programs. *American Archivist, 51*, 380-89.

______. (1991). *SAA Directory of Archival Education 1991-1992.* Chicago: Society of American Archivists.

______. (1993). Draft Guidelines for the Development of a Curriculum for a Masters of Archival Studies. Chicago: Society of American Archivists.

Sola Pool, I. de (1983). *Technologies of Freedom* Cambridge: Belknap Press of Harvard University Press.

Stielow, F. J. (1991a). Archival Redux and Redeemed: Definition and Context Toward a General Theory. *American Archivist, 54*, 14-26.

______. (1991b). Archival Theory and the Preservation of Electronic Media. *Ohio Archivist, 22*, 3-7.

______. (1993). The Impact of Information Technology on Archival Theory: A Discourse on an Automation Pedagogy. *Journal of Education for Library and Information Science, 34*, 48-65.

Stout, L. J. (1990). The Penn State Electronic Records Appraisal Project: A Jumping-Off Point. Unpublished paper presented to the Mellon Fellowship Symposium, Ann Arbor, Michigan.

Subramanyam, K. (1986). Information Technology and Library Education. In A. Kent (Ed.) *Encyclopedia of Library and Information Science* (vol. 41, suppl. 6, pp. 161-93). New York: Marcel Dekker, Inc.

Szary, Richard (1989). Technical Requirements and Prospects for Authority Control in the SIBIS-Archives Database. In *Archives and Authority Control: Proceedings of a Seminar Sponsored by the Smithsonian Institution, October 27, 1987*, ed. Avra Michelson, Archives and Museum Informatics Technical Report (no. 6, pp. 41-45). Pittsburgh: Archives and Museum Informatics.

Thexton, J. E. (1974). Archival Potential of Machine-Readable Records in Business. *American Archivist, 37*, 37-42.

Thibodeau, K. (1991). To Be or Not to Be: Archives for Electronic Records. *Archival Management of Electronic Records*, Archives and Museum Informatics Technical Report (no. 13, pp. 1-13). Pittsburgh: Archives & Museum Informatics.

United Nations, Advisory Committee for the Coordination of Information Systems, Technical Panel on Records Management (1989). *Electronic Records Guidelines: A Manual for Policy Development.* New York: United Nations.

______. (1990). *Management of Electronic Records.* New York: United Nations.

U.S. Congress, Office of Technology Assessment (1988). *Informing the Nation: Federal Information Dissemination in an Electronic Age.* Washington, DC: Government Printing Office.

U.S. House Committee on Government Operations (1990). *Taking a Byte Out of History: The Archival Preservation of Federal Computer Records.* Washington, DC: U.S. Government Printing Office.

U.S. National Academy of Public Administration (1989). *The Effects of Electronic Recordkeeping on the Historical Record of the U.S. Government: A Report for the National Archives and Records Administration.* Washington, DC: National Academy of Public Administration.

Veres, J. G., III; M. A. Lahey; and R. Buckly (1987). A Practical Rationale for Using Multimethod Job Analyses. *Public Personnel Management, 16*, 153-57.

Walker, W. (1989). Records Managers and Archivists: A Survey of Roles. *Records Management Quarterly, 23*, pp. 18-20, 45.

Wallace, P. E. (1981). Career-Ladder Positions and Task Performance as Viewed by Records Management Professionals. *Records Management Quarterly, 15*, 44-52.

Warner, R. and F. X. Blouin (1979). Some Implications of Records in Machine-Readable Form for Traditional Archival Practice. In *Archivists and Machine-Readable Records* (pp. 242-48). Chicago: Society of American Archivists.

Weber, L. B. (Ed.). (1984). *Documenting America: Assessing the Condition of Historical Records in the States.* Albany: National Association of State Archives and Records Administrators and the National Historical Publications and Records Commission.

______. (1988). Educating Archivists for Automation. *Library Trends, 36*, 501-18.

Webster, F. and K. Robins (1986). *Information Technology: A Luddite Analysis.* Norwood, NJ: Ablex Publishing Corporation.

Weisner, M. (1991). The Computer for the 21st Century. *Scientific American, 265*, pp. 94-95, 98-102, 104.

White, H. S. and M. Paris (1985). Employer Preferences and the Library Education Curriculum. *Library Quarterly, 55*, 1-33.

Williams, R. (1987). Records Management Education: An IRM Perspective. *Records Management Quarterly, 21*, 36-40, 54.

Wood, E. B. (1967). From the Information Soapbox: Information Handling Dialectically Considered. *American Archivist, 30*, 311-20.

Yates, J. (1989). *Control Through Communication: The Rise of System in American Management.* Baltimore: Johns Hopkins University Press.

Yoo, J. (1988). An Exploratory Study of Academic Librarians' Attitudes Toward Computer Technology and Their Relationship to Library Science Education. PhD dissertation, University of Pittsburgh School of Library and Information Science.

Zuboff, S. (1988). *In the Age of the Smart Machine: The Future of Work and Power.* New York: Basic Books.

Index

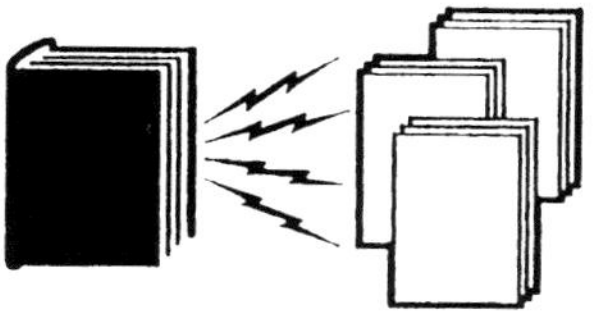

Haworth DOCUMENT DELIVERY SERVICE

and Local Photocopying Royalty Payment Form

This new service provides (a) a single-article order form for any article from a Haworth journal and (b) a convenient royalty payment form for local photocopying (not applicable to photocopies intended for resale).

- *Time Saving:* No running around from library to library to find a specific article.
- *Cost Effective:* All costs are kept down to a minimum.
- *Fast Delivery:* Choose from several options, including same-day FAX.
- *No Copyright Hassles:* You will be supplied by the original publisher.
- *Easy Payment:* Choose from several easy payment methods.

Open Accounts Welcome for . . .

- Library Interlibrary Loan Departments
- Library Network/Consortia Wishing to Provide Single-Article Services
- Indexing/Abstracting Services with Single Article Provision Services
- Document Provision Brokers and Freelance Information Service Providers

MAIL or *FAX* THIS ENTIRE ORDER FORM TO:

Attn: **Marianne Arnold**
Haworth Document Delivery Service
The Haworth Press, Inc.
10 Alice Street
Binghamton, NY 13904-1580

or FAX: (607) 722-1424
or CALL: 1-800-3-HAWORTH
(1-800-342-9678; 9am-5pm EST)

PLEASE SEND ME PHOTOCOPIES OF THE FOLLOWING SINGLE ARTICLES:

1) Journal Title: ______________________________
Vol/Issue/Year: ______________ Starting & Ending Pages: ______________
Article Title: ______________________________
____

2) Journal Title: ______________________________
Vol/Issue/Year: ______________ Starting & Ending Pages: ______________
Article Title: ______________________________
____

3) Journal Title: ______________________________
Vol/Issue/Year: ______________ Starting & Ending Pages: ______________
Article Title: ______________________________
____

4) Journal Title: ______________________________
Vol/Issue/Year: ______________ Starting & Ending Pages: ______________
Article Title: ______________________________
____

(See other side for Costs and Payment Information)

COSTS: Please figure your cost to order quality copies of an article.

1. Set-up charge per article: $8.00
   ($8.00 × number of separate articles) __________
2. Photocopying charge for each article:
   - 1-10 pages: $1.00 __________
   - 11-19 pages: $3.00 __________
   - 20-29 pages: $5.00 __________
   - 30+ pages: $2.00/10 pages __________
3. Flexicover (optional): $2.00/article __________
4. Postage & Handling: US: $1.00 for the first article/
   $.50 each additional article __________
   Federal Express: $25.00 __________
   Outside US: $2.00 for first article/
   $.50 each additional article __________
5. Same-day FAX service: $.35 per page __________
6. Local Photocopying Royalty Payment: should you wish to copy the article yourself. Not intended for photocopies made for resale. $1.50 per article per copy
   (i.e. 10 articles x $1.50 each = $15.00) __________

GRAND TOTAL: __________

METHOD OF PAYMENT: (please check one)

❑ Check enclosed ❑ Please ship and bill. PO # __________
(sorry we can ship and bill to bookstores only! All others must pre-pay)

❑ Charge to my credit card: ❑ Visa; ❑ MasterCard; ❑ American Express;

Account Number: __________ Expiration date: __________

Signature: ✗ __________ Name: __________

Institution: __________ Address: __________

City: __________ State: __________ Zip: __________

Phone Number: __________ FAX Number: __________

MAIL or *FAX* THIS ENTIRE ORDER FORM TO:

Attn: **Marianne Arnold**
Haworth Document Delivery Service
The Haworth Press, Inc.
10 Alice Street
Binghamton, NY 13904-1580

or FAX: (607) 722-1424
or CALL: 1-800-3-HAWORTH
(1-800-342-9678; 9am-5pm EST)